THE
GHOST LIMB

THE
GHOST LIMB

Alternative Protestants
and the
Spirit of 1798

Claire Mitchell

First published November 2022

Beyond the Pale Books
Teach Basil
2 Hannahstown Hill
Belfast BT17 0LT

www.beyondthepalebooks.com

© 2022 Claire Mitchell has asserted her right under the Copyright, Designs and Patents Act 1988 to be identified as the author of this work.

All rights reserved. No part of this work may be reproduced in any form or by any means, electronic or mechanical, including photocopy, without permission from the publisher.

ISBN 978-1-914318-19-1 (paperback)

Printed in Belfast by GPS Colour Graphics Ltd.

Out of a healed past a healed present will grow. Out of a re-realized past a re-realized present will emerge.

John Moriarty, *Dreamtime*

[Ulster Protestants have been denied parts] of their history, such as the radical struggles of the Presbyterians or the labor movement. Regaining that won't happen in history class. It will only happen by fighting in your corner and discovering that someone else was here before you.

Bernadette Devlin-McAliskey, *Jacobin*

I am reconciled to my Lundyism. There are a lot of us, I like the company, and we are not planning to flee.

Susan McKay, *Northern Protestants: On Shifting Ground*

Contents

Acknowledgements ix

Beginnings

1. A County Down Bar 3
2. The Ghost Limb 5
3. 1798 17
4. The Dreamtime 25
5. How to Find a Spirit 35

Hidden Histories

6. The Battle of Antrim 41
7. Dis/Inheritance 48
8. The Entries 57
9. Lockdown in Moneyreagh 67

Language

10. The Magic Door 79
11. Seol Beag 87
12. A Bridge to Scotland 97
13. Larne Language 105

Faith

14. Counter-cultural Christians 117
15. The Abbey 127
16. The Father and the Mother 135
17. Karen the Baptist 144

Political Activism

18. Beatnik Aristocracy	157
19. Bald's Yard	165
20. Foremothers and Feminism	175
21. Cara Van Parke	185
22. Republican Planter	195
23. The Woods	203
24. We Will Be the New Ireland	213

Endings

25. The Past and the Future	221
26. The Betsy Gray Café	235
Bibliography	239

Acknowledgements

In many ways, I feel that this book has communal authorship. While I lent my mind, time and hands to record it, it only exists as a cross-pollinating conversation with others, spanning many years. It is also a conversation over time, with so many who have walked this road before us.

I can find no words expansive enough to express how thankful I am to everyone who has given of their stories to make this book. Nobody undertook it lightly. And yet, nobody flinched from the task. The wider story only has power because of their courage.

A number of people quite literally took this book's journey alongside me, visiting 1798 sites, bouncing around ideas, reading early drafts, suggesting changes, pushing me further, giving practical advice. I will be forever grateful to Lisa Rea Currie, Will Jordan, Angeline King, Stephen McCracken, Gemma Reid, Stephen Baker, Ian Mitchell and Pamela Mitchell for their company throughout the fever dream. I am also indebted to Linda Ervine, Rev. Karen Sethuraman, Kellie Turtle, Roland Spottiswoode, Rev. Cheryl Meban, Maurice Macartney, Stephen Donnan-Dalzell, Seán Napier and Heather Wilson for their insight, comradeship, openness and generosity.

Many others helped me think about the themes of the book, and our conversations underpin it in many ways. Niamh Puirséil, John Gray, Deaglán Ó Mocháin, Caoimhe Ní Chathail, Colm Ó Dóghair, Paul Kelly, Jonny Currie, Billy Mitchell RIP, Wes Forsythe, Catherine Mazs, Ian Falls, Bill Kirk and Fiona McShane. Thanks to Colum Ó Ruairc and Andrew Holmes for pointers with the research. Huge thanks to all at Reclaim the Enlightenment, Turas and Naíscoil na Seolta for allowing me to be a part of their worlds. Also to Brian O'Neill and all at Slugger O'Toole for giving me the push to write this. I am very grateful to Robbie McVeigh, Bill Rolston and Mike Tomlinson at Beyond the Pale Books for their wisdom and encouragement.

All my love and thanks to my ever-patient husband and children, who carry me, and who have visited enough graveyards to last a lifetime.

Beginnings

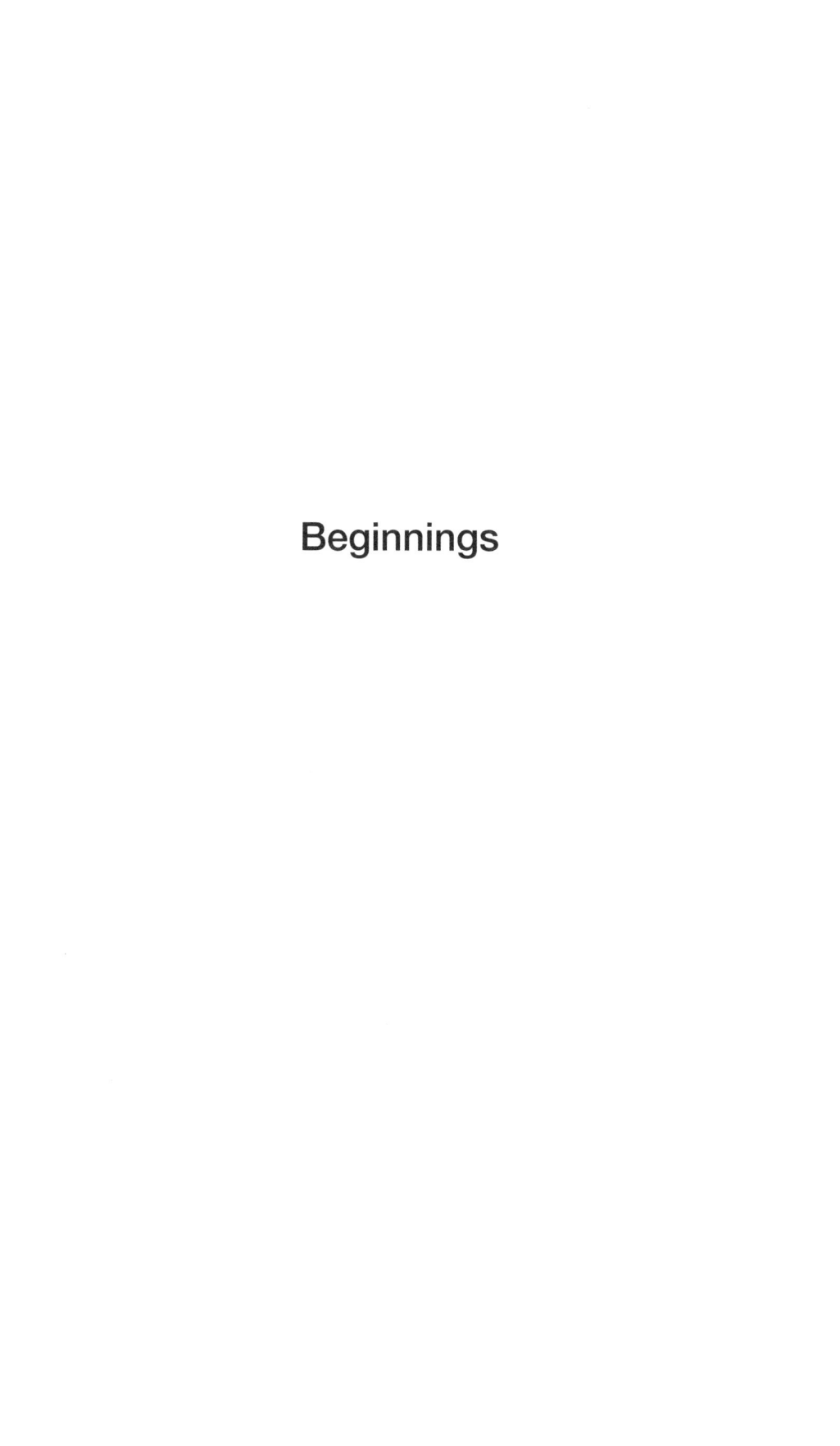

1

A County Down Bar

On a stone-cold night, late in 2019, the Strangford Green Party gather around a crackling pub fire in County Down. We'd done well in the recent election. In our strongly Protestant, unionist area, we'd proposed to our neighbours – 'what if we could do politics a different way?' And many agreed.

We are joined by friends from the town. The Guinness is flowing. A local Gaeltacht is jokingly established in broken Irish by a few of us Protestant learners and a Catholic Gaeilgeoir friend. We slur our Irish words out loud, in fits of laughter. Not trying to hide them, as we often do in the harsh light of day.

People drift in and out of the pub. Layers of coats pile up. The whiskey is out now. We huddle around the fire talking about what happened to radical Protestant politics in Northern Ireland. Amongst us are trade unionists, environmentalists, socialists. Many have been involved in northern politics for years, in the civil rights movement, the Labour Party and the Ecology Party. There is fond talk of activism in England, a place where the craft of resistance was learned. And eventually, as is so often the case these days, the chat veers to Irish unity. But not to nationalism. Instead, how a new Ireland might be shaped by activism, class analysis, environmentalism.

A guitar is produced from a back room. I am wondering what songs will be safe territory, as the pub is mixed along religious, class and every other line you can think of. Christy Moore is the answer that comes back. Galway girl. REM's 'Losing My Religion'.

An elderly Englishman from the Newcastle pits joins us. People propping up the bar begin to dance. Speeches are being made now in between tunes.

THE GHOST LIMB

About how certain songs are shared by all of us, but some of us have lost touch with our histories. Cheers go up. I look nervously around, but all is well. A Scottish woman sings a ballad in a voice so raw that it finishes us off. We end the night pledging to come and campaign with her in the next Scottish independence referendum.

Maybe you have these kind of nights all the time. But I've had few and far between in the North of Ireland, or in the South for that matter. And I've put the hours in.

It leaves me even more optimistic than usual that the radical heart of the Protestant north still beats.

And, you know, this is how it always happens. Ordinary people meeting in pubs and around kitchen tables, dreaming dreams and hatching plans. Throughout centuries, people like you and me quietly talking, singing, connecting, encountering one another's ideas. Deciding to be a bit braver. To say a bit more. Breaking down barriers. Until ideas build into waves that cannot be held back.

And then taking these ideas back out into the world. Turning them into actions. Having wider conversations. Listening to what comes back. Organising. Campaigning. Writing. Voting. Protesting. Changing what can be changed. Celebrating achievements back in the bar. Looping and repeating down through the generations.

Who sat on these bar stools 200, 20, two years ago, and what plans did they hatch?

We weave through time, us alternative Protestants, dissenters, misfits and radicals.[1] We've been at it for centuries. We haven't got the society we want yet. And so, we keep going.

---

[1] On the meaning of 'alternative Protestants', see footnote 6 on page 8.

2
The Ghost Limb

Where did the spirit of 1798 go? Did northern Protestants forget their history? Who are the keepers of the flame?

This book started as a quest to find the spirit of 1798 amongst 21st century northern Protestants. I wanted to know what became of the anti-sectarian passion that once loomed so large in Irish politics. That inspired the United Irishmen, creating bonds between Catholic, Protestant and Dissenter. I needed to find out if that radical spirit of brotherhood and sisterhood still existed today. To reconnect to an older history. To give myself hope that there's a destination beyond anger, where we can find the good in each other again.

And I found the spirit of 1798 in generous abundance. But, at some point, it became another kind of quest too. A personal exploration of an absence in my own identity. A ghost limb. A hidden compartment that I could not quite access. And I am not the same person as when I began.

I did not feel the ghost limb when I lived in Dublin. The dislocation happened when I moved back to Belfast. To the land of Lundy[2] and binary choice. Where you just are what you are. And by default, you cannot be what you are not. Tick the form, pick a side, or we'll pick it for you.

Northern Ireland is still a divided society. Many northern Protestants feel British and unionist. But some of us walk a different path. Umbilically tied to the island of Ireland. Back north, it feels precarious to be a Protestant who feels so culturally Irish. One foot in each camp. Trying to be whole as a person, while my heart and mind stretch across two sides of a divide.

---

[2] Robert Lundy was a Scottish, Protestant, British army officer who was city Governor at the beginning of the Siege of Derry in 1689. As King James' forces approached Derry, Lundy surrendered the city and fled.

THE GHOST LIMB

The words of Kerry writer, John Moriarty, follow me around: 'Out of a healed past a healed present will grow'. A portal in my imagination opens. Moriarty says, 'we need people who can live in our cultural Dreamtime, people who go walkabout, creatively within the old myths, people who go walkabout into the unknown' (1999: viii). As I read his words, I somehow know what I have to do. A ghost limb can't be healed by the wringing of hands. I must act.

'Ok', I reply silently to Moriarty's ghost, 'I will try it'.

I begin walking.

The Dreamtime that calls me is 1798. I pick up the worn paths of those who walked here before me. I am not the first to seek the wisdom of the United Irishmen, and I will not be the last. My gut tells me if I spend time with this history, it might help me understand the ghost limb. That I might be able to learn from northern Protestants who wrestled with all this before me. Who found healing in equality, fraternity and solidarity with their Catholic friends and fellow travellers on this island.

In search of the spirit of 1798, I visit every site I can find of the United Irish rebellion. Walk on the same cobbles the United Irishmen walked on. Lay my warm hands on their cool, damp headstones. But I know that I need to talk to the living as well as the dead, if I am to manifest hope.

So I ask my friends to start walking with me. Frosty walks, with flasks of tea and hiking boots. We travel through open fields, back alleys, cemeteries, golf courses and forests. Winter walks become spring walks, revelling in new life and birdsong. Summer walks, foraging for sorrel and dozing in the sun at Movilla Abbey. Autumn walks, mizzling rain sticking hair to our heads as we follow the breadcrumbs.

We are looking for clues in the landscape that might help us feel at home. That might tell us: 'you're not the first people here to feel this way. This place does have room for you.'

I have been walking like this for two years now. And as my friends and I search for the spirit of 1798, I begin to reconnect with my Protestant heritage. It bears little resemblance to the current PUL (Protestant-Unionist-Loyalist) amalgamation.[3] But nor is it an historical identity, pickled in a jar. It is modern

---

[3] The terms PUL (Protestant-Unionist-Loyalist) and CNR (Catholic-Nationalist-Republican) are relatively recent inventions. They first appeared in peace and reconciliation work and academia from the late 1990s, as people searched for alternatives to religious labels to describe

and immediate. Radical and future-facing. I feel like I am laying down new sediment on top of old. Because 'Protestant' has never been a static identity. It evolves over time. I can feel this evolution within my own self. And as I give myself permission to reimagine my belonging, I realise that the ghost limb has begun to ease.

* * *

Historian Guy Beiner writes about how the 1798 rebellion in Ulster has been disremembered.[4] How it is an historical moment that our binary northern politics has been unable to deal with.

In the 1790s in Ireland, Catholics, Protestants and Dissenters began to work together. They did not want to be governed by a remote British state, but dreamed of French Revolution-style liberty, equality and fraternity, here on this island. They rebelled in 1798 to gain self-rule. It was not successful.

The United Irish movement was far from perfect. But it means something to me that we tried. Because it demolishes the idea that there are 'two sides' of an inevitable divide.

The failure of 1798 left layers of trauma from which we never recovered. The rebellion was violent. It was even more violently suppressed. United Irishmen were imprisoned, executed and exiled. Homes and whole villages were burned to the ground. Some were never rebuilt. Amidst this chaos, the story of 1798 became hushed. People buried illegal mementoes of 1798 underground. They buried memories of 1798 within their own selves. Stories were whispered to family and friends. But publicly, people feared to speak of it.

---

communities. They were originally designed to show that there were variations, not uniformity, within ethnic axes. A broad and inclusive term where you could be P, U or L and still be meaningfully described as part of a particular community. Both terms began to be used in community relations evaluations from the 2000s, which needed to categorise participants so they could show that they were getting people of different traditions in the same room. The term PUL started to filter into internet usage and real life in the early 2010s. It was taken up by some unionist and loyalist groups as a self-description, sometimes used to over-claim representativeness and a communal coherence that does not exist. There was little uptake for the term CNR on the ground. Today the terms are still used as shorthand to describe community blocs. But they are highly contested, as they have come to be used in ways that lack nuance, failing to capture the everyday mixing and mingling between people from all backgrounds, and the overlap of categories.

[4] 'Disremember' is a specific word that is different to forgetting. Guy Beiner (2018: 30) draws on a range of sources to show that it was common in Ulster speech, implying a disinclination to remember, a sense of buying secrets which can only be excavated with some difficulty.

THE GHOST LIMB

Ever since 1798, anti-sectarian movements in Ireland, and specifically the north, have struggled for oxygen. Those wielding power have found sectarianism more useful. Wave the flag, stir the passions, get the votes. 1798 has been dismissed as an anomaly.

But it was not an anomaly. Relationships between Catholics and Protestants have always existed in this place, expanding and contracting according to political circumstances. Anti-sectarian politics have always existed. Northern Protestants' Irishness has always existed. But all of these things have been interrupted, sometimes deliberately erased, disremembered.

Because after partition, and during the Troubles in Northern Ireland, people started to define as one thing or the other. Identities became packaged up. Protestants began to detach from the idea of the island as a political entity. Radical northern Protestant traditions contracted. Dissenters dropped out of mainstream narratives.

Ironically the 1998 peace Agreement embedded this pattern. Our new system of government institutionalised Unionist and Nationalist identities, squeezing out other voices.[5] The labels PUL (Protestant-Unionist-Loyalist) and CNR (Catholic-Nationalist-Republican) were invented. Initially intended as diverse categories, they decayed into old simplicities, leaving little room for nuance, for identities that would not fit in a box. All of us were crunched through the sectarian machine. Our shared historical experiences shrank from view, while our differences were amplified.

Many northern Protestants walk around with this dissonance. We know that our lives are anti-sectarian. Many of us feel Irish. We prioritise class and equality above ethnicity and empire. But we cannot see this reflected in our politics. Many of us move through the world disjointedly. Censoring ourselves. Ill at ease.

The truth is that alternative Protestants often walk on eggshells.[6] Had one

---

[5] On the first day each newly-elected Northern Ireland Assembly meets, MLAs (Members of the Legislative Assembly) must designate themselves as Unionist or Nationalist to allow for cross-community voting on certain issues. Those who do not designate this way are considered to be 'Others'. Only those who are Unionist or Nationalist are counted for votes on Speakers, budgets, Standing Orders and are able to raise a Petition of Concern. The rise of the Alliance Party in recent years has highlighted the exclusion of Others from current governance arrangements.

[6] I have used the term 'alternative Protestants' throughout the book as a loose and broad way of describing people in Northern Ireland from a Protestant background who have politics that is not traditionally unionist or loyalist. It's an imprecise term, and one that I haven't seen used

yank too many of the Lundy leash.[7] For being traitors, betrayers, letting the side down. Sometimes experiencing pressure, threats or worse, on account of stepping outside traditional PUL boundaries. 'Who fears to speak of '98?' is a question many northern Protestants still ask in the 21st century.

But a silence that doesn't feel authentic can gnaw away at you. It can become the elephant in the room, to the point where the feeling keeps nagging you, reminding you that something is out of balance.

I came to feel this deeply in my own life. That there were things about my history as a northern Protestant that I had lost a connection with. My heart felt an absence. An Irishness that was awkward and incomplete. A homeless politics. But these existed as feelings. Like a ghost limb. It was not something that I was able to articulate.

When I read Beiner's book, I feel the ghost limb stir. I begin to understand how 1798, and all of the dissenting and radical Protestant histories that came before and after it, are links in a chain. I begin to wonder if my ghost limb could be the persistence of social memory. A politics that has always existed, but has often been silenced. And I wonder what would happen if I pulled on this thread. If it might connect me to my heart's stories?

* * *

I first heard of the United Irishmen when I was 20, when I took Tom Bartlett's class in University College Dublin. This history clicked with everything I understood about my life in the North. I was having too good a time to dwell on it. But it was an important breadcrumb in the long trail of my story.

As Beiner awakens my ghost limb more than 20 years later, I start to trace more breadcrumbs back through the course of my life, trying to get to the root of this feeling.

---

elsewhere. I initially planned to write about 'Dissenting Protestants', as a nod to 1798, but it became clear that this was an historical term with a specific theological meaning and would not be appropriate as a catch-all description (although I still use dissent in the sense of having opinions that differ from the norm). I use the term 'radical Protestants' most often in relation to the political left. While the term 'Protestant' is religious in origin, I use it loosely here, as very imperfect shorthand for people who share some aspects of a particular communal experience in the North, be that through churches, schools or family politics. The book explores language and labels in depth, so these terms are best seen as broad starting points.

[7] To be called a Lundy today implies that, like Governor Robert Lundy in Derry in 1689, one has betrayed the Protestant community. The Lundy leash is a phrase, originally coined by Colm Ó Dóghair, that describes the sense of a Protestant being pulled back into line by the PUL community.

Much of the trail leads back to my parents, whose politics were left-wing, pacifist and anti-colonial. They were not raised with these beliefs. But they developed them, as a response to the unfolding Troubles in Northern Ireland. We discussed politics daily at the dinner table. I watched my parents have difficult political conversations with wider family, and observed the contexts in which they learned to keep quiet.

Alternative politics led my family into the charismatic church. This was a religious movement straddling both Protestant evangelical and Catholic worlds in Ireland. While it was a theologically conservative space, my family gravitated to the hippies and boundary crossers that it also contained. Religiously, as well as politically, I was raised with the idea that 'Protestant' and 'Catholic' were human constructs. All that mattered was your relationship with God. I left the church in my teens, and my parents became Quakers. But that fusion of faith and anti-sectarianism that was central to 1798 was foundational in my life too.

The mixing. Another breadcrumb. No family in the North is homogenous. There were deep shades of Orange in our wider family. Orangemen and women, British soldiers, a UUP election agent, a B Special, RUC officers. Yet, both sides of our family had mixed marriages. Some families fell out because of the mixing. Others did not. I found a signed copy of the Ulster Solemn League and Covenant in my Protestant granny's Gaelic League Irish dancing book. These things sat together in my family history. Often in tension. Sometimes in silence. But my political consciousness was shaped by the melding of cultural traditions.

As I follow the trail of my Irishness backwards, I become painfully aware of early manifestations of the ghost limb. While my family was steeped in British left-wing politics, our cultural orientation was to the island of Ireland. Our passports were Irish. But I had few methods to express this identity. I sought out Irish history books, to fill in the gaps from school. Sometimes I walked to the local Catholic chapel and quietly lit a candle, wondering if it would somehow fuse a connection. I listened to Irish language radio, not understanding a word. I experienced my Irishness as a rich inner world. But it had no social scaffolds.

At 18, I crossed the Irish border for university. Living in Dublin for eight years cemented my feeling of this island as home. I studied politics, but mostly drank pints, went to gigs and enjoyed the lightness of my escape from a divided society. I could feel myself physically relax when I crossed the border south, and tighten when I crossed it back north. I don't know if I would have felt the ghost limb so deeply if I did not have this lightness to compare it to. Another breadcrumb on the trail.

I did my PhD on religion and politics in Northern Ireland in University College Dublin. My post-doctoral and early academic work was on evangelicalism. These experiences gave me a new affection for my northern Protestant tribe. More aware of its complexity. I felt so anchored within this tradition. But so deeply disturbed by the violent and oppressive elements within it, that I could not fully embrace it. So, I resigned myself to Otherness and Neitherness.[8] I thought this was my lot.

While I never intended to move back north, the Sociology Department in Queen's University Belfast offered me a lecturing job in the early 2000s and I took it. The sweet amnesia of Dublin ebbed away, and I was immediately thrown back into categorisation. Where I would live. Who my friends were. What bars to drink in and which taxis to get home. Finances and familiarity led me to Protestant east Belfast, streets away from my childhood church.

Soon after I moved home, Billy Mitchell from the Red Hand Commando – a loyalist paramilitary organisation – invited me to help document the group's transition from conflict to peace. David Ervine, and this wider project, were still very much alive then. While my personal politics were socialist, environmentalist and increasingly republican, I voted for the Progressive Unionist Party (PUP) during these years, because they were offering left-wing, feminist politics.[9] I also knew that political change happened at peace

---

[8] Living in Northern Ireland requires you to declare your religious background frequently, for example, for school applications, for equality monitoring in workplaces, or for peace-building schemes. Generally, you can be Catholic, Protestant or a variety of things which can end up being recategorised as Other. The term Neither is most commonly found in political and opinion surveys, for example the Northern Ireland Life and Times Survey, which often asks if a person is Nationalist, Unionist or Neither. In 2021, 38 per cent of respondents to this survey described themselves as Neither.

[9] The Progressive Unionist Party, PUP, was founded in 1979 and was linked to the UVF and the Red Hand Commando – loyalist paramilitary groups. The party was led by David Ervine between 2002-2007 and Dawn Purvis from 2007-2010. Both Ervine and Purvis were progressive socialists whose aim was to give working class Protestants political representation while steering loyalist paramilitaries away from violence. The PUP was one of the first political parties in the North to support reproductive rights. Since that time, the PUP has become more

walls, not glassy shopping malls.

My career came crashing down in the late 2000s when I picked up a virus that I never recovered from. My health was so ragged that I left the job I loved, to give my body a fighting chance. I slept and slept. Crawled up and down stairs. I battled with the benefits system and sold my sociology books on Ebay to buy food. Class politics cut to the bone.

My life was so culturally and religiously mixed by this point, that I may have been happy identifying as a former Protestant, Other and Neither for the long haul. But politics did not stand still. Brexit, and all the turmoil that came in its wake, changed me. I felt the democratic deficit press in heavily. I voted to Remain in the EU, but this did not drive me. I watched the UK become increasingly authoritarian and partisan. Careless of our delicate peace. My desire to reclaim my power as a citizen boiled and brewed. As I trace my ghost limb back in time, I understand this now as the moment of chrysalis.

After two babies and ten years out of work, my health began to improve a little. I tentatively began to write again about what I knew – Protestantism, faith, conflict and politics. It didn't take long to feel the yank of the Lundy leash. My home address, photos and phone numbers were put online by fringe loyalists, who encouraged people to call to my house and critique my writing. I locked the doors and windows tightly after that, hugging my small children inside.

I do not tell you this for sympathy, but to help explain the reflex to self-censorship. To highlight the modern mechanisms of Lundying, which every person in this book has experienced in one way or another. Unionists and loyalists experience it too, if they challenge the wrong person. In the end, I believe (although I do not know for sure) that it was the quiet words of loyalists who helped bring an end to it. Reaffirming what I already knew. That my tribe was various. Full of goodness as well as anger. In a strange way, this community gatekeeping helped me to articulate the ghost limb. I understood the processes of silencing more deeply.

And the stubborn Ulsterwoman in me kept writing.

As I slowly recovered small patches of health, my life broadened out in other ways. I joined the Green Party in Northern Ireland, which I found to be full of radicalism and diversity. I started attending an Irish language class. I made friends with my neighbours and discovered our shared interest of

---

conservative, and a significant number of loyalists continue to be involved in various forms of violence.

history. My friend Lisa and I started to take our kids heritage hoking after sunny school pick-ups to see what we could find. I felt so rooted in the landscapes of east Belfast and the Ards Peninsula. So thrilled with each fragment of radical history we stumbled upon, with each alternative story of belonging told. I collected them up like little treasures in a magpie's nest.

Until this point, I was wearing my Otherness and Neitherness defiantly. Two fingers up to our broken inheritance. But, I also found myself starting to ask, what is the soul of an identity which is a negation? To be defined by absence. I craved deeper roots. I wanted to restore belonging. To identify positively with my history, rather than opt out. I wondered if I was the only person to feel this way, or if others were also reaching for a different kind of connection.

I do not think I believe in God, or fate, or magic, although I am open to all three. I do believe that humans tell stories backwards. Starting from the present feeling, seeking sense in the past. But as I trace back the trail of breadcrumbs, I cannot help but feel a sense of things converging. There were so many echoes of 1798 in how my family, and I, had been living. So many traces of the United Irishmen in the landscape around me. It was as though my seeking willed a portal to open, which I stepped through without hesitation.

I met Bill Kirk, a documentary photographer from Newtownards, at a First Communion. The following week, I got a call from the local pub to say Bill had left a book there for me. It was Bill Wilsdon's *Sites of the 1798 Rising in Antrim and Down* (1997). Once again, encountering this history made direct contact with my gut. I began to work my way through Wilsdon's pages. The Belfast Entries. Clifton House. Betsy Gray's cottage. Movilla Abbey. Bangor Abbey. Greyabbey. Ballynahinch. Downpatrick.

As I visited the sites of 1798, I found that other people were on these trails too. A snowball of stories and connections began to form. My understanding of place began to shift dramatically. I have lived all my northern life in unionist majority areas, where identity is proclaimed loudly in red, white and blue. But, I realised, other histories exist here too. Right under my feet. Histories that make sense of my own story.

At some point, it dawned on me that I was not a free-floating member of a rootless tribe. I had been walking in the furrows of alternative Protestants all along. The P detached from the UL. Our lives fully intertwined with Catholics and all the people in our worlds as we found them. We were not members of any club. There was no weekly ritual, no uniform, no secret code by which we could recognise one another. There were no pikes being forged. No website designed.

But, I realised, we exist.

We exist and we are everywhere. We have stories to tell that aren't often heard. Stories that might be important for an island in a state of transition. Stories of alternative politics that may be healing in some way. Stories which take power away from the straitjackets of orange and green. Which unlock a tumbling, radical, dissenting Protestant history. And which give us back our power to define ourselves meaningfully as part of – not versus – one another.

I had finally found a way of being Protestant in the North of Ireland that I could relate to. I added '1798-style Dissenter' to my Twitter bio. I tentatively started to tick the Protestant box on paperwork. I still do not know if this is progress or regress. If it is a destination, or a rest stop on a longer journey. That defiant Otherness is still part of me. But I allowed myself to feel the pain of that Otherness. To walk towards reconnection with my heritage. And slowly, I began to feel more at home, both in my own skin and in the place where I lived.

The more I walked and talked with my friends, the more my synapses flickered. I began to feel like we should tell our story out loud, rather than nursing our ghost limbs alone. I proposed that we go on an intentional journey of thought and conversation together, roping in others for wisdom and inspiration along the way. To go walkabout in the Dreamtime. Puzzle through the questions that followed me around: what happened to the spirit of 1798? What is the ghost limb? Are diverse and dissenting Protestants something we might still be? Could answering these questions restore connection? Help build political change?

* * *

Mostly, this book is one of friendship. In its writing, I have walked and talked with old friends and new. I have learned songs and sung them with people. I've been to classes, bars, churches, kitchens, meetings, gigs, protests, main streets and back alleys. Walked a lot of dogs. I have listened to the wisdom of the school gate and the town sages. There's been a lot of laughing, some tears. I have celebrated Bastille Day like the United Irishmen before us. Conjured their ghosts and laid flowers on their graves. I've combed through a lifetime of stories from living in this place. Tuned into feelings, my own and those of others. I've written about matters of the heart as much as the intellect.

This book was mostly written during the global COVID-19 pandemic of 2020-22, with all the intensity and questioning that brought. We were all swept up in a global crisis, to which the solution was to stay at home. The upheaval outside my front door felt like a premonition – if it is acceptable to use magical language for a logical thought – of our future lives. How climate crisis may bind us to our island once again.

The COVID-19 pandemic itself became a lurking character in the book. Brexit too was lurking. Scotland was restless. The question of Irish unity was fomenting. Ulster unionism was in crisis. This forced me to face the sharp realities of future politics. To write into this moment with a strange, dogged urgency.

As we couldn't travel during this period, the pandemic also dictated the shape of the book. It forced the work outdoors. Mostly, I went for walks with people in locations that were meaningful to them. This brought an unexpected and lovely rootedness to the material. A clear sense of time and place. Occasionally, circumstances directed conversations online, or later, to a coffee shop. But most conversations took place walking through the counties of Down and Antrim. These locations were not something I planned. But, as these places were focal points for the 1798 United Irish rebellion, it seems serendipitous.

From the beginning of my research for this book, I carried chalk in my pocket. I started to leave a small mark, '1798', wherever I went. Sometimes I added 'We Exist'. Usually I did this in quiet, wild places. Out of sight. On a wall or a tree. Once I was caught chalkless in a Belfast alleyway and used an antacid. I scrawled 1798 on a Larne street overlooking the site where some of the first shots of the northern rebellion were fired. I didn't know why I was doing this at first. Other than it felt good to reclaim a tiny piece of space for this alternative story of dissent. As it turned out, breaking silences and reclaiming space would become a central theme in the book.

* * *

This book is stories and stories are not immovable truths. They are held in our minds, our families, our relationships and our current politics. This book is in no way an authoritative history of 1798. Nor a sociological study of a defined group. It is a journey of thought and identity. And it is simply the story that nagged me to tell it. It is for you to decide what feels authentic and what makes sense.

THE GHOST LIMB

My hope is that you will feel like you've had a night out where conversation and ideas open up in a way that you weren't even looking for. That you will feel like you have stepped inside a vibrant subculture that you perhaps didn't know existed, even if you are part of some strand of it. My hope is also that you might take some words into your own heart and help keep them safe, for we may have need of them in the future.

You can read this book as short stories, in whatever sequence you please. Most chapters tell the story of one person, with fragments of time and place woven through. Some chapters are my own stories.

You are invited to join the dots. Although some of the dots may not join. Some people in this book think differently to one another. This is not a story of an homogenous tribe. We change over time. We lose some things – for example, pikes. And we amplify other things – for example, women's voices. We change within our own selves over lifetimes. But for many people in this book, deeper values of solidarity, openness and island, prevail.

There is no way to thank the people in this book that could ever be big enough. Friends who have given generously of their lives to help tell this story. My own family, who raised me to dissent. All the black sheep and the boundary crossers whose shoulders we stand on. Dissenters in politics, faith, culture, language and activism. We hold each other up in friendship, radical empathy and hope.

All my life has been lived in this matrix of relationships. I have come to believe that these might be places in which the spirit of 1798 lives and breathes today. That all of the people in this book show us different ways to connect to an alternative Protestant heritage, should we want it.

Memory is a creative act. For most people, it is a construction of current identity. And so, this book is a personal restoration. One northern Protestant remembering, re-naming and celebrating their heritage. Exploring what this means in conversation with others. Gently pulling back the political undergrowth. Finding my way back to a tradition whose radical heart still beats.

This book is a chalk mark on a wall. To say, 'We Exist'.

So here we are. Telling stories about our resistance, our silences, our small braveries, our hopes for this island. Joining our voices to explore and understand the ghost limb. Perhaps even to receive healing.

3
1798

I spend half the time with my eyes closed, in imaginary conversation with ghosts. I like to run my fingertips along old stone walls. To lie in the grass and wonder who lay there before me. To converse in my mind with biological and spiritual ancestors. Telling myself stories about their lives. I spend the other half of my time with eyes wide open in the land of the living. A mass of heat and questions. I love conversation, easily flowing or awkwardly stuttered out. Stories stick to me like burrs. Connection matters. But I like walking beside people in silence and difference as well as communion.

The reason I tell you all this is to explain how I came to walk along this path. It is also to excuse myself from the expectation of being any kind of historian. I do not want the burden of it. While my academic training underpins me in many ways, this book is an act of conversation, curiosity, imagination, identity and story.

I will try in this chapter to tell you why 1798 matters so much to me. The ideas that shape my present tense so strongly. The people that I have come to love. I will try to do this with as much accuracy as possible. But my relationship to these histories is in the gut and the heart as well as the mind. It is better to think of me as a student and a learner. Someone who dwells in a broken present. Someone who dreams of a better future.

But these dreams must have something to root themselves into. So I will lay some core and crust.

* * *

For a comprehensive history of 1798, I would recommend reading everything John Gray has written, reading ATQ Stewart, Kevin Whelan, Daire Keogh, Nancy Curtin, David Dickson, Marianne Elliott, Thomas Packenham, Fergus Whelan, John Gibney, Tom Bartlett et al's collection of bi-centennial essays; reading Ian McBride and Andrew Holmes for the religious nuance; Jim Smyth for an analysis of social class; and the myriad of biographies that give depth and frailty to these people of myth and legend (for example, Thomas Bartlett, Kenneth L. Dawson, Mary McNeill and Fergus Whelan). Roger Courtney is an interesting read about a selection of Presbyterian reverends who have carried the flame over time.[10]

The handbook for how 1798 has been dis/remembered has been written by Guy Beiner. Beiner encourages us to look at a wider range of sources. From oral historians like Richard Madden to antiquarians such as Francis Joseph Bigger. He encourages us to look at vernacular histories in novels like Wesley Guard Lyttle's *Betsy Gray or Hearts of Down* and Samuel McSkimin's history of Carrickfergus. Some of these sources have been criticised for romanticism and/or bias. Whilst this is undoubtedly the case, my experience is also that these works contain local clues that often perform well in a 21st century fact-check. Clues that may otherwise have been lost.

For those starting from a blank canvas, here are some basic brushstrokes to help understand why this history carries so much meaning today.

Ireland in the 18th century was a not a good place to be a Catholic or a Dissenter. Dissenters were Protestants who refused to conform with the established Church of Ireland. Most commonly these were Presbyterians who had come from Scotland to Ireland during the Plantation of Ulster, or as Highland Clearance refugees, or seeking work.

The Penal Laws put belt and braces on Protestant ascendancy rule. Presbyterians were denied property rights, their marriages were illegal, their children were not recognised as legitimate, they were barred from all public offices. The Penal Laws were not quite as bad for Presbyterians as they were for Catholics. However, frustration brewed, especially as they looked to Scotland where Presbyterianism had itself become the established church.

---

[10] Full details of all these publications and others throughout the book are provided in the bibliography at the end.

Many Dissenters turned their hand to business and thrived in the new Belfast. But Irish trade was continually stunted by the English parliament, which did not appreciate the competition. Things loosened up with late 18th century reforms. But the Irish parliament was highly elitist, and always second fiddle to London. The Volunteers – a local militia – formed in 1778 to push for more local power, and won concessions. But the pace of reform could not keep up with demand.

Despite reforms, many Presbyterians continued to distrust authority. They were influenced by Enlightenment thinkers such as Francis Hutcheson who believed that political authority was based on the consent of the people. Exiled brethren in America cross-pollinated anti-colonial, democratic and revolutionary ideas. By the time of the French Revolution in 1789, many Dissenters had become radicalised, demanding a deeper kind of democratic representation.

Of course not all religious Dissenters were United Irishmen. One fifth of Presbyterian ministers (an equal number of liberals and conservatives) were implicated in the rebellion (McBride 1998: 232-4). And not all United Irishmen were Dissenters. Many were Catholics. Wolfe Tone was an Anglican. However, the spread of religious Dissent and United Irish politics are not separate historical moments. They grew around one other. Drawing from a common well of Enlightenment thought.

William Drennan, a doctor and son of a Belfast Presbyterian reverend, had been writing in the 1790s about how reform in Ireland could only be achieved by complete separation from England. Drennan was an Anglophile, married to an English Dissenter. But his analysis in the 1790s was that Ireland would have to detach from England to achieve real democracy.

At the same time, Dubliner Theobald Wolfe Tone was writing about Catholic Emancipation (Tone 1791). A cluster of former Volunteers began to meet secretly in pubs in the Belfast Entries in 1791. Tone suggested that they call themselves the Society of United Irishmen. Drennan wrote an oath, where members pledged to advance 'a brotherhood of affection, an identity of interests, a communion of rights and a union of power among Irishmen of all religious persuasions'.

Branches of the United Irishmen began to emerge in Dublin, Antrim, Down and across the island. The *Northern Star* newspaper was set up in Belfast, edited by Sam Neilson. Henry Joy McCracken and weaver James

Hope worked on the ground, ferrying messages between Belfast and Dublin. Relationships were formed with the Defenders, a Catholic agrarian society. Thomas Russell from Cork was a key recruiter. Wolfe Tone focused on roping in French support. Things were starting to come together.

Belfast was buzzing with radical thought during these years. Tom Paine's *The Rights of Man* was said to be the Koran of Belfast (Gray 2017: 4). Fergus Whelan tells us how in 1792 many windows in Belfast were lit up to celebrate the French Revolution using transparencies – paper cut-outs with a light behind – shining over the dark streets with slogans such as '*Vive la République*', 'Church and State separated' and 'Union amongst Irishmen' (Whelan 2020: 102). I love to imagine a dark unlit city, these messages radiating light from the houses.

The next year, the French Revolution took a chaotic turn. The Irish parliament moved quickly to offer some reforms to middle-class Catholics, while suppressing the Volunteers and building their own state militia. Some of the gradualist reformers took the hint. But the radicals decided to go the other way. By the time the Society of United Irishmen was banned in 1794, momentum had built to overthrow the establishment.

Arrests and exile ensued. Sectarian violence simmered. Guy Beiner (2018: 46-88) calls this period 'pre-forgetting' – the state's attempt to shut the idea down before it even got going. But it was not fully effective. By 1797, the government estimated there were 117,917 United Irish members in Ulster (Curtin 1985: 125). And an estimated 280,000 island-wide (Holmes 2018: 135).

Rebellion finally broke out on 23rd May 1798 in Dublin, and was easily quashed. Later that month, there was another attempt in Wexford, accompanied by sectarian violence at Scullabogue.[11] On 7th June 1798, and despite French support not materialising, the northerners went for it, full revolution, based on the original non-sectarian principles. Some areas in Down and Antrim were held for a time, but within a week, the rebellion had been put down. Wexford was lost on Vinegar Hill at the end of June. The French made it to Mayo in August, but they were beaten back in Longford in

---

[11] At least 100 people were burned in a barn at Scullabogue, most of them Protestants, an event which has become known as the primary rebel atrocity. As usual, things were not black and white. Around 20 of those burned were loyalist Catholics, and three of the 17 rebel guards charged were Protestants. See Gahan 1996.

September. Robert Emmet tried to relaunch the rebellion in 1803, but it was quickly suppressed.

* * *

The crackdown on the United Irishmen came fast and hard. It was particularly brutal in the north (Pakenham 1997: 284). Public hangings. Heads on spikes in town squares, hair blowing in the wind. Deliberately cruel punishments, like the hanging of Rev. James Porter outside his own Presbyterian church in Greyabbey. Some luckier souls, whose family had connections or money, were banished instead, draining Ulster of its radical thinkers (Beiner 2018: 123). Houses and villages were burned. Some were never rebuilt. Killings and floggings were routine, reaching people who had just tangential connections to the rebels. Beiner says even 'poets had to be constantly on their guard' as book clubs and literary societies became suspect' (2018: 179).

This suppression by terror was effective. Within a short space of time, some former rebels had joined the Orange Order or state forces (although were never fully trusted). Signatures of loyalty were collected from Catholics as well as Dissenters (Beiner 2018: 96). Amnesty in return for amnesia. Beiner (2018: 17) calls this 'wilful forgetting'.

But the state could not fully suppress the memory of 1798. Some United Irishmen became outlaws. Some working class members joined the mainly Catholic agrarian Defenders. Plenty more held on to their anti-sectarian ideals, but they talked about their ideas more quietly now. Dates were tweaked on gravestones to hide the truth. Identifying details were often concealed in memoirs.

Even amongst those who had not supported the rebellion, there was often a level of respect and sympathy for those who had. There was widespread resentment towards the brutality of the crackdown. Many families quietly held on to heirlooms, mementoes and relics of the rebellion. I meet many people today who have kept these objects safe. 1798 loomed large in folk memory, if not official history.

Over the centuries, as many people would lay claim to 1798 as would deny it. Its commemoration became popular with Catholic nationalists, which aggrieved some Protestant unionists who felt the nationalist version was a misrepresentation. At other points, unionists claimed the United Irishmen as misguided brethren. Memorials were cyclically erected, contested, destroyed, replaced. A cycle which continues still.

It's in this context that 'The Memory of the Dead', a poem and song about 1798, was published by the nationalist newspaper, *The Nation*, in 1843.

> Who fears to speak of Ninety-Eight
> Who blushes at the name?
> When cowards mock the patriot's fate,
> Who hangs his head in shame?

It was published anonymously. While it is a call to speak of '98, it also gets to the heart of the silence. The author, a Protestant scholar John Kells Ingram (1900: 253), only put his own name to it in 1900, having previously feared for the safety of his children.

All this fear. All this silence. You wouldn't be long developing a ghost limb.

* * *

But don't we have enough battles in Ireland already? Is that not precisely our problem? What does it add to the future to incorporate another historical rebellion into our sense of selves?

What 1798 means in this part of Ireland is so much more than rebellion *per se*. In Eamon McMahon's words, the rebellion was 'only one expression – albeit the most militant – of a broader evolution of critical social thought' (2017: 17). And it's these ideas that linger. The hopefulness of this anti-sectarian moment. The porousness of the binary. The call for deeper democracy. The religious freedom. The resistance to being controlled by a remote state with other priorities. 1798 was scaffolded by brilliant men and women who lived radical lives both before and after the rebellion. And, for me, that's where the heart of this historical moment beats.

But there's a trap in there as well.

Marianne Elliott writes in the new forward to Mary McNeill's (2019: xi) biography of Mary Ann McCracken, that 'it is easy to romanticise the 1790s – long seen as one of the great might-have-beens of Irish history'. She is right to warn us.

Some years ago, a very good friend, Wes Forsythe, lent me some books about 1798. As he handed them over, he offered me a similar word of caution:

> This is good stuff. But don't get sucked down a rabbit hole. It's a well-worn path. I've seen too many lose the run of themselves.

Wes' words constantly travel with me as I navigate my pilgrimages to the 1798 sites. He forced me to ask, what is relevant and important about this now? What is romanticism? What is cliché?

Guy Beiner's work is just as much about starry eyed co-option of 1798 as it is the silencing of it. It's a moment that has been suppressed, denied, whitewashed, customised, shoe-horned. None of us should claim to be its true heirs.

But the ghost limb grumbles on. Ignoring this history is not an option for me. I need the wisdom and the hope of it. What I can do though is mine a little deeper into what this history means to many of us. Eyes wide open as possible. Resisting seduction. In the knowledge that some of the truth of it ultimately may evade us. And that all history is a retelling shaped in the present moment.

4

The Dreamtime

No tradition should ever be pickled in time. Cultures are living, breathing organisms which must be allowed to adapt and grow. We do not need to take everything from the past with us into the 21st century. We must give ourselves permission to explore this history, to see what still makes sense, what is useful for now, so we can bring the very best of it into the future.

So far I have laid out the bare facts of 1798 as I find them. I will keep grasping for accuracy. But journeys through time come with feelings too. Heart and gut strapped in for the ride.

As I write, things are chaotic with the pandemic. A haze of a new virus variant fills the air. Infection and vaccine surge through my body. John Moriarty's *Dreamtime* sits on my bedside table. The swirliness of each thing meets the other. Moriarty's *Dreamtime* is based on the aboriginal concept of *altjeringa*, when the world was dreamed into being. It's a headspace that Moriarty visits in the book, seeking wisdom in folklore, spirituality and the Otherworld. He likens it to an aisling, an Irish poetic tradition that speaks of a vision or dream-vision. Manchán Magan (2020) finds enlightenment in a similar way, allowing himself to see the scim, the veil between worlds, as he communes with lost Irish words.

These methods do not quite feel accessible to me. I am no Celtic bard. I am an unemployed sociologist at the school gate. But yet I find myself drawn into the possibilities that these writers offer.

What I take from their work is that there are stories beneath the stories. Meanings inside the silences that we have formed. That dreaming can help construct reality. They encourage me to think about time as cyclical, where ideas loop around. The past in the present. This makes sense to me.

THE GHOST LIMB

I will try to meet these visionaries half way. I will go walkabout in the 1798 Dreamtime. Try to navigate this history with heart and imagination.

* * *

The pikes. The pikes were made by local blacksmiths in small forges. They were no match for the fully kitted out British military. In many ways, pikes are a symbol of the resistance of the oppressed. Hand hammered tools of impossible hope. But people were also killed with those pikes. It was not an even match. Kevin Whelan (1998: 55) estimates that 30,000 died during the rebellion, 28,000 of whom were on the side of the rebels. Many more were conscripted, exiled and banished to penal colonies. The state used its power brutally, without restraint. Yet, I have an unsettled relationship with the pikes. Teenagers should not have to die to make things right.

My friend Will sends me a screenshot from Madden's book, about a pub near my house that was burned down by the military on account of a rumour that a United Irishman had a drink there. Taking the United Irish oath was made punishable by death in 1796. I think of the pub we have our Green Party meetings in. If this was the 1790s, the pub could be burned and we could be killed. And what do you do if that keeps happening?

The United Irishmen lived in a context of extreme persecution. They had limited means of achieving change. But I was raised as a pacifist, and that blood runs deep.

I try to imagine myself in the 1790s, in a deeply anti-democratic state. With no rights as a citizen. Land confiscated. Barred from many aspects of life, my language denied, my religion persecuted. Reform was on the way, but could my family wait? There can also be a violence in waiting too long. People die from that too. Would my thoughts be different if I was a man or a woman, rich or poor? I suspect some versions of me would have lifted a pike. But my imagination strains.

What I can see with clearer eyes, is that 1798 did not succeed. The failure of the rebellion, and the brutality of its suppression, enabled conservative and sectarian politics for generations. It drove the ideas underground. Nearly all those who write about this period acknowledge that the 1798 rebellion was not a happy beginning for Irish republicanism. Violence can slow progress down as well as speed it up. Violence spirals. It spills down generations. We carry the trauma around centuries later in our bodies and minds.

THE DREAMTIME

21st century Ireland is a different context and time than the 1790s. We have access to politics in ways our antecedents never did. I have a 1798 commemorative badge with an image of crossed pikes. I wear it often. But I have made my own badges now, and have replaced the pikes with crossed pens. We live in troubled times globally. It may be unwise to ink out lines that may not make sense in the future. But the pen is where my own heart lies. I believe in the power of stories.

* * *

When I think of 1798, I feel waves of testosterone wash over me. All those stories of vivid, drunken nights, making resolutions, swearing oaths. I want to go to the pub in the 1790s and make resolutions too. Stand on my chair toasting the oath, beer spilling from my tankard. But I am unsure if a woman is allowed in the pub. And I wonder who will mind my kids.

History is good at celebrating battles and balls. But it's not necessarily the men's history that defines this moment. When I think of the 1790s, I think of women like Martha Drennan and Mary Ann McCracken. As a woman reading this history, I find them no less radical than my 21st century sisters. It's these women I want to fall into step beside.

Martha 'Matty' Drennan is one of my favourites. She's often remembered as the wife of leading Belfast United Irishman, Sam McTier. Matty's letters to her famous brother, William Drennan, show what a fine thing her mind was (see Agnew 1998). Directing action by planting ideas. In a painting, she wears a loose white shirt and headband over brown curls. She looks unpinned with a glint in her eye.

Which is possibly why Matty worked the way she did. Boldly and radically. Advocating for women's health, helping establish a maternity hospital in Belfast, arguing for the admission of unmarried mothers and prostitutes (Agnew 1998, vol. 1: 115). She ran a school in her home for local girls who could not otherwise afford an education. A pioneer of women's rights, working on issues that still have not dated. I think of my foremothers who got lost or in trouble, who had husbands who legged it. I will their paths to cross with Matty's.

John Gray (2020: 2) talks about Mary Ann McCracken as 'a revolutionary [...] as a feminist before the term was invented, and as a social reformer'. He says that Mary Ann McCracken pushed the boundaries of what was possible for women to do in male-run organisations. The bronze statue of Mary Ann

McCracken planned for Belfast City Hall will depict her handing out anti-slavery literature at the docks, something she did into her eighties.

Mary McNeill's biography underlines Mary Ann's radical empathy. Things she fought for at Belfast's Poor House (Clifton House) included: soap, skipping ropes, candles to read at night, girls' education, trips, play, good quality jobs, window blinds for patients in full sun, milk – as buttermilk was too acidic for the kids' stomachs (McNeill 2019: 249). She fought for human dignity. She had a strong Presbyterian faith, but none of her work came with religious strings attached. I imagine myself in Clifton House, having a candle where I hadn't one before. Remembering when my own babies had acid reflux.

Walking through the Dreamtime is not a romance. It's blood and bone. It would be ahistorical to separate out the women's good works and contrast these to the men's violence. Most of these women supported the rebellion. Many women ferried arms, spied and fought – Molly Weston, Suzy Toole, Betsy Gray, Rose Mullan. But honing in on the range of women's ideas and work deepens my understanding of this political moment. It gives me another way to think about 1798. It makes me interrogate what is revolutionary.

* * *

There's a display of objects from Betsy Gray's cottage in the North Down Museum in Bangor. Betsy Gray was a United Irishwoman from Six Roads Ends in County Down. She fought and was killed in 1798 at the Battle of Ballynahinch. The display contains a metal plate, a cut wine glass, a little metal sugar bowl and dainty sugar tongs. These domestic objects help me visualise Betsy Gray's social class. Neither tremendously rich, nor tremendously poor.

As I sip from mug after mug of tea, I imagine how United Irishmen and women took theirs. What it might tell me about how wealth, poverty and class shaped their politics. How many had servants make their tea? How many boiled the leaves hard, to take the edge off their hunger? How many saved up for a fancy revolutionary teapot or a little pair of sugar tongs? How many followed Mary Ann McCracken's example and boycotted sugar as the product of slavery?

A lot of leading figures in the United Irish movement were Presbyterian entrepreneurs, conservative in their politics, driven by business concerns. The impulse of some of the wealthy United Irishmen was to resist social change;

the *Northern Star* newspaper warned against early unionisation of workers and calls for higher wages (Gray 2018a: 11).

James Hope, a leading United Irishman and weaver, was incredibly critical of this conservative impulse. He told Madden:

> None of our leaders seemed to me perfectly acquainted with the main cause of social derangement [...] except Neilson, McCracken, Russel[l] and Emmet. It was my settled opinion that the condition of the labouring class was the fundamental question at issue between the rulers and the people, and that there could be no solid foundation for liberty [until] the right of deriving a subsistence from the soil on which their labour they expended. (Madden 1842: 242)

Hope felt that the milder reformers were simply commercial and aristocratic interests determining which set of people, British or Irish, they could prey on. The parallels with James Connolly's analysis in 1916 are striking. Later, John Hewitt called on the socialists of Ulster to celebrate James Hope, as a pre-Marx Marxist (in Clyde 1987: 133-7).

Hope was far from alone. John Gray (2018a: 6) shows how the *sans culottes* – weavers and artisans, bricklayers and carpenters – were pressing forward from below in the early 1790s. Early trade unions, calls for fair wages, withdrawal of labour and tenants' rights concerns impacted the evolution of the movement. Breandán Ó Buachalla (2003) says that the Gaelic poetry of the time captures the unrest from below that helped fuel political mobilisation. Carol Baraniuk (2019) highlights a passion for social fairness in United Irishman James Orr's Ulster Scots poetry. Nancy Curtin (1985: 468) talks about the United Irishmen's overlap with the Jacobin Clubs, politically radical places, where mechanics, petty shopkeepers and farmers worked beside merchants. These kinds of combinations were unprecedented at the time.

I've not been able to trace any line of my family back to the 1790s. But I have two young girls of eight and nine sewing muslin in County Antrim in 1859. Generations of my family hackled flax and wound bobbins in the Belfast textile industry, made shoes and stitched clothes. I do not find it a stretch to believe that some of their great/great/great grandparents would have been drawn to the most viable method of achieving change in working conditions at the time.

The 1790s were a jumbled period. Ideas were being worked out as people went along. It seems wise to sit with these multiple stories. There were kernels of early socialist radicalism in the United Irishmen. There were kernels of deep conservatism. And much in between. But that is ok. We are not a re-enactment society. We are not bound by the past. We are just walking in the Dreamtime, drinking tea, looking for stories, seeking wisdom.

* * *

The 1790s were an extraordinary moment of anti-sectarian togetherness. But all of the groups I am part of today are held together imperfectly, with internal tensions. The United Irishmen were no different.

Many people tell me that their favourite thing about 1798 is that it was a secular rebellion. But some of the leaders of the northern United Irishmen were extremely religiously conservative (Roulston 2008: 90-8). Many were incredibly hostile towards the Catholic Church. Historian Andrew Holmes (2018: 135) asks the difficult question: did some Dissenters actually see the 1798 rebellion as a way to usher in their version of theocracy? And the same question can be applied to the Catholic Defenders. Awkwardly, I think that some may have done.

I do not put Belfast Presbyterian William Drennan in this category, but he troubles me. For William, opposition to the Catholic Church spilled over into ideas about Catholics themselves. I cannot imagine ever liking a man who could write that Newry was full of 'pigs and papists' (quoted in Whelan 2020: 50). Fergus Whelan unpicks the knot, showing how Drennan was opposed to all hierarchies – Catholic, Anglican and Orange. How Drennan became an advocate for Catholic rights to vote and bear arms, later making consistent alliances with Catholic radicals. A man on a journey. But I still would not want to go to his dinner parties.

United Irish Catholic priest, Father James Coigly (1798), gives me a similar feeling. Despite finding United Irish Dissenters enlightened, and being an important persuader for cross-community unity in the run-up to 1798, Coigly distinguishes his own ancestry of ancient Irish tribes from those who were descended from plundering settlers. I feel Coigly might be the type to post disdainful late-night comments about Planters on Twitter, deleting them the next day.

What should we do with such anti-Catholicism, such ethno-nationalism? I pick these things up and acknowledge them. Then place them back down again. They are of no use to me.

Because there are other things in the 1798 Dreamtime that bring my soul alive. No amount of caveats remove the power of the fact that United Irishmen and women radically challenged sectarianism. They formed real, lasting and deep friendships across religious divides. Knowing this is like a balm rubbed into my ghost limb.

Wolfe Tone, a Dublin Anglican, argued for Catholic emancipation from the beginning (Tone 1791: 7). I imagine hearing these words in 1791, sharply intaking my breath:

> I am a Protestant of the Church of Ireland, as by law established, and have again and again taken all the customary oaths by which we secure and appropriate to ourselves all degrees and professions, save one, to the utter exclusion of our Catholic Brethren. I am, therefore, no further interested in the event, than as a mere lover of justice, and a steady detester of tyranny, whether exercised by one man or one million.

In modern terms, Tone is identifying his own privilege and calling for equal rights. It is sometimes hard to locate this sentiment in the 2020s, never mind 1791.

And it was not just words. The Volunteers had been working together across religious divides for many years. Jim Smyth (1993) shows how the United Irishmen and the mainly Catholic agrarian Defenders worked together throughout the 1790s, minds often meeting on socio-economic grievances. A Masonic element to the United Irishmen facilitated social mixing between Catholics and Protestants. The women's committees Mary Ann McCracken was involved with, from education to famine relief, were deeply and deliberately non-sectarian (Gray 2020: 28-9). Even William Drennan's coffin was carried by six Protestants and six Catholics, with people from all social classes attending the funeral (Whelan 2020: 283). I like this tangled redemption.

The United Irishmen generated an anti-sectarian momentum that shattered social norms at the time. A momentum which I don't think we ever regained. However, it created so many lines that can be traced to the present. Cross-community activism in the Fenian Society, the Gaelic League, the civil rights movement, trade unions, reconciliation work during the Troubles. Ideas looping through time. Links in a long historical chain. A trail of breadcrumbs that we can choose to follow.

* * *

THE GHOST LIMB

Wolfe Tone says something else that gets to me (Tone 1791: 9). That Ireland being ruled by England feels like an amputated right hand. None of this subtle ghost limb stuff. Tone is describing the abject sense of powerlessness that comes from not having democratic control over your own life. Most days in Northern Ireland, I feel like this too.

The United Irish goal was to bring deeper democracy to citizens. Most United Irishmen were not nationalists in any ethnic sense. They were republicans – against divine right, monarchy, empire and colony, and in favour of citizens' rights to govern themselves. They were deeply in tune with democratic thinking in France, America, Scotland and England. Outward looking internationalists.

The vocabulary is too modern, but to me, many United Irishmen were early anti-racists. They had a sense of global ethics, which is clearly seen in their opposition to slavery. In 1791, Belfast Presbyterian United Irishman and watch-maker, Thomas McCabe, invited freed slave and author Olaudah Equiano to Ireland to give public talks. Equiano stayed with the *Northern Star's* editor Samuel Neilson, and his book sold well in radical Belfast (*Belfast Telegraph* June 2020). I picture Mary Ann McCracken today, handing out leaflets outside Larne House detention centre, demanding a humane asylum system. Matching refugees with spare rooms across the city.

Of course not all United Irishmen live up to my expectations. Some became rich on the spoils of the British Empire. While slave ships never docked in Belfast, much of the wealth of the city was built on slavery (Rodgers 2007). United Irishman, William Tennant, for example, was a sugar merchant. I acknowledge the contradiction. But I am not bound by Tennant or his friends. Such knowledge stops romanticism. But it does not stop me channelling the radicalism of Thomas McCabe, Samuel Neilson and Mary Ann McCracken.

The United Irishmen's anti-colonial values spoke to local issues as well as global. As I write, friends are organising an event to mark the 230th anniversary of the 1792 Belfast Harper's Assembly. In the planning of the new event, I am transported to the 1790s. I imagine Edward Bunting gathering harpers, most of them blind, to play in the Assembly Rooms in order to annotate and preserve the music. I laugh out loud when I think how Wolfe Tone hated the music, possibly due to a hangover. But what lingers with me, is that many Protestants in the United Irish orbit deliberately made space to celebrate the subordinated, Irish, culture. In the context of colonial power relations, this solidarity is compelling. This is why the Irish language movement is so important to me in the 2020s. I think reparations have still not been made.

But there is a puzzle here. Because as anti-imperial as the United Irishmen were, after the Act of Union between Britain and Ireland was passed in 1800, many worked within the new political context to achieve the reforms they wanted. Was this a blunting of their radicalism? A pragmatic realism? Or did they have a set of values that are not attached to a nation-state per se? A lot of former United Irishmen continued to be anti-imperial and anti-colonial, for example in opposing the Boer War. But maximum democracy and social reform is what they were after. And many took different opinions on where this might be achieved, depending on the political moment.

The United Irish analysis in the 1790s, and mine now, is that politics on this island offers us the best chance of realising these values. During the COVID-19 pandemic, Northern Ireland was bound by the purse strings and policies of London. The DUP did not try to hide this, and I am shocked to hear them confess the amputated right hand so bluntly.

And so, Irish reunification, in some shape or form, has always made sense to me. Bigger fish, smaller pond. Republic not monarchy. Leaving a state which is constitutionally rooted in empire and feudalism for a state that at least attempted to be a people's republic. For some this is self-evident to the point of being non-negotiable. For others it is too romantic, given how conservative the Irish Free State became, and can still be. But it does not stop me dreaming of a Second Republic, with a new constitution, re-made by all on the island today.

Whatever the constitutional arrangement, there's something deeper here to be learned. Entry to the United Irish project, dishonourable exceptions aside, was never based on DNA. Most United Irishmen were about fictive kinship. A set of values that they opted into. A brotherhood and sisterhood of all fellow travellers who found themselves here, sharing this island. How could you not have this analysis, if you'd just sailed in from the Straits of Moyle?

Of all the ideas washing around the 1798 Dreamtime, I'm drawn to this the most. It feels like a magic key. When I hold the quality of democracy and the power of citizens at the front of my mind, my compass is set. It is my guiding star, against which I evaluate all my prejudices, ideas, fears and feelings. I do not care whoever has laid claim to this soil. Viking, Celt, Planter or modern migrant. All who find themselves here are us. The question is how can people here thrive? I slip this magic key in my pocket and take it with me.

* * *

Is it any wonder then, the ghost limb? The absent feeling? For a northern Protestant like me, who dreams of a better politics. Walking around with all of these ideas underfoot. Ideas that live below the ground. Feeling their tremors. Sensing their pull. But not quite being able to make out their features. Seeing so little of them in our governance.

Yet, here they are. Mary Ann, Matty, James, Henry Joy. Believing in the things that I believe in. Living their lives in pursuit of these ideas, centuries ago. Walking in the same streets I walk through today. Running their fingertips along these same walls. Imperfect radicals. Flawed, like all of us. In a movement that had internal contradictions. With a project that failed. But who filled this place up with radical empathy and hope.

And I think of all those who have retraced their steps before me. The folklorists, the writers, the poets, the descendants, the exiles. All of the people since 1798 who have stood on their shoulders. With ideas that are often subterranean. Seldom spoken without consequence. The land reformers and tenants' rights advocates, the Christian socialists, suffragettes and trade unionists, the anti-poverty and equality campaigners, the Irish language preservationists, the Ulster Scots free-thinkers, the New Ireland movement, the hippies and the peace-makers.

Links in a chain between then and now. And when I think of these people, I feel somehow connected to the chain. Ideas looping through time. I think maybe I am not so alone in my difference. I know that there must be others out there too.

And this is how it began. The walking and the talking. The thinking and dreaming. As I set out to search for the spirit of 1798 today.

5

How to Find a Spirit

How do you find an historical spirit? I did not know at first. I spent a long time retracing the steps of the United Irishmen, wandering around graveyards, reading history books. I learned a lot, but not much about the present. I needed to talk to the living, if I was to truly unlock these lost social memories. So I decided to talk to my friends about the different ways they were living their lives as Protestants outside the traditional PUL package. I contacted some other people, whose work or voice inspired me, to see if they could help untangle this journey of thought. To explore how they connected heritage to present and future.

Not all of the people in the following pages spend their time thinking about the United Irishmen. Most of them are normal people who do not try to commune with radical ancestors (although a disproportionate amount of them do). Not all feel the ghost limb. I realised it would be a very slim book if I was to go around asking people what they thought about politics in the 1790s or an imaginary limb. Instead, I felt that answers might emerge if we just talked about our lives. I did not ask everyone in this book the same questions. Sometimes I barely asked any questions. I just told people loosely what the book was about, and asked if they might have a story to share. Most chapters that follow are simply someone's story on their own terms.

People talked to me about who they were. Who had inspired them. Their relationships. Their sense of self and place in the North. Their hopes for the future. Often, 1798 came up naturally and where it did, we explored it. But some of the chapters that follow do not reference 1798 as an historical event. Sometimes people would laugh with me, asking what on earth their story had to do with the United Irishmen. But, to my mind everyone in this book embodies the values and energy of that moment in one way or another. Sometimes I saw this in people's political ideas. Often, it was the way they refused to live lives hemmed in by sectarian divides. Always, it was a disposition to question the way things are and a fearlessness about doing things their own way.

My hunch was that the spirit of 1798 might be found in the following places: amongst people who love history and heritage; in the contemporary language movements – both Irish and Ulster Scots; in faith communities and churches; in the nooks and crannies of activism and politics. Most of these are overlapping worlds that I am, or have been, part of. So I knew intuitively who I wanted to speak to, although I did not know what they might choose to tell me. The chapters are grouped into loose sections, each spending time in one part of the alternative Protestant ecosystem.

All of the stories are told by people who live in Protestant majority areas, east of the Bann in Northern Ireland. In a different moment in time, I would have talked to Protestants west of the Bann too, to see what experiences were shared and what differed. I initially planned to talk to southern Protestants, but COVID-19 made travel difficult. This omission weighs on me, especially given the all-island nature of United Irish politics. But I know there is also value in honing in on the depth of a particular experience, and a realism in recognising how deeply northern Protestants have been shaped by partition.

Most conversations in the book took place on long walks through Down and Antrim. Some were told over WhatsApp messages or Zoom calls, whatever means we could find to connect as the COVID-19 pandemic surged and receded. Nearly all were a part of a much longer conversation, before and after the interview, sometimes lasting many years. Lots of the ideas in the book came from late night DMs, tipsy WhatsApps, bleary-eyed school pickups, hectic playdates, forest walks, history events, tours and classes, political meetings, chats in the kitchen, the town square and pub. The book is deeply embedded in living my life as a modern dissenting Protestant, rather than deciding to do a study about it.

The fact that all of the people in this book were so immediate to me, socially and geographically, is interesting to consider. I am a poor networker. I have a hidden disability and love being at home. Yet it was not difficult to find people to participate. This makes me wonder if this book could be written many times over, with many different voices. If alternative Protestant stories were so accessible to me, they are likely to be accessible to other people too.

All participants in the book were offered anonymity, and nobody took it. Everyone read their story before publication, adding and taking away things until it felt authentic. Some of these stories are very personal, others follow a train of thought, or describe a set of specific experiences. I just went with whatever people felt comfortable talking about. Some of my own stories are here too.

Everyone I talked to gave me a jigsaw piece. A few years after I had begun to search for the spirit of 1798, I knew that I had found it. I started to slot the jigsaw pieces together. I understood that while we may lose words for a history, the memories of it often linger. Many of us walk in the United Irishmen's furrows without realising. Because ideas have been passed down through the generations. Somehow we absorb them, through family (or disagreement with family), through books, language, liturgy and landscape, through stories, conversation and song. Sometimes the ideas come naturally to people as a logical and humane response to our age-old problems. As I digested what my friends shared with me, the ghost limb began to ease.

Something I was not expecting before I set out was to find such a diverse community of people who were actively following the trail of historical breadcrumbs. As I was writing this book, a 1798 walking tour was established in Belfast. A Betsy Gray café opened in Six Road Ends. A 1798 play was staged in the Belfast Entries. We celebrated Bastille Day in St Joe's in Sailortown. We laid wreaths to mark William Orr's hanging. There was a celebration of Mary Ann McCracken's life in Clifton House. A Mary Ann walking tour was launched. I would learn later that these are just the most recent iterations of local people seeking out these conversations.[12] It was just my time to stumble upon them.

And this is where the book begins. With historical adventures and adventurers. People who, in their own ways, are channelling the spirit of 1798. Consciously engaging with these histories to see what we can learn about the present.

---

[12] Guy Beiner (2018: 538-603) charts the extent of activity in the 21st century. Peter Collins (2004) has provided a detailed account of bicentenary activities in 1998.

Hidden Histories

This section of the book is directly concerned with the remembrance, and disremembrance, of 1798. We take a tour of the Battle of Antrim, where we see a variety of people struggle to make sense of one another, and work out how to share this history. Stephen McCracken talks about how religion and politics fractured his family, yet his 1798 ancestors inspire his work. Gemma Reid walks me through a street art project in the Belfast Entries, where a lot of 1798 was planned, and we have wider conversations about historical erasure and rediscovery. Will Jordan explores Moneyreagh over lockdown and uncovers a radical Protestant history right under his feet.

6

The Battle of Antrim

6 June 2021

Portadown is protesting today. Speeches are being made against the sea border.[13] The new UUP leader, Doug Beattie, who looks to be a liberal reforming unionist, attends to observe the protest. While he is meeting loyalists privately to hear their concerns, Beattie distances himself from the men in balaclavas who illegally march through the town after the Portadown demonstration. COVID-19 restrictions against mass gatherings are still in place. Loyalism is angry today and political unionism is in disarray.

On the same day, 30 people attend a tour of the Battle of Antrim, hosted by Reclaim the Enlightenment, a society that celebrates the histories of the 1790s. We drive in convoy from cemetery to fort. Coffee is dispensed from the boot of Stephen McCracken's car. We queue up to buy 1798 pamphlets from John Gray's boot. We merge and challenge ideas of our shared history.

When I set out on this Battle of Antrim tour, I expected a guide to take us to various locations and provide information and historical facts. This does happen. But it is so much more than a tour. Over a long afternoon, it emerges as a raw and spontaneous conversation. Between Catholic, Protestant, Dissenter and heathen. People make impromptu speeches and interjections. Together we struggle with what 1798 could mean today.

Memory can be heavy and light at the same time. I think many of us are still working out how to hold these in balance.

---

[13] The 'sea border' refers to the trade border that was implemented between Britain and Northern Ireland after Brexit, as agreed in the Ireland/Northern Ireland Protocol of the Brexit Withdrawal Agreement in February 2020. The Protocol required extra customs checks and paperwork for goods and animals crossing the Irish Sea, so that Northern Ireland could continue to comply with EU single-market regulations.

THE GHOST LIMB

* * *

We spill out of our cars at Mallusk cemetery, and gather loosely around the grave of James Hope. Hope was a weaver, a self-taught scholar, a 'man of no property', and one of my favourite United Irishmen. I am excited because one of Hope's descendants is with us. A lovely, understated man, who has only recently discovered this ancestry.

The first words of the tour are his. He tells us how his family made the discovery, and how he was making sense of it all. It was a shock for them – family stories of unionism and loyalism were more familiar. He reads out fiercely beautiful testimony about James Hope's character, focusing on Hope's values, how he would not take a senior position in the rebellion, preferring to stand with the ordinary people. How he is remembered for his strong views on equality and against poverty.

Next it is my turn, and I stumble over a few words about Rose Mullan, James Hope's wife, who was also active in the United Irish movement. I have recently joined Reclaim the Enlightenment and am happy to have the chance to speak about the women.

Rose played an active role in both the 1798 rebellion in the north, and later in Dublin, helping Robert Emmet prepare for the second rebellion in 1803. She carried messages as well as ammunition under her cloak. I feel awkward saying this in front of James Hope's descendant, drawing attention to the ammunition like that. But it didn't feel right to skip over it either. I talk about the fact that Rose, like James, was loyal to her friends, open-minded and clever. Although Rose was a Presbyterian, her four children were baptised by a Catholic priest. She loved Rabbie Burns' poetry. I say that Rose, who James called his Rosebud, was loved and remembered.

Just behind James and Rose's memorial is FJ Bigger's grave. Bigger was a key figure in the Irish cultural revival, and we meet him properly later in this book. Historian Mark Doherty talks about Bigger's life, his antiquarianism, wide social circles, his lifelong dedication to preserving and promoting Irish culture. It was Bigger who added the inscription to Rose on the Hopes' memorial in 1901. One of many memorials that he would organise, restore, repair or erect for the United Irishmen more than 100 years after the rebellion. Because it was too politically controversial to memorialise them at the time.

The Celtic cross on the top of Bigger's grave is made from a noticeably different, modern looking granite, to the base. The original cross was destroyed by a loyalist bomb in 1971 and ultimately replaced by the local council in 2013 (Graham). The irony of Bigger's own grave being destroyed, when he had repaired the graves of so many others, feels cruel.

Marty McManus takes to his feet then, making an impromptu speech. Marty is a former Sinn Féin councillor, now working on archeological projects. He wants to draw attention to the Old Irish inscription on one of the Hope's gravestones. It is such antiquated Irish that an expert had to be flown in from London to translate it. It translates as 'until the dawn of the day'. Marty points out the Irish language on Bigger's gravestone as well. I trace my fingers over the worn letters, without being able to make them out.

There is emotion in Marty's voice. He says he is disillusioned with politics. That it is great to love these histories of 1798, but what does it mean in the present? That he cannot see a way that we can tangibly change our broken politics. He says that we just have to look at how the Irish language is denigrated by many unionists today. That this history is hidden. It is as if the fading lettering, the indecipherable Old Irish, are metaphors for history slipping away from us. Mark Doherty suggests that the current Irish language revival amongst northern Protestants is a good place to look for the spirit of 1798.

The questions are left hanging.

* * *

Thank God James Hope's descendant has a good sense of direction, because my own is terrible. I follow his red car down winding back roads until we arrive at Roughfort. We spill out onto the road, pinning ourselves to side walls and hedges, trying not to block other cars passing.

A crumbling, roofless Orange Hall with a Union Jack flag sits opposite a Liberty Tree. The United Irishmen used to plant oak trees as a symbol of freedom, and this is thought to be one. Roughfort was one of the assembly points for the Battle of Antrim. Stephen McCracken – one of the tour organisers – starts to tell us about the history of the site. He likes to think that the Orange Hall was built on this specific site as a nod to 1798, rather than in opposition to it.[14] When I get home, I read Peter Collins' book on the

---

[14] The Orange Order is a Protestant fraternal organisation, primarily based in Northern Ireland, but with a presence in Scotland, England, the Republic of Ireland and throughout the world. The Order was founded in 1795, in the run-up to 1798, in no small part because of opposition

commemoration of 1798 and discover that the Orange Order marked the rebellion's 1998 bicentenary with exhibitions, catalogues, re-enactments and dinners (Colllins 2004: 88-90). Later, I am offered the use of an Orange Hall for my own 1798 meetings. I am surprised to learn of the Order's affinity with this history.

A few local Orangemen do not seem to approve though. Some of us have climbed up onto a roadside wall to get a good photograph of the Liberty Tree without the cars. The Orange Hall is set back a metre or two from the wall.

A white van pulls up in the middle of our group, and two men get out. They come over and tell us to get off the wall and away from the Orange Hall. The guides quickly say that we will now move on to the next site. We have only been there five minutes.

'I'm sorry', I say to one of the men as he asked me to stand down, 'I was just taking a photograph of the tree'.

'I know exactly what you are doing', he replies.

* * *

William Orr's memorial is the next site we visit. Nestled in a beautiful and quiet cemetery at Templepatrick, adjoining the UUP's Danny Kinahan's ancestral home.

There are some murmurings about what had just happened at Roughfort. It seems to have rattled Marty. When I get home I google Marty and learn that in 2014, a 1798 bus tour to Antrim from the Féile (a west Belfast festival, with roots in the republican community) was attacked by 100 loyalists, and had to leave the town (*Irish News* August 2014). Marty tells us that he has run many 1798 tours for loyalists and republicans over the years, and describes how meaningful they have been in bringing people together. I

---

to the United Irish aims of Catholic emancipation and repeal of the Penal Laws. It remains prominent today, although has declined in membership and increased in age profile. It is heavily associated with political unionism and loyalism, and continues to march each year in celebration of various Protestant historical victories in Ireland, for example at the Battle of the Boyne in 1690. The Orange Order is a religious organisation. Rules state that members must be Protestants and must not marry Catholics. As a result, it is often criticised for being sectarian and exclusionary. In 2019, the Scottish Orange Order removed the stipulation that members cannot enter a Catholic Church for weddings, funerals and other occasions. At the time of writing, this rule has not changed in Northern Ireland, but in practice, it is often ignored. Members and supporters argue that The Order exists to defend religious liberties and maintain Protestant traditions.

understand where he is coming from then. Seeing the potential of the message, despairing about the silencing.

There is talk of United Irish graves being hidden around Antrim and Down, dates changed. The '8' in 1798 doctored to cover things up. United Irish names added to gravestones many years afterwards. Oblique references to people's lives with no detail of the circumstances of their death. Erasure. Self-protection.

Marty is a great admirer of William Orr, a United Irish rebel who was executed in 1797, in an attempt to shut the rebellion down before it began. We will come back here and lay wreaths on the anniversary of Orr's hanging. Marty tells us how a memorial stone had been installed by Reverend Hoey and other parishioners from the adjacent Non-subscribing Presbyterian Church. How the stone was installed exactly 200 years after William Orr's hanging, on the very hour of his death. A film crew from RTÉ had attended. Again, Marty laments the loss of this history. Maybe he has seen the news from Portadown.

Others speak up with a different view. John Gray, former Librarian of the Linen Hall Library, current chair of Reclaim the Enlightenment and historian of the 1790s, makes the point that many of us do not feel so gloomy. That Reclaim the Enlightenment's events are incredibly popular. That here we are today, many Protestants and Dissenters amongst us, actively connecting with, and telling others about, our United Irish history. How the very story that has just been told about Reverend Hoey shows the persistence of 1798 ideals. John Gray notes how this church did the opposite of historical erasure. They organised a celebration and invited the media. It was a very public honouring of William Orr.

Someone else speaks up then. I am not recording, so I paraphrase what he said:

> I am a former British soldier. I used to be an Orangeman. All of us here today are born and will die in Ireland. We are all the same. I will be a United Irishman until the day that I die. And so will my children.

Just at this moment, the last member of our tour group belatedly arrives. Another former Orangeman and history lover. He stayed behind to talk to the men at Roughfort. As a former structural engineer, he gave them some advice about the condition of the Hall. They swapped names and numbers and he tells us he has just offered to help the men apply for funding for a heritage scheme run by the Ulster-Scots Agency. To the rest of us he says, 'these are people who we need to reach out to, who we need to connect with over this history'.

Stephen McCracken interjects that while researching the Battle of Antrim for his own books, he had a lot of positive contact with Orangemen, and whilst interpretations differ, he has found openness in talking about this historical moment. Many Orange Order members are, after all, descended from United Irishmen and women. Some showed him pikes and weapons from 1798, still in their possession.

I talk to some of the women in the group about the cultural blending and sometimes political fracturing in our families. I think most of us have this to some degree.

And it just all sits like this together. In all its complication. The silencing. And the reaching out. The heaviness of history. And the positive counter of connection.

* * *

When I get home, I continue to brood over the Orange connection that came up so much at Roughfort. While we had older family members in the Orange Order, my parents kept us away from it. During the Twelfth of July, we would often join the exodus of Catholics and middle class Protestants to the south. I was a teenager when Drumcree flared up.[15] Orange sashes blended with orange fires in my mind. Years later, I was doing fieldwork for my PhD about religion and politics in Northern Ireland and I physically could not bring myself outdoors to observe the Twelfth. I sat in the house with each heavy drum beat from the bands knotting my stomach further, telling me, 'this is not your place'.[16]

Although I would later go on to attend many Twelfths, initially for work and later for neighbourliness, getting kicked out of Roughfort taps into the

---

[15] Drumcree, in Portadown, has been one of the most contentious Orange Order marches in recent history. In the 1990s, part of the July parade was routed through the mostly Catholic Garvaghy Road, leaving residents feeling hemmed in and intimidated. In 1995, after residents protested, the march was stopped by the RUC. More than 1000 Orangemen refused to move and a stand off with the police ensued. Riots followed. The march was eventually allowed through with no music, with the UUP's David Trimble and the DUP's Ian Paisley Senior at the helm. In 1996, the Garvaghy Road section of the march was also banned. Loyalists flooded into the area, and after much violence locally and across the North – riots, barricades and fires – the Orangemen were allowed to march. 1997 was also chaotic. A number of Catholics were killed by loyalist paramilitaries during this time. Since 2001, the situation has been calmer.

[16] The Orange Order and the loyalist bands are largely separate entities. Loyalist paramilitaries are another entity again. It is important to be able to distinguish between them, while also acknowledging that, in some times and places, the distinctions blur.

part of me that associates the Orange Order with exclusion. But Stephen takes a different approach. Instead of withdrawing, he met with the Orange Order a few weeks after Roughfort, to discuss what had happened. He brought his friend, an Orange Order Grand Master, with him. The meeting went well. After some difficult debate, there was resolution. And new relationships. They would work together on future heritage projects in Antrim. The Orangemen told Stephen about the work they were doing in the community – a free lunch kitchen, a badminton club and their hopes to establish a childcare facility. They offered the use of their Hall as a stop for refreshments on future tours. A few of them said they would like to come on the tours. A few weeks after that again, Stephen sends me a photograph from their Facebook page. It is a picture of himself and the man who asked us to leave Roughfort, together in the Hall. It reads: 'Thank you to Stephen McCracken [for the] kind donations of Suki drinks to be enjoyed at the funday tomorrow'.

The Orangemen tell Stephen that the Orange Hall at Roughfort had been burned down in the 1970s, and the memory of that is still with them. I realise when I hear this that I should have been more aware of the contentiousness of our presence, and more respectful of the site. I feel bad for climbing on the wall. Stephen apologises for those of us who had trespassed. And the Orangemen accept that we felt intimidated. A lesson learned. That to share a history is more than words. It means listening to others, as you try to carve out a voice of your own.

* * *

Going on the Battle of Antrim tour feels like walking around in Guy Beiner's book. Hiding and erasure. Contestation. Bridges and connection. Consciously walking alongside people in the 1798 Dreamtime, trying to re-realise the present.

'Is it always like this?' I ask Stephen. He says, 'Yes, it often is'. As I go on to take more tours, I will see this for myself.

And so these histories, and our relationships to them, layer up like sediments of earth. Although we will all go home to our separate lives, and our different politics, here we all are now, having these conversations with one another. Digging deeper into these historical sites, and into our own imagination of ourselves. Perhaps being a little bit changed in the process.

7

Dis/Inheritance

Stephen McCracken is a direct descendant of Belfast's United Irish McCracken family. He runs tours of 1798 sites in Antrim and all over the North. Stephen has written a number of books about the United Irish movement – important families, the battles and the exiles – and is the Secretary of Reclaim the Enlightenment.

Given Stephen's expertise in 1798 and his ancestry, I talk to him about writing this book and ask if he might have a story to share. 'I do have a story', he says, 'and I don't mind telling it'.

It is not the story I am expecting. I doubt it is a story he ever expected to be telling either.

* * *

As I research this book, I meet people who trace their ancestry back to United Irish figures. Invariably there are differences of opinions within families, with people processing their histories in different ways. This is how Northern Ireland works. Most families are culturally blended and diverse in one way or another. Sometimes these differences can be held lightly. But differences can also create silences and fractures.

Stephen was raised in a rural part of County Derry/Londonderry in a Presbyterian home. As a child, he was an Apprentice Boy. Being in the army, or being a police officer, were some of his potential career plans. His family were deeply religious, and in this part of the world, Stephen says, 'the politics comes with the territory'.

Stephen grew up surrounded by historical artefacts. He and his siblings used to play with old swords they found in the loft. Some of Mary Ann

DIS/INHERITANCE

McCracken's possessions are sitting in his garage. At one point when we're talking, Stephen runs to the garage to grab some Reichmarks he'd found in an old tin. When I see him at Zoom meetings, there are antique pistols mounted on the wall behind him. Stephen's approach to history is that he likes to see the original documents. You would, wouldn't you? Growing up with a living history all around you like this.

But while Stephen always knew about the link to the McCracken family, it was a history carried in objects, rather than in stories or conversation:

> The McCrackens weren't really talked about at all in the family. My granny had a picture of the United Irishmen up on her wall, one handed down over generations. One of my uncles has stuff from Mary Ann's house.

Stephen sends me the pictures of a centrepiece later. A gorgeous elongated pyramid with Henry Joy McCracken, Wolfe Tone and (Stephen thinks) William Tennant on the sides.

> We've always known it. It's always been in your back of your head that we're from that family in Belfast. But it's never been talked about. Just fallen by the wayside.
>
> This is what always happens. Once you get a change of circumstances. Like with the Act of Union, and then you have another one with the partition of Ireland. And then the Troubles. Everything previous to that gets forgotten, and left behind. We didn't talk about it.

I wondered when Stephen started to make the connection with 1798 himself, and what that looked like, given his deep interest in this history today:

> I suppose I started to make the connection myself at secondary school. I went to Coleraine Inst and everyone would say, 'do you know Henry Joy McCracken?' And I'd say, 'oh yeah, he's a part of the family'. One of my uncles is called Henry Joy McCracken, and then a grand Uncle too. It's a name that has gone down the family. But I didn't really know who he was until I started with it myself.
>
> Then I went and read more. ATQ Stewart's book (*A Deeper Silence*) came out when I was in upper sixth, and I think that's when I got interested and started to really work out that Presbyterians were involved, and that this history was for everyone.

THE GHOST LIMB

* * *

After school, Stephen went to university in Dundee. Given his preference for the original document, rather than third party interpretation, the following is what happened next, in Stephen's own words:

When I went to university, for the first few years I stuck to my own. I was told what church to go to, and that there'd be a man called Joe there waiting for me.

And after a while, I just thought 'stuff this, I'm going to explore a bit'. And then I fell in with some Irish ones from Tyrone. My best friend is a girl from Tyrone. I started playing Gaelic football as well, and I was good at it. So the last few years of Dundee was just hanging out with the Gaelic ones. I went to church for a few years, but you really had to give it all your time to fit in, and I didn't really want to do that. You don't want a church and religion to control your life.

Growing up, and at school, religion did dictate to us. Where I lived was about 90/10 Catholic/Protestant. Growing up, my next door neighbour was a young Roman Catholic boy. But when you get to upper sixth, he's doing Gaelic, and going out in Limavady, and I'm going out in Coleraine. There's a split there.

But then you go to university, and so much changes. It can explode your mind, if you're willing to let it. I was, and I'm thankful for it.

There was a priest in Dundee called Eugene O'Sullivan. We used to have great nights out after the football, and he'd ask me questions about my life. And then one night he came in with a Henry Joy McCracken five pound note and gave me it. I was the only Protestant in the room. It was just very, very thoughtful. When I left university, he was still the team coach and he was also the university chaplain, and he wrote me this big fancy reference. It was brilliant. I couldn't ask for more. The others would call him Father. But where I came from, you just don't do that. So I just called him Mr O'Sullivan or Eugene.

After university, I spent six months in Toronto and Canada, which was a big eye-opener because everything is so mixed. Then I went back to Dundee for a few years. By then I was moving away from religion.

I didn't know that I'd come back to Northern Ireland. I remember growing up, there was a shooting on the bus in Castlerock. The UDA shot three boys and our bus was passing at that time. The screams. You still hear it today. And Halloween night. Growing up, we couldn't celebrate Halloween because of the shootings at Greysteel. They happened on Halloween night, [the UDA] came in to the Rising Sun Bar and killed eight people, and they said 'trick or treat' before they shot people. So we could never say 'trick or treat' again; it was just too raw.

So I never wanted to come back to Belfast. But I was offered a good job in finance. I worked there for two or three years. And then my dad got hurt, so I had to go home to the farm. But while I was in Belfast, I'd got going with my wife. She was a Roman Catholic. And we had a wean [child] together, so that wasn't so good, coming from a strict Protestant background. After the wean, I proposed. We were at the farm for a few years. We did up a big house on the farm, spent a lot of money on it. Then started building a new house on the land.

And then we went to Cyprus to get married.

We were told, 'you'll be thrown out. Once you get married, you'll not be allowed in there'. These were local Catholics who worked for my family down the generations. And I just kind of dismissed it. I didn't believe them.

We baptised our daughter in the Roman Catholic Church. It didn't go down too well at all. Soon after we got married, everything changed. We were asked to politely leave. And I was disinherited. It all had to go through the solicitors. Because once I'd gone back to the farm, I'd been put as a partner in the whole business.

So we were thrown out. We went back to the Presbyterian Church. I was friendly with our minister and he was trying to negotiate, saying for us to come back. But, I was just 'I can't, you know'; we'd been totally thrown out of this whole area.

My parents did come to the wedding. They were on a cruise and they stopped off for it. And it was ok for about six months afterwards. But then the realisation must have kicked in that the farm may not stay Protestant. It may eventually go Roman Catholic. And they couldn't cope with that. And that was the driving issue of us getting out.

You have to put it into perspective. The 17th and 18th century Presbyterians, they didn't have that tie to the land. Some were only here a generation or two. So a lot of Presbyterians then, they were just able to up and leave. But now hundreds of years have passed, and one hundred years of Northern Ireland, and they just want to keep the land now.

But I got over it. Because you have to just get into that mindset, or else you would lose your mind.

That was ten years ago. I've not seen them since. I never heard tell of any of my family for the last ten years. In fact, a cousin emailed me last year to ask if I was going to my granda's funeral the next day. I didn't know he had died.

I'm the only one in the family who got away from that pull of the church and of Protestantism, when I went away. I don't see myself as anything now. Just in the middle.

But you know I'm far better for it. You have to be free. You can't be held down by anybody telling you what to do. When I left the rank, it was funny, it was like all that stress left.

I asked if all this had affected the way Stephen felt about people, if it made him more wary:

No. It's actually made me more open. I can talk to people more. 90 per cent of the farmers I work with are Protestants. They know what happened, and we can talk about anything. It was in the news a bit at the time. The rural population of Protestants are civil people. I wouldn't even see people in religious ways any more.

* * *

In 2020s Northern Ireland, there is definitely something of 1798 in the air. New tours are being launched. A statue of Mary Ann McCracken is coming to Belfast City Hall. New societies have been formed. Stephen is enthusiastic about pretty much any project that celebrates this history.

But there are layers in Stephen's reactions to how 1798 history is talked about. He says that the political editor of the *Belfast Telegraph*, Suzanne Breen, wrote a great article about the planned statue of Mary Ann McCracken (*Belfast Telegraph* May 2021). But 'when [Suzanne] tweeted about it, she put in the word republican'.[17] Stephen struggled with that. Many others will struggle with this language throughout the book too. Stephen says:

---

[17] https://twitter.com/SuzyJourno/status/1389467145134911488?s=20&t=XxsIkmmiAjCyKvRbxKRIaw

> Mary Ann, she was a republican, pre-Union. And then 20 years into the Union, she does have a change of mind in her letters; she says it's not so bad. She doesn't say anywhere she's a republican, so we don't have the right to second-guess someone like that. Republicanism is a hard word.

Those last four words get to the heart of things. Stephen asks me whether I think of myself as a republican. Which I think I do. I am definitely a republican in the sense of being opposed to monarchy and believing in citizens' democracy. And I am a republican in the context of 1790s Ireland. But it's difficult in the 2020s to identify as a republican without a bit of hesitancy. Because the fractures of Irish history, especially the Troubles, created a disconnection with republicanism for a lot of Protestants. And although most people in this book are doing very active identity work, deliberately crossing divides, republican is a destination where only a few of us have landed so far.

A new interpretative centre in Belfast is being planned. The aim is to acquire Belfast's historic Assembly Rooms, and install a project that explores the United Irish and other Enlightenment histories of the building. While Reclaim the Enlightenment has had the goal of saving the Assembly Rooms for a long time, new impetus came in 2021 from the United Irish Historical Society. Stephen bristled at Sinn Féin councillor Jim McVeigh's initial framing of the issue when he said, 'We're very excited about the idea of the visitor centre in particular, because if you talk to some people within the Protestant community they haven't a clue about the radical Presbyterians of 1798' (Belfast Media Group August 2020).

Of course Jim is hitting on something very real here. This book is about that very absence. But I think it can be difficult to hear the idea that your community doesn't have a clue, when you are a Presbyterian like Stephen whose life's work has been to promote awareness of 1798. And knowing what a high price has been paid for your own lack of sectarianism.

Ever since Stephen and I talked about the United Irish Historical Society, I thought I might contact Jim and try to invite myself along. But the invitation from him came first, via Seán Napier, who I talk to in chapter 22. Stephen and I didn't have to think about it too long before we found ourselves in Henry Joy's bar in Belfast city centre, with Catholics, Protestants, Dissenters and others, talking openly about ideas and frictions, exploring what goals we shared in common.

THE GHOST LIMB

Stephen and I talk afterwards about how good it felt to be there. That it would be the greatest tragedy of all if 1798 was to be remembered separately by Protestants and Catholics, as has so often been the case historically. I think the challenge for all of us who love 1798, is to get in the same room and do the work that our ancestors started.

When I ask Stephen what role has 1798 played in his life over the last 10 years, he says:

> I think it's opened up my mind to other people. Henry Joy was a member of the Defenders in Armagh. I've started to work with more republicans. I was chatting to Danny Morrison last week. Opening up your mind to other ways of doing things. 1798 was over 200 years ago. A lot has changed since then. And you have to be open to changes in society and politics.

The morning after we talk, Stephen sends me a photo of his breakfast. A fine looking Ulster fry, cooked for him by Bobby Sands' former cellmate. And this is the work of the modern United Irish, I think. To welcome friendship. To break bread with one another. To be open to changing our minds. To continually look for goals that are shared.

* * *

Stephen says his politics are 'somewhere in the middle' politically these days. I'd characterise him as a thran Antrim Ulster Scot, driven by anti-sectarianism and a strong sense of justice.

The idea of a united Ireland does not bother Stephen. Nor is he particularly an advocate. Andrew Trimble, an ex-Ulster rugby player, went to school with Stephen. Trimble had been on Claire Byrne's political talk show on RTÉ a few weeks before we spoke, saying that he did not mind either way about the constitutional question, as long as things were done sensitively. Stephen sees himself in a similar place to Trimble, saying 'we don't care either way':

> My views have changed a lot regarding a united Ireland. People have been telling me for the last 30 years we'll have a united Ireland. I think we'll have to go for a federal approach. I think there are good people in the SDLP and Sinn Féin. I just take each individual as they are. I'd vote for the person rather than the party.
>
> I've played around with this in my head. I don't think it matters. If you

don't have money worries, you can go wherever you want. I could go one way or another, as long as I can still get my groceries.

I've got a lot of friends from Galway and Mayo. My best man was from Wexford. In some ways I think it would be really good to have a united Ireland. But there's some things that would have to change for that to be considered by certain people up here. One thing would be 'The Soldier's Song', the national anthem. Another would be the flag issue. I never liked the Irish flag, but maybe that's because it's bred into me.

I say I like the symbolism of the flag, which is about unity of the different traditions on this island. Stephen thinks hardly anyone knows what the symbolism is. Interestingly, this is the only time the flag and anthem arise in this book. Most other people I speak with are more interested in the social and economic aspects of constitutional change.

Stephen and I end up talking about digital money and transformation of the financial system. He thinks the development of digital currency will change the unity and union debate completely. We are in uncharted waters.

* * *

One of the things I learned from Stephen, in the time I've known him, is not to dismiss anyone else's voice as you raise your own. This is how I have always tried to live. But, as I watch Stephen in real life, I understand this in a new way. Particularly when it comes to 1798 history.

I am drawn to the inclusiveness of Stephen's work. Like him, I've found that there's an affinity for 1798 even amongst those who were historically on the 'other side' of the rebellion. I've met ordinary unionists, people from the Orange Order, the DUP, plenty of loyalists, who relate to aspects of this history, and Stephen has introduced me to many more. On his 1798 tours, Stephen hands the mic to Irish republicans and former British soldiers, Ulster Scots poets and Irish language speakers, anyone and everyone who comes with an open heart and knowledge to share.

Stephen's exploration of 1798 is always blunt, honest and he is a stickler for historical accuracy. There is zero romanticism about his work. He is happy to call out United Irishmen for hypocrisy, for example those who took slaves. His book with Colum O'Ruairc (2020) highlights many examples of this, Henry Joy McCracken's uncle in the Bahamas being among them. This is a hugely important reminder to not slip into myth. While we may take inspiration from 1798, its ambassadors did not always live up to their own ideals.

Stephen is a man of documents and records. But he is also someone who has a deep ability to relate to people from all walks of life by the simple (but difficult) habit of a truly open mind. I cannot help but pull Stephen into my magical thinking. The McCracken spirit is in him. That uncanny ability to bring people along on his journey. An unwavering commitment to anti-sectarian principles, whilst seeking out new relationships with people that challenge his views. Personal adversity has caused Stephen to dig deep into the marrow of 1798, finding generosity rather than anger in the longer timeline of his family story.

I am deviating too far from historical fact now for Stephen to be happy with me. But I sense Henry Joy and Mary Ann may have travelled through the world like this too. Rallying, gathering up, standing firm, listening, persuading. No better spirits to channel.

8

The Entries

Gemma and I meet at Cole's Entry, at the back of Belfast's In-Shops, famous for its cheap coffee, carpets and hemp merchandise. It's Friday afternoon. Usually the bars are filling up about now, with people having post-work pints. But COVID-19. We almost have the city to ourselves. Sharing quiet streets with drug users and occasional locals wandering past shuttered shops.

I've asked Gemma to walk me through the Entries, to show me a recent street art project that she had a hand in bringing to life.

A few hours later, I stand outside the In-Shops blinking back tears.

What Gemma shows me, moves me at some visceral level. They have made a street art love poem to radical Belfast, to the counter-cultural underground, to the people and ideals of 1798, to dreams dreamt in secret alleyways. The Entries and the alleys are the arteries of the city. Off the beaten track. Their stories told in this project – as they have been for centuries – in code.

Until recently, 1798 history has been barely recognised in Belfast city centre. There is a handful of plaques and a few paintings down a quiet alley. A statue of Mary Ann McCracken, proposed by Alliance councillor Michael Long, is planned. But most of the significant sites remain unmarked, overlaid with new development or dereliction. There's been a very public silencing of this history, and indeed most histories in Belfast city centre, where 'neutrality' has often been seen as a marker of progress (Switzer and McDowell 2009).

The artworks that now live in the Entries and alleys will be interpreted by people in different ways. On the surface, they might seem to tell stories of industry, linen and empire. Some will see a conceptual art project. Others will wish that the theme of 1798 was more obvious. All of these readings make sense to me. But today, I interpret it as an arm around my shoulder, a quiet word in my ear:

> You are meant to be here. You are a link in a long chain of people who have felt the way you feel. Who whispered radical words in back allies. Who built this city. Who identified its troubles. Who spent their lives fighting for equality and against sectarianism. Keep going.

* * *

Gemma explains how the project came about with a Belfast City Council tender for creative place-making. The Primark fire in 2019 had dampened a lot of life in the city centre. Large areas were cordoned off for safety reasons. The ghost streets were reminiscent of the silent city during the Belfast Blitz, or the Ring of Steel during the Troubles. By 2020, Belfast City Council was wondering how to regenerate the city centre. A particularly visionary Council officer suggested turning people's attention towards the Entries. Once vibrant places that decades of neglect, violence and absentee landlords had sucked the life out of. Places that offered new routes through the city, a new way of understanding it.

To imagine Belfast's Entries, think of a built-up city. Think about small, narrow alleys running between main streets, creating an invisible network of connections. The alleys run along old Plantation plot lines between big merchant houses. In the 18th century, they were the beating heart of the city. Lots of small shops, taverns, warehouses and homes. Their entrances are often marked with a narrow stone arch and metalwork bearing their name – Joy's Entry, Pottinger's Entry, Sugarhouse Entry.

The Entries were a big part of my teenagehood. The Dr. Marten's shop, vintage stores, cheap all-you-can-eat lunches in the Northern Star pub, sneaky cigarettes down the side of the In-Shops. Crusties, goths and punks. Listening to the Pixies in Castle Arcade. Subcultures have always thrived here.

Some friends of mine from the creative collectives Daisy Chain Inc. and Form Native won the Belfast City Council tender. It's my childhood friend, Gemma Reid, from Daisy Chain Inc. who is showing me around today. Their suggestion was that the Council commission street art, which they felt would be a Belfast-appropriate way to do regeneration. A city that always wears its feelings on the walls.

THE ENTRIES

Each artist responded to a creative brief, which explored the history and character of the Entries. The brief gave a few nudges about how the Volunteers and United Irishmen met in the pubs of the Entries in the 1790s. That their *Northern Star* newspaper was published here. That the Entries are steeped in radical politics, protest and dissent.

As time passes, I will come to understand that different people relate to the art in different ways. That references to the United Irishmen in the alleys are not simply historical. They tap into live and current politics. The artworks I see today will provoke rich and passionate debate. Conversations which will come to profoundly shape my understanding of 1798 in the present.

* * *

At Pottinger's Entry, the artist Nomad Clan has painted a giant white pelican, in an oval of sea and sky, against a brick red wall. Gemma explains:

> The Pottingers were a Presbyterian merchant family, wealthy and influential members of Belfast Society. Their home, offices, warehouse and stables were here in the Entry. The pelican is from the Pottinger family crest. You can also see Asian inspired flowers. A descendant of theirs, Henry Pottinger, led East India expeditions through what is now Pakistan and Iran. He ended up negotiating Hong Kong for the British and became the first British governor there.

There's an industrial bin in front of the wall panel. We lug it out of the way, to reveal a picture of Henry Pottinger. But that isn't all. Gemma says:

> Gail [McConnell, Belfast poet] wrote short poems for each Entry. I like this panel. We had to word it carefully, but the relationship between Belfast and empire is in there.
>
> The Pottingers were Planters. They come here at the right time to make a fortune, through trade with the expanding British Empire. They become diplomatically very powerful in later generations. Sugar was an important trade, established here around the same time, in Sugarhouse Entry, which is just over there. Local abolitionists, including Mary Ann McCracken wouldn't eat anything with sugar, as it was produced on slave-worked colonial plantations.
>
> And this is how Gail picked up on it:

THE GHOST LIMB

A story of empire made and remade:
enterprise, power and colonial trade.

It was a careful negotiation. Getting the balance right with only a few words to play with. Staying true to the complexity of the past, but also being aware that we are touching on sensitive subjects. There's not an immediate connection between what's there in the panels and the artwork. But it's there, if you take the time to find it, you know.

This theme emerges time and again throughout the project. Gemma says that Belfast artist, Peter Strain, was interested in drawing lesser-known characters from the Entries. In a quiet alleyway, Peter has painted Barney Maglone. Gemma tells me:

> Barney Maglone was his pen name, but his real name was Robert A. Wilson. He wrote for the *Morning News* in the 1920s and 1930s, which was one of the first penny papers in Ireland. He was a big advocate for workers' rights. A Protestant-born Gaelic speaker. He hung out in the bars down here all the time.

A pen name, I think to myself. Just like so many of the United Irishmen who used pseudonyms. Just like I nearly did when the threats started. A long line of people who have had to live with a divided self, just in case it's not safe. This city gives and it takes away.

* * *

Joy's Entry is named after Francis Joy, who was a merchant and a trader. Francis founded the *Belfast News Letter* in 1737, Belfast's first newspaper. Under his leadership, the newspaper was progressive and critical of the government. But after it was sold out of the family in 1795, it became increasingly conservative.

Gemma points out Gail's lines. They're some of her favourites.

> *Trace stories told in code and hint*
> *in lines of brick and steel and print.*

She says:

> Gail has woven in so many layers of meaning in just these few words. There is the reference to newspapers and what a subversive tool they were in the 18th and 19th centuries. They were vital to radical politics at that time,

because they spread new ideas so effectively. Here in the Entries is where the radicals were meeting and talking, and writing. Sometimes their writing had to be disguised in code. But the poem also makes reference to the codes and hints of the past that can still be read in the built fabric of the Entries today. It's beautiful.

This theme picks up again in Wilson's Court. The verse there contains one of the most explicit references to the radical politics of the Entries.

> *With its radical ideals, the Northern Star*
> *spread United Irish politics near and far.*

The *Northern Star*, founded by United Irishmen in 1792 and edited by Samuel Neilson, quickly became one of the most widely-read papers in Ireland. By 1797, Gemma's panel points out that 'even possession of the paper was regarded by the government as evidence of seditious intent'. And that eventually 'a mob of Monaghan militiamen, anxious to demonstrate their loyalty [...] destroyed the printing press that produced the *Northern Star* and threw the pieces out on this street'.

Gemma tells me to look up. On a tall thin wall in front of us, there's a pink, blue and purple geometric maze stretching up to the sky:

> That's Rob Hilken's piece. It blew me away. When you see it in the sunlight, that whole wall just glitters. It's gorgeous. This is about Samuel Neilson. The Northern Star was printed here in Wilson's Court for a while. And it was spoken about as a planet of light and heat, as this force for change in the world, dispelling myths and prejudices. So that's Rob's tribute to that. Light and heat.
>
> It would be hard to get the meaning from it, unless you knew.
>
> But when you know, you know.

Something else strikes me about Joy's Entry. There are some new bars here, which proudly reference Henry Joy McCracken, one of Belfast's leading United Irishmen, who grew up around this Entry. Henry Joy was executed in 1798 outside the old Market House on High Street.

The website of Henry's Bar says it was established in 1798. In reality it's built on the old site of McCracken's bar, which has been a licensed premises since 1892. Beside Henry's is the Jailhouse Bar. Once the site of Mary Ann McCracken's muslin shop, the Jailhouse bar became derelict, until it was renovated in 2018 by a local pub chain. These are bars of the new school. Their Instagram pages are dominated by bright cocktails and ads for whiskey tasting nights. Large screens show major sporting events.

But these are not generic sports bars. There is something different about them. Their United Irish theme is loud and proud. Barrels outside the pub are emblazoned with the name 'Henry'. Websites for both bars have old pictures suggesting 1798 plotting. The Jailhouse's website invites customers to 'take a closer look and see what history and tales you can find while you sip on tipples and nibble on rations. Time Served Well'.

There's a statue of Henry Joy McCracken outside Henry's Bar, with his name at the bottom. No other details. Gemma and I go up and give it a knock. It sounds hollow, made from fibreglass. In the context of official institutions being so wary of commemorating 1798, and the absence of these histories in Belfast, it seems that people have taken matters into their own hands.

Comparing the assertive 1798 cocktail bars and the encoded street art is jarring. The easy confidence of the bars sits in contrast with the difficult historical conversations being started on the walls outside. Each reflecting different facets of this moment of vibrant historical rediscovery. Each, perhaps, informing the other.

* * *

Just before Joy's Entry spits you out onto High street, there is a large wall painting of Olaudah Equiano. Gemma continues:

> Olaudah Equiano was an ex-slave who became a prominent member of the British abolitionist movement. He came to Belfast in May 1791 and stayed with Samuel Neilson. He travelled around promoting his autobiography, which was one of the earliest books to be published by a black African writer and became hugely popular. So, right when the United Irishmen are being founded, and Samuel Nielson was running the *Northern Star* newspaper, Olaudah Equiano is here. The artist – Dreph – wanted to honour the fact that Equiano was here, to put his face up in the public space, in Belfast. This went up just before the Black Lives Matter protests in the city.

Another connection between past, present and future. And a reminder that Belfast's history has many of the tools we need to design a better way of life in the present.

THE ENTRIES

We walk past another painting with a black face, a long thin banner above Crown Entry.

> This is another one of Peter Strain's. The words are from Louis MacNiece:
> 'A city built on mud, a culture built on profit, free speech nipped in the bud, the minority always guilty.'
>
> That's pretty powerful.
>
> Louis MacNeice is describing Belfast as a place where it's always the minority that loses out. Peter chose to put a black person there to say – this issue is as important now as when Louis MacNiece wrote about it in the 1930s. That was painted before Black Lives Matter too. And I'm so glad it's there.

Another artist, Rebekah McBride, focused on the life that used to be in the Entries:

> The Entries were once really busy places, humming with activity. There used to be little shop fronts all along here. People would hang out small painted boards outside to show what trade they were.
>
> Rebecca wanted to go back to that. So she painted all these little signs. It's kind of honouring all the trades that used to be in here. And she was really interested in the United Irishmen as advocates for equality. So the signs are all hand painted, and she's put gold leaf on one letter in each one. If you find them, and add them all together, it spells out the word equality.
>
> Like you're never going to get that unless you know about it. But it's magical.

* * *

There's far more in the Entries than I've been able to write about here. A reference to 'rebellion planned' at Crown Entry. A giant redshank bird at Cole's Entry. An old Plantation map in Castle Arcade with a quote from Cathal O'Byrne, that Belfast is 'in the mud and of the mud'. Both speak to Belfast's precarious relationship with nature. There are paintings of Belfast's punk scene – mohicans, Stiff Little Fingers and a raised fist. A female Phoenix-like figure of Belfast, portrayed like a masthead of a ship. There's an itinerant fiddler called Cocky Bendy, about whom I have outstanding questions.

Street art is not permanent. It is not declarative. All of these pieces are open to interpretation, and raise more questions than they answer. Art in the Entries will not solve the problems of the city.

But I feel such a strong sense of belonging to the city today with Gemma. Gemma says:

> These Entries are spaces in between. Between the traditional boundaries of our society, where radical things can happen. This is the Belfast I know and feel a connection to. Even though I don't live in Belfast anymore, the fact that I have made a mark here in some way is really special to me. Those panels are going to be here for a while. My words are on the wall. Only some people will notice them. Even less might take the time to stop and read them. But they're there.

Many of us in the North feel that we live somewhere where public space is already taken. It's been coloured in, in a way that we did not get to choose. Flags on lampposts transmit the message, 'this is our place, not your place'. Murals, the mighty Belfast culture whose language street art speaks, have only recently begun to reflect diverse subcultures outside the two dominant traditions.

In a talk about the Entries project, my friend Adam Turkington of Daisy Chain Inc. describes how the first walls his children saw every day had paramilitaries painted on them. How he never felt like there were any walls for him until the Teenage Dreams graffiti appeared under a Belfast motorway bridge.[18] Adam talks about a mural in Dublin that says, 'Do Not Be Afraid'. How seeing this message on a wall imperceptibly, but inevitably, infuses into people's daily lives.

It feels good to see these quiet marks on the walls. It does not bring 1798 into the mainstream. But it sends signals between those who recognise them. That this is our place too.

* * *

Public art does its job well when it starts conversations.

I send pictures to Seán Napier when I get home from my day with Gemma. Seán is confused by the images. He types back immediately, 'why is it all so

---

[18] When John Peel, an alternative music DJ, died in 2004, giant graffiti appeared under a motorway bridge in east Belfast that memorialised Peel and referenced a lyric in The Undertones song 'Teenage Kicks'.

subtle?' This is my first sign that others may not read the art in the same way as I did.

Seán Napier is a republican who runs a 1798 walking tour in Belfast with Colm Ó Dóghair. They are frustrated at the quietness of the Entries artwork. As they bring tour groups through the city, they say there is little to show people. No statues, few plaques, barely any of the buildings have been preserved. For Colm, this speaks to the history of unacknowledged unionist domination in the North. The fact that the Overton Window is at a place where being subtle and nuanced is the norm. That radical politics must always be muted. Colm and Seán want to change this. Many radical Protestants say this too, that the 1790s – one of our most enlightened political moments in terms of democracy, anti-slavery, celebration of Irish culture – should be remembered loudly.

A year after my day with Gemma, I am at a meeting of the United Irish Historical Society in Henry Joy's pub. Colm puts it this way: 'They used the word equality. But then they made the letters small. And then they hid it'. This hits me like lightning. To have experienced inequality in this city, to finally feel that there was a chance to speak, and how to him, it felt inadequate.

I say to Colm and Seán that I think the codedness of the art is almost part of our DNA in this place. Its subtlety feels like a second skin to me. I've spent much of my life working out how much can be said, and where. I felt that the art tapped into something deeply authentic about our history. Radical politics hidden down side alleys in the cultural underground.

Colm and Seán ask me to dream bigger. They say that deeply ingrained codedness is something that should be challenged, not accepted. That we should strive to be as radical and confident as the United Irishmen themselves. That we should not feel the need to celebrate all histories equally, because some are more relevant, more inspiring, than others. I hear what they're saying, and it stays with me.

This conversation is of course not about the artists. It's about the political context in which public art takes place. Would Belfast City Council have approved anything more overt? Was that the job of this project? How do you convey the imperial and conservative context of the Entries – for example the colonial sugar trade – in artwork that is purely confident and celebratory? Is that ahistorical? The Belfast Entries project was about urban regeneration.

The art in the Entries can only carry so much of the load in addressing the omission of 1798 from the city's built heritage.

But the conversation the Entries artwork is provoking is vital. Their existence has made many of us ask harder questions about politics and public space. The work has underlined that Belfast has not been an equal place to live, and that this inequality continues to be knitted into the architecture of the city. That the city centre has been designed as a 'neutral' shared space, with few references to even the Troubles. That a culture of caution and code is deeply embedded within our public bodies, and within our own selves.

But, as Catherine Switzer and Sarah McDowell (2009: 350) point out, official silences in Belfast city centre do not always reflect people's mental maps. Sites connected to 1798, like the Entries, still carry meaning for a lot of people. We are only beginning to work out how to recognise this. While it is not always easy to find answers, it is good work to be doing.

I also love the challenge of the question – how else can we write the 1790s back into the story of the city? And I love that many of us – Protestant, Catholic, Dissenter, heathen and Other – have decided to ask these questions together.

9
Lockdown in Moneyreagh

While everyone else is wrapping presents on Christmas Eve 2020, Will and I are walking around the graveyard of Moneyreagh Non-subscribing Presbyterian Church,[19] drinking tea from a flask, and talking about our lives. Winter sun beams down and frozen grass crinkles under our feet as we squint at the gravestones.

Something important for Will happened here in 2020 and I want to ask him about it.

During the COVID-19 lockdowns, we were all digging deeper into our local landscapes, because we were trapped at home. All life became local. For some, this meant looping nearby streets and parks. But for others, a deeper kind of discovery beckoned.

'I just feel comfortable in my own skin now', Will says.

> I used to feel like I was out of place, out of step. But I don't feel like I'm cosplaying republicanism any more. I've become comfortable with my Protestant identity. Being a Dissenter and a Presbyterian. Because being a Protestant has shaped me so much. Being able to combine that with my Irish cultural identity and my politics is everything.

If anyone gets the ghost limb, it's Will. In many ways, this is a journey of thought that we have taken together.

* * *

---
[19] The Non-subscribing Presbyterian Church of Ireland is a Unitarian Church. It is generally liberal in theology, stressing the importance of individual conscience. It is part of the General Assembly of Unitarian and Free Christian Churches.

THE GHOST LIMB

Will Jordan is a friend of mine in his early thirties. Raised in a Presbyterian, unionist home. He lives in the council house joined to the one he grew up in, in Moneyreagh village. Ian Paisley senior was a regular guest to the house he lives in now.

Moneyreagh is a predominantly Protestant village near Comber, in County Down. It's a small place, with under 1,500 residents. It's the kind of village where the DUP have been ascendant, with the centrist Alliance Party more recently nipping at their heels.

Social life in Moneyreagh in the 1990s and 2000s was church, Boys' Brigade, Orange Order and the occasional Ulster Scots event. It was a deeply Protestant, conservative and unionist world. Will grew up on a diet of BBC, and felt very British. On family holidays, he felt Donegal was like 'a foreign country... You just grow in a different universe, where you don't feel Irish'.

Yet Will always suspected he thought a bit differently to his family. Much of his story is a search for the information that makes sense of these feelings. There was a curious streak in him: 'I always felt that there was something wrong with sectarianism, despite the fact that I never met someone from a Catholic background until I was 18, at Tech.' Will started to become aware of class politics. One of his daily tasks at a dull desk job was to comb the local newspapers. Columns by Derry socialist, Eamonn McCann, about the Iraq War and international leftist politics, began to catch his eye.

The relevance of these ideas soon hit home. In 2012, Belfast City Council limited the number of days the Union Jack could be flown at City Hall, and Northern Ireland exploded, as it often does, into chaos. Loyalists protested on the streets almost daily, blocking roads, rioting, attacking the offices and homes of non-unionist politicians. It was a clenched time. Will was upset with the protesters' violence. But he was uncomfortable with the reaction to the loyalists too. People began to mock the protesters' working class accents, saying 'fleg' instead of flag. There was a sneer in it.

> At the next election I voted for the [loyalist] Progressive Unionist Party [PUP], who had a candidate who was very left-wing, progressive, forward-thinking. I felt really comfortable with that.

This kind of solidarity with those marginalised by social class comes up so often in this book. An empathy for loyalist culture and points of pain, despite our often differing political analyses. Many of us have voted for the PUP in the eras of David Ervine and Dawn Purvis.

The next step for Will was beginning to question Northern Ireland's constitutional status. His take on this is typically United Irish. For him, it's not about nationalism, blood or soil. It comes down to the North's democratic deficit.

> As soon as I was able to vote, I was looking at who the cross-community candidates were.
>
> But it soon became more of a practical thing. Realising how little power we have in the North, and how it's impossible to have left-wing politics when you're getting pocket money from London and haven't any real control over the big decisions.
>
> I know that Ireland has a lot of problems. The health system is not ideal. But you can push for change quicker. You've more power. You've a bigger voice.

Will's politics were now beginning to diverge significantly from his family's, with cross-cultural friendships, class politics and constitutional flexibility. But there was another puzzle piece that would not fit for a long time. And that was his identity. Will's feelings about Irishness. Like so many of us, Will shelved these feelings, identifying as Other and Neither. Opting out of it all:

> I was becoming more and more interested in Irish culture. But I would never have been open about that. Because it's so deeply ingrained in you, that it's wrong to go against what you're told, or what you grew up with.
>
> I also sort of felt like it was cultural appropriation.

While Will had always been drawn to the Irish language, he also worried that he had no business being near it. Family and teachers told him so. Even a nationalist acquaintance had said to him that Irish was a language of liberation, and sure wasn't he so privileged as a Protestant that he didn't need liberating.

> But then I became aware of what Linda Ervine was doing. I went to a talk she did one night about Protestants and the Irish language.

Linda, a Protestant Irish language activist who tells her own story in chapter 11, talked that night about Irish being woven through our place names, how Presbyterians were at the heart of the Gaelic Revival. She told stories about all the Protestants and unionist Irish speakers who signed the Ulster Covenant and fought in the World Wars. And, as before, Will gave himself permission to explore this new thought more deeply.

He started to listen to Motherfoclóir, an English language podcast about the Irish language. He downloaded the Duolingo app, took Irish language classes in real life. He earned a silver fáinne – a badge of progress in the Irish language.

Then, as with so many of us, came Will's discovery of the United Irishmen:

> Around the same time as hearing Linda, I started looking into the history of the United Irishmen. That's when I really started to feel comfortable that I wasn't culturally appropriating. That this is a history that belonged to me too.
>
> Reading about people like James Hope [a United Irish Presbyterian weaver] in Madden's book, I connected with that. I remember having a pint in Kelly's Cellars in Belfast then, and seeing a poster on a wall about the United Irishmen. That's when I started to look into it.

Will went on to research and drink his way around the Belfast Entries, and wrote an essay about it, knitting together 1790s revolutionary politics and reviews of beer (Mac Siúrtáin). He concluded that Kelly's Cellar's claim to 1798 lineage was unlikely, but that you should go anyway.

And this is where Will found himself in March 2020, when COVID-19 changed our lives forever.

* * *

During lockdown there wasn't much traffic on the roads. It was good cycling weather.

'It all started with townland names', Will says. Armed with his bike, PRONI historical maps, and a few websites, he set out to find old landmarks, raths, anything of interest.[20]

He points to Tullyhubbert: 'That's where the water tower is. In Irish it's Tulaigh Thiobrad, which means hillock of the well. The 1950s water tower is where the well was.'

Moneyreagh is Monadh Riabhach. The grey speckled bog land.

---

[20] http://logainm.ie; http://placenamesni.org

But these small discoveries were the tip of the iceberg. By the time of the pandemic, Will had already experienced a lot of identity change. But he still had a feeling, like so many of us, that he was dislocated from the place where he lived. A Moneyreagh misfit, quite alone in his difference. All this was to change.

'It was here, in this graveyard', Will says. 'That was the moment things really took off for me.'

* * *

One day in April, Will was idling around Moneyreagh, taking a photograph of a blue plaque on a building beside the Manse celebrating Robert Huddleston, an Ulster Scots poet. The minister was gardening and called over to Will: 'There's a lot of information about Huddleston, as well as his grave, in the church grounds if you look'.

Will was predisposed to this minister, having noticed that Moneyreagh's Presbyterian Non-subscribers are a liberal congregation. Their website says they are 'open-minded and open-armed,' and specifically welcome people from any 'religious background, age, gender, ethnicity or sexual orientation'.[21] A rare invitation in Northern Ireland.

Will went to look in the graveyard. He found Huddleston. And then he stumbled across Fletcher Blakely's gravestone.

Will googles Blakely – a Presbyterian farmer's son from County Down, who was the minister at Moneyreagh from 1809–1857. Blakely trained at Glasgow Divinity School, which was the source of so much of Ulster's Enlightenment thinking at the time. Theologically, under Blakely, Moneyreagh came to be seen as 'a radiating centre of liberal thought and Unitarian doctrine' (Crozier 1875: 135). People liked Blakely. He was charismatic and spoke plainly. He was enthusiastic about education. He advocated for tenants' rights.

Some synapses start to fire in Will's head. Moneyreagh – a radiating centre of liberal thought? This was unexpected. Will hunts down a pamphlet with a history of the Church to begin the unraveling (MacMillan 1969).

From April to June 2020, Will sends me updates of his discoveries. The following is – with his permission – a transcription of his Twitter DMs. I've

---

[21] http://www.moneyreaghnonsubscribers.com/

added some background, mostly from materials he collected during this time and allowed me to borrow.

> *29 April 2020*
>
> Digging into Rev Harold Rylett now who is a very interesting character.
>
> This Moneyreagh book is giving me all sorts of nuggets I can't believe. Like I do believe it, but it's blowing me away.
>
> For instance, apparently this radical preacher Harold Rylett has Michael Davitt [from the Irish Republican Brotherhood] speaking in the Moneyreagh church while he was campaigning for the Land League.
>
> And Parnell too allegedly. Speaking about Home Rule.

Michael Davitt and Charles Stewart Parnell were leading figures in Irish nationalism in the 19th century. Invited to speak in this place that Will always assumed was a unionist stronghold. This challenges so much of what we think we know about the Protestant north. I am as surprised as Will to learn of it.

Harold Rylett was born in England and led Moneyreagh church from 1879–1884 (MacMillan 1969: 52-3). He was a social reformer like Blakely, interested in agricultural reform and labourers' rights. He became the chief organiser of the Land League in Ulster, criticising the Orange Order for backing landlords rather than tenants (Courtney 2013: 266). The Non-subscribing Presbyterian magazine in 1936 (page 112) described Moneyreagh during this time as 'an Island of Radicalism in a Sea of Unionism'.

> *30 April 2020*
>
> The radical Moneyreagh folk have really got my mind buzzing today (may also be to do with the six cups of coffee I've drunk!). I've kicked over a stone I didn't know existed. Rev. Richard Lyttle is a fascinating guy. The Moneyreagh school hall that I did PE in, school plays in and played a gig in later in life, is named after an nationalist Irish language enthusiast who advocated for tenants' rights, women's rights, home rule and was regularly denounced by unionist newspapers. He preached nationalist doctrine from the pulpit in Moneyreagh church and had the church's newsletter printed in the *Irish News*. I mean where has this info been all my life?!

Rev. Richard Lyttle, from Dromore in County Down, served in Moneyreagh from 1889 to 1905. While Lyttle annoyed some church sextons, and occasional stones were thrown through the windows of meetings, the local congregation seems to have largely supported him (Thompson 1986).

Like many Dissenters, Lyttle wasn't anti-English. But he was anti-colonial, opposing the Boer War. He was critical of Queen Victoria for not being interested in Ireland. He thought Home Rule for Ireland presented the best chance of compulsory purchase of farms from landlords. He cultivated the community's 1798 heritage, helping Alice Milligan and Ethna Carberry set up the Irish Women's Association in 1894, supporting Moneyreagh women in their decoration of 1798 graves at the 1898 centenary. He established a Gaelic League branch in Moneyreagh (Maume 2009).

All of this radical Protestant history right under Will's feet. Disremembered. Histories which make direct contact with his 21st century gut.

> *30 April 2020*
> It's amazing that it was lockdown that forced me to actually look at my own patch's history. I've been reading Belfast history for years now, I just always thought that nothing ever happened here.
>
> I've a list of five Moneyreagh radicals so far.
>
> Including two from 1798.
>
> And four of them Unitarian Reverends.
>
> The local community association does a lot of stuff about Robert Huddleston, who was an Ulster Scots poet. But there's nothing at all on Lyttle – bar the old school and church buildings named after him. But there's no info about him.
>
> I assume it's because it's such a repressed history.
>
> *3 May 2020*
> What a whirlwind of a week. I know I should be beyond the whole cultural appropriation worry by this stage and 'Irishness' is not defined by the beliefs of my ancestry. But still, I feel a little less like a cosplayer today than before. And my mind is blown by the thought of a radical history in my very conservative, very loyal village.
>
> *5th May 2020*
> Well now, is thon Gaeilge I spy on the 1900 map of Monadh Riabhach?
>
> Seems to be marking the entrance of the graveyard – beside the Unitarian church. This would have been during the time our new pal Rev. Lyttle was minister.

> Roilig is graveyard it seems.
> Vanished [in later maps].

We think what happened is that when the Ordnance Survey Map of 1900 was being created, input was sought from important local figures. This was the time that Lyttle was active in the Gaelic League. It's likely that he submitted 'Roilig' for inclusion. When the map was updated, this was overwritten with English.

> *7 June 2020*
> Like it's wild that people who want to know about 1798 have to actively go looking for it. I knew nothing about it bar Wolfe Tone's name (and that's because of the band) until I was in my late twenties.

As Will was making these discoveries, he was also reading Guy Beiner's book. The book helped him, like me, to understand how many Protestants became disconnected from 1798 history.

> *9 June 2020*
> I wouldn't be comfortable now with people saying I have no claim to these beliefs or this republican heritage. Just because some of my family rejected that heritage. So much heritage was rejected after 1800. Guy Beiner's book talks about how so many people who were out fighting in the rebellion were wearing Orange sashes a few years later, because of the culture of fear.
>   What staggers me most is the repression of all this. It was thought-policed out of existence. To the point where 200 years later, people like me can feel uncomfortable about pursuing this path.

And that's it. The mental block. The thought-policing. Imposed by others and by our own selves. But then there's the counter point. The ghost limb. That gut feeling which compels so many of us to take the awkward, lesser travelled path. Just to see where it might lead.

The Moneyreagh DMs wind down in June, as lockdown measures ease. But it feels like Will's exploration of lost heritage, like my own, may continue for some time yet.

***

Will is very close to his family, many of who still live around Moneyreagh. But he doesn't talk to them much about politics.

> I think a lot of us just have to be sensitive about what we say. Not because we're ashamed or want to hide anything. But because a lot of my dad's generation would associate republicanism with the IRA; they had friends and family who were killed. And I wouldn't want to hurt them. Even though I don't associate those two things.

Will's doing a diploma in Irish now at the University of Ulster. He held back from telling his parents about his Irish until recently. But, as it turned out, they were happy for him.

As we empty the dregs of cold tea from our cups, Will weaves past, present and future together.

> I may be from a Scottish Planter background, but my family has been here for hundreds of years. Just like people from an Irish Gael background, their families have been here for centuries too, maybe a few millennia. Just like anyone who has come here from the Middle East escaping war, gaining Irish citizenship, they're Irish too.

And he's right. Ethno-nationalism doesn't mean a lot in the context of the continual movement of people over millennia, and in the 21st century.

Will's girlfriend is from West Belfast. Maybe he'll move there himself one day.

> But I'll always feel a tie to Moneyreagh. Learning about its radical history gave me more of a tie than I'd ever felt before. I never felt that close to this place, because I felt it would reject me. I felt like I was out of place. Out of step with the history. Realising that it's always been there has made me feel more comfortable in my own skin again.
>
> Learning about 1798, and the history of Moneyreagh after 1798, is more about me than the history really. It's about me becoming more comfortable with my own identity. And that I'm not culturally appropriating. That it's as much my history as anyone else's. That my love for the Irish language is not unique.
>
> I'm glad there is that radical strain. Because it does make me believe in a bit of change. It does make me believe that this spirit can emerge again. I think it is starting to emerge.

Standing in the graveyard, looking at Will in his 'Drop Seeds, Not Bombs' hoodie, I know that he is right. Something *is* starting to emerge. And I know he's not alone in the village in his connection to a diverse past. There are Protestants from Moneyreagh in my Irish language class. There were large handfuls of Alliance and nationalist SDLP votes in the Moneyreagh boxes at the last election. The head teacher, Roy Greer, recently published a book on Con O'Neill (Greer 2019). All of this shows an engagement with the past and the present as a tapestry, rather than a monoculture.

Some people in this book can tell stories about radical ancestors whose furrows they walk in. Others plough their own furrow. There was nobody in Will's family whose template he was following. A radical spirit is not in the blood. Protestant Irishness is a fictive kinship which can be opted into. As with so many of us, Will has made an active choice to engage with his ghost limb. And this is where it led. To the Non-subscribing Presbyterian Church graveyard in Moneyreagh. To an identity at peace with itself.

This journey of discovery is not just about the past. The graveyard is a place to pass through for enlightenment, not a place to fester. Will has broken out of the social and cultural segregation so many of us are raised with. He is an environmentalist, for whom the Irish language connects past, present and future natural worlds. He is active in environmental politics. An anti-racist who identifies with immigrants putting down roots, just like his own family did. He channels the wisdom of the Dreamtime into an active political life. United Irish incarnate.

Language

A lot of my exploration of the ghost limb has taken place in the world of language and landscape. This section focuses on my personal experiences with the Irish language and Ulster Scots, both of which have offered me ways of connecting with northern Protestant identity, and in which I have found alternative political frameworks. Linda Ervine describes her own ghost limb, talking about the Irish language, island and social class. And Angeline King talks about her experiences of living in Larne, a place rich with social and linguistic diversity.

10

The Magic Door

I'd been collecting little fragments of Irish since I was a teenager. A line of a poem or scrap of a song. In the evenings, I listened to Irish language radio in my bedroom. I didn't understand a word, but the sounds made me feel something. I'd always felt like there was an Irish-language-shaped space in my heart. A hidden compartment that I couldn't quite access. But I'd never known what to do with these feelings. How to make contact.

This seems strange to me now. I could have taken a bus across town and signed up for a class at Cultúrlann[22] anytime when I moved back to Belfast. But the blockage was deeper. Irish was never taught at my state schools. I'd never heard of a class in the parts of town where I lived. And I think this unconsciously led to a feeling that Irish was out of reach, that, as a Protestant, it was not really for me. I recognise this now as the ghost limb. The sense of feeling both connected to, and disconnected from, the language.

As I began to identify and articulate the ghost limb in more recent times, I became restless. I knew in my bones that there was richness here, if I could find a way to restore the connection.

Late one night, my friend Lisa sends me a message. She's researching her genealogy. She's found Protestant relatives who are recorded as having Irish in the 1901 census. Her grandmother remembers Irish being spoken in the house.

I needed to find out if this was my story too. I began my own genealogical adventures. The first stories gave themselves up easily. Official stories from the family canon, that drew a smooth line from past to present. I traced back my tree through four, eight, sixteen, thirty-two families. And I was astonished

---

[22] Cultúrlann McAdam Ó Fiaich is an Irish language cultural centre in The Gaeltacht Quarter in west Belfast. It was opened in 1991.

at the purity of my Protestant line, the brick wall of English language, my many, many Scottish antecedents.

Yet I knew that my genealogy must be more diverse than it seemed. My own family unit's sense of Irishness must come from somewhere. I thought about my Newry Protestant granny's cabinet in the good room, filled with Irish dancing trophies. I knew we had mixed marriage families dotted around. In my bones, I knew that there were stories beneath the surface that might help make sense of my Irish ghost limb. And so, I kept digging.

* * *

It's 2019 and I'm sitting in a packed classroom in the Lower Newtownards Road in east Belfast. It's full of Protestants learning Irish at the pioneering Turas project, set up by Linda Ervine, who tells her story in the next chapter.

Aodán, this week's teacher, slowly untangles a lifetime of hidden meanings about the way we speak. So many of the little words that are 'wrong' come from Irish: 'They're like dreams', he says 'they're hard to remember sometimes'.

But yet the muscle memory is there. We're not starting from scratch. Irish has 67 phonemes – or sounds – 22 more than English. 'But you'll know some of them already', Aodán says. 'Maghera, Lough, you have those sounds'.

'Maith sibh' means 'you' plural; more than one of you. We don't have a word for this in English. It's a bare 'you' whether you're talking to one or one hundred people: 'So when we say "youse" or "youssuns",' Aodán explains, 'it's trying to look for a meaning of "you" plural that we had in Irish'.

I learn later that a lot of our speech is Hiberno-English, where Irish words and grammar underpin the way we speak English on this island. Rounded out with Ulster Scots and even bits of Shelta too, the language of the Traveller community (Dolan 2020).

One of the first things we talk about in class each year is place-names. The connection is immediate. As I'm in the bunrang (beginner's class) so often, I can report that Ballyhackamore is consistently a hit. Ballyhackamore is a leafy area of east Belfast, known for its cafe and restaurant culture. Baile an Chacamair, townland of the slob land or mud flat. Or in local slang, cack meaning poo.

In the COVID-19 2020 Zoom class year, Rosemary is not on mute. She repeats 'townland of the big poo' over and over again, chuckling under her breath. Ripples of laughter spread around the class. Pure enjoyment of our connection with place.

As I sit in these Irish classes at Turas, I look around the room, imagining the reasons other people have come here. Wondering if they have a ghost limb too? If the classes help to ease it?

Every week I ask someone different, 'why are you here?'

Some people tell me they see Irish as a hobby and they like to keep their minds active. Some are brushing up on bits of Irish they picked up at school or from grandparents. Others are trying to keep up with their kids at the Gaelscoils. Many learners are here after discovering Protestants' long relationship with the language in Ireland (Ó Snodaigh 1995). At class, I find out that the Church of Ireland printed Bibles and prayer books and held church services in Irish. That Presbyterians helped set up the Gaelic League. That the first president of Belfast's Gaelic League, Dr John St. Clair Boyd, was a unionist (McCoy 2019).

Other people have deeply personal reasons for taking the class. One man I spoke with described his family as very unionist, Orange, conservative and evangelical. He said he had always felt like a black sheep. In his words, he was here to 'challenge boundaries and divisions within his own heart'. His family did not know he was taking the class. I think about this man often.

Researching in the early 1990s, Gordon McCoy (1997) found that learning Irish was especially difficult for working class Protestants, who felt like they were on the front line of the conflict, and faced social sanctions for associating with the 'other side'. In an animation produced by Turas, Ivor, a unionist lorry driver, says he used to see Irish as 'the enemy's language'.[23] But when he followed his curiosity and joined a class, he found that learning Irish 'was like walking through a magic door'. Ivor says that 'after a few times of going, all the nonsense that I had in my head went away'.[24]

Another learner from a 'staunchly Protestant background', Chris, said they did not have a word of Irish until they walked through the doors at Turas.[25] A few years later, Chris proposed to their wife in Irish. They said this was 'like marrying the two sides of me'. That Irish class gave them a sense of being at home in a way that they had only experienced before in the LGBTQ+ community. Chris likened this to putting on a cosy jumper.

I feel like this when I walk through Turas' doors too. Like I am at home.

---

[23] Turas, *Ulster Gaeilge*: Ivor, https://qft.vhx.tv/free/videos/ulster-gaeilge-ivor

[24] 'Unionist man's love for the Irish language brought to life in animation', Irish News, 3 March, 2021.

[25] Turas, *Ulster Gaeilge*: Chris, https://qft.vhx.tv/videos/ulster-gaeilge-chris

One of my favourite phrases in Irish is 'an maith leat do chuid oibre?' It is a way to ask 'do you like your job?' But it translates as 'do you like your share of the work?' There is something communitarian about this. It hasn't been updated from a time when people worked their patches of land together. It might be said that this harks back to the past. For me, it is also a language which imagines another way of being, and offers possibilities for the future.

As I take more classes, I begin to understand how umbilically connected the Irish language is to its environment. My townland is named after holly bushes, which grow ludicrously well in our garden. In a series of videos from Protestant Irish learners in Derry, Helen talks about what it meant to her to discover that Doire means oak-grove or oak-wood, which opened up a new understanding of her local ecology.[26] Helen says:

> In class, we also marked the various transitions, like St Brigid's day, Imbolc, really reconnecting back into the Celtic calendar in a way. And it's lovely then when you start to feel yourself part of those cycles, and you start to notice the Solstices, the change in the light, you start to feel more connected to your place.

One of the most beautiful things I've read in recent years is Manchán Magan's *Thirty Two Words For Field: Lost Words of the Irish Landscape*. He tells us that in Irish there is not just a 'field'. But rather 32 different words which describe the type of land of the field, its purpose, boundaries, how it is worked.

Something that sticks with me is the black seaweed that we call 'wrack' in English. It has many micro-local typologies in Irish, each describing different nutritional and agricultural properties, the different weather conditions it washes up in. My mum's people were wrack gatherers in Kilkeel. The relevance of this information is immediate. It seems like we may need to know all this again in a more ecologically attuned future.

Helen goes further and adds a political dimension. She says that she has found learning Irish restorative and empowering. That we do not need to accept the identities put upon us. How Irish can be a way of decolonising our minds. She does not elaborate in the video, and I am left chewing over the question of what this might mean for northern Protestants.

I attend a talk in Irish one night for the 50th anniversary of Bloody Sunday.

---

[26] https://www.culturlann.org/culture/droichead/discovering-irish

Feargal Mac Ionnrachtaigh talks about how the Irish language connects with class struggle and grassroots empowerment across the North. He links this to experiences of colonisation. How colonisation batters your sense of self-worth, and how the Irish language has helped restore confidence amongst working class Catholic communities. This gives me a new understanding of how the language can be a form of connection with self, community, history and activism.

While the current revival of the Irish language amongst northern Protestants might seem quite depoliticised, my sense is that many people I meet seek Irish out as part of a wider journey of connection with the island. Sometimes that journey is a conscious attempt to shake off the cultural programming of a divided society. To intentionally seek out inclusive spaces. I think for some northern Protestants, it can be about making a stand with an historically subordinated culture. Choosing to do our share of the work.

* * *

At some point after starting Irish classes, I stopped looking for the language in my own family history. I'd made peace with Irish as a present-tense exploration. I was happy to be in a space where others were shedding stereotypes and mingling cultural traditions. Connecting with the language of the island where I lived, its contours so intimately described by these words, was more than enough for me.

But then, after having made my peace, I found a connection in the most unexpected of places.

I'd left researching my paternal grandmother's line until last. My Newtownards granny never spoke about her life before marriage, and nobody seemed to have much information. But some clues were preserved in the records.

The Gibbney family lived on Belfast's Shankill Road in the 1900s. Presbyterians and Anglicans. House painters and linen weavers. Dora, my great-grandmother, is a Gibbney. In the 1901 census, her big brother Archie and his whole family speak Irish as their first language. Archie's brother James, his wife and brother-in-law are all recorded as speaking Irish and English the same year.[27] Another brother Samuel marries RoseAnn.

---

[27] Many Protestants' entries of Irish speaking are scribbled out in the 1901 and 1911 censuses, most likely by a census official. Archie and his children's Irish was left intact, and his wife Elizabeth is recorded as speaking both Irish and English. James and his family do have their Irish scribbled out. While the reason for the alterations is not known, there are various theories.

RoseAnn's family in County Antrim only speak Irish. And so it goes on.

Gibbney. Ó Gibne. Gibne. A lock of hair? A family keepsake.

Eoghan Ó Néill found that as many people were recorded speaking Irish in the Shankill as in the Falls in the 1911 census. Up to 17 per cent in some streets (*Belfast Telegraph* April 2012). I checked my family's staunchly Protestant streets in 1901 and 1911. Between 13-15 per cent of people are recorded as speaking Irish. Had I found it? The invisible cord that had been pulling me towards the language?

One of the earliest branches of the Gaelic League was set up on the Shankill Road (Ó Snodaigh 1995: 91). Did the Gibbneys come into contact with it? Did Maria, the Gibbney's mum, bring Irish to industrial Belfast from the rural Sperrins? The wider Gibbney family had many Catholic intermarriages, and I wonder if this might be how they had Irish in their lives. It begins to sink in that the history of the Irish language in the North was perhaps woven through my family history too.

But just as I think I have found the thread, I lose it again. By 1911, the Irish language is gone from my family's official records. Did they lose their Irish by accident? Or was it disremembered? My Gibbneys weren't all that literate. There are no diaries or letters for me to cross-reference how they spoke. It is difficult to excavate the histories of the poor. I am left only with questions. Wandering around the Dreamtime, imagining their lives.

Of course the erasure of Irish started much further back, with the Penal Laws. People were punished for speaking it. Urban living diluted the language over time and Irish became concentrated in more rural areas. The Catholic Church was patchy in its support (Ó Ciosáin 2015). An Gorta Mór, the Great Hunger, took a grave toll on the language, as speakers died and emigrated.

As National Schools were set up across Ireland in the 19th century, English

---

Ulster Scots expert Mark Thompson thinks that many people who said they spoke Irish on the census had an awareness that they did not speak proper English, and so they called it 'Irish'. But in Antrim and Down, Thompson thinks it's more likely that they spoke Ulster Scots, which wasn't an option on the census (http://clydesburn.blogspot.com/). Areas that have large Ulster Scots speaking populations today of course had them 100 years ago. I think there is much value in this theory. On the other hand, if I compare the records from Belfast's Shankill Road and Falls Road, it does not make sense to me that most Protestants' Irish was scribbled out and most Catholics' Irish was not. Life was not that compartmentalised. Plenty of marriages were mixed, including in my own family. Linguistic mingling has always been a feature of speech in this part of Ireland. It also seems wise not to rule out the idea that some people's Irish was scribbled out for political reasons.

was promoted as the proper way to speak and get ahead. In the first decades of the 1900s, unionist MPs described Irish as a useless language, a waste of money, with seditious tendencies (Andrews 1997). The parallels with the present are striking. After partition, unionist politicians began to remove Irish language teaching from schools. Between 1924 and 1927, the number of primary schools teaching Irish in the North halved (Mac Póilin 2006: 114-35). In 1987, a report found 40 per cent of Catholics in Northern Ireland aged 16–24 had some knowledge of Irish, compared to 0 per cent of Protestants (Sweeney 1987). So there was a near extinction of the Irish language amongst Protestants during the Troubles.

I think about my Gibbneys' language loss. I pore over newspaper archives and see how politically heated the Shankill was becoming in the years between 1901 and 1911. Their Catholic neighbour was shot for 'talking back' to a British soldier. A mural of King Billy was painted on the gable wall of their street. Half of the family signed the Ulster Solemn League and Covenant. Large Orange Order demonstrations were taking place in neighbouring streets. I can imagine why it might have been socially astute and politically expedient to Anglicise during these years. How it might have been safer to swallow those words.

My own granny, half Gibbney, never talked about her upbringing. She presented as middle-class, a devout Presbyterian, strongly unionist. There were no hearthside stories. No trace of the Irish. The Troubles provided yet another reason to stay quiet about the Irish, that is if she ever knew about it in the first place.

Finding the Gibbney's Irish leaves me with many questions. I wonder how the relatively recent presence of the language trickled down through our family. If we unconsciously picked up some kind of intergenerational thread. Were fragments of code passed on by accident? A trail of breadcrumbs. Did our Hiberno-English speech contain the social memories for us? Leaving just enough to decipher later?

And that's the Irish ghost limb, I think. A cultural reservoir that lies off the beaten track. A thread that can connect us to our heart's stories, if we wish to pull it.

* * *

Ideas loop around. And so does the language. While Irish was nearly extinguished amongst northern Protestants during the Troubles, the muscle memory lingered. The sounds stayed on our tongues as we said where we lived, Magherafelt, Ahoghill, Cregagh. A dedicated community of Irish language activists kept the torch lit throughout these years. Tending to a language that, as we would rediscover, belonged to us all.

Aodán Mac Póilin puts it well when he says that, '[l]anguages and their cultures are not static; they do not live in libraries or theme-parks. They live in communities, in a constant dynamic between a complex past and a complex present' (Mac Póilin 2018: 16). Our fragile peace opened up a window where it became possible to explore our shared heritage again. Many of the barriers to Protestants accessing the Irish language have dropped. Are dropping. Slowly.

And here we are in the 2020s in Northern Ireland. Hundreds, maybe thousands, of Protestants learning Irish. Struggling with fadas and séimhiús and how to pronounce 'is deas bualadh leat'. 'It is nice to meet you'. Tracing our fingers over the lost words. Trying to work out what they mean for us.

I haven't yet made much progress with the language. As my love for Irish is not matched by my linguistic ability. Eternal bunrang of the addled mind.

But, in a way, I think that's where I'm meant to be. With people who are on a similar journey. Feeling these little jolts of recognition and rediscovery together. Getting under the bonnet of our own histories. Piecing together how the Irish and the Ulsterness intertwine.

In so many ways, Irish has helped bring me back to a Protestant identity, after feeling so Neither and Other. Because I had found a way of being Protestant on the island that I could relate to. The language soothes my ghost limb. It slips its hand into mine as we walk through the landscape, naming its features. It creates little revolutions in my mind as ideas of being and sharing are transformed. 'Out of a healed past a healed present will grow', says Moriarty. I am beginning to understand what he means now.

11

Seol Beag
(A Little Sail)

It is four days since we announced that Naíscoil na Seolta, a new integrated Irish-medium nursery school, will be opening in the grounds of Braniel Primary School in east Belfast. Linda Ervine and others have been teaching Irish in the primary school, and it emerged that a purpose-built nursery space was available on site. There had been little to no objection to Irish classes in the school, so the naíscoil committee (of which I am a member) decided to go for it.

Sixteen toddlers, from all backgrounds, learning Irish together in a mobile classroom. Dearcán beag – a little acorn. But it feels important. We hope it will be the first step towards setting up an integrated Irish-medium primary school in east Belfast. We choose a school motto – 'páistí sona ag foghlaim le chéile' – 'happy children learning together'. 'Naíscoil na Seolta' means 'nursery of the sails'. A nod to east Belfast's shipbuilding history, and a hopeful image of little boats sailing off on a journey together.

A few extra flags have gone up outside the school gates since the announcement. Some people on Facebook are threatening to picket. But there is a lot of support. One parent messages to say that he is a confident loyalist, that his child loves the Irish classes in the primary school, and that the nursery presents no threat to his identity. He signs up for an adult Irish class that weekend. Diane Dawson, Braniel Primary's head teacher, is unwavering in her enthusiasm for having the naíscoil on her grounds. It sits side by side with the Northern Ireland centenary party the school is having the following week, with red, white and blue lemonade for the kids.

Linda Ervine has seen it all before. Having set up Turas, an Irish language and cultural hub, on the Lower Newtownards Road in Protestant east Belfast in the mid-2010s, she knows that change is hard. That breaking down cultural barriers takes time. But, as she says, for every person complaining, or out on the street protesting, there are many hundreds of others who either do not care or are actually quite interested. As we head up to her house to fetch some naíscoil paperwork, Linda reflects, 'the reality of this place is so much nicer than it seems'.

* * *

Linda Ervine is a well-known Protestant Irish language activist from east Belfast. I would love to see her face reading that line when she was a teenager. Because this was never a life that a young Linda would have imagined.

Born on the Lower Newtownards Road into quite a fractured family, pregnant at 15 and struggling with her mental health, Linda never had big expectations for her future. But there's a grit and a fight in her. A glint in her eye. Her pursuit of education, and later her discovery of the Irish language, would change her life as she knew it.

To understand Linda's journey, it's best to start at the beginning. Her family lived disjointedly, and she spent a lot of time living with her grandparents. But the common threads that tied her family together were anti-sectarianism and socialism. Both of these are a product of her family's early experiences of intermarriage on one hand, and the grind of poverty on the other. Linda says:

> I'm a Presbyterian, because my mother had me christened. Her own mother was Catholic. My daddy's side were all Church of Ireland, but they were all atheists and communists. It's an interesting mix.
>
> I always felt very disconnected because of the family politics. There was always a sense of being not one thing or another. My mummy and daddy split up when I was young. At one point I went to live with my daddy in Twinbrook, and this whole other narrative opened up. I went to a Catholic school there for a while. As a child, life was very fragmented, and I found it all very confusing. I loved the bonfires and the bands. But we weren't Orange Order. I never signed up to any of that.
>
> My first husband was from the Newtownards Road. His father was a socialist. He actually joined the army because he was being tortured to join the paramilitaries. And he hated all that. He wasn't sectarian. We always felt very outside of politics here.
>
> During the 1980s, we were very interested in English politics, because it was Labour and Thatcher. He was a factory worker, and lost his job, so we were very hard hit by it all.

This blend of anti-sectarianism and socialism still shapes Linda's ideas about the world. Her analysis of where we find ourselves is typically United Irish:

> I have no time for hatred of anything British. My grandfather was English. I'm much more interested in how we can recognise our mixed history, and think of ways to work together in the future. My early politics was all formed around the English socialist tradition. I really do value the link between these islands.
>
> But also, I've always seen myself as Irish. Because obviously I was born in Ireland. I've always felt like I belonged on this island.

Yet, Linda has a frustration about being Protestant and Irish, which I'm not sure existed in 1798. It's a strange kind of self-alienation that I share. A disconnection from Irishness that doesn't feel right.

> In many ways, I think Protestants are the forgotten Irish. I'm not from the South, I'm not Catholic, I'm not nationalist. So my Irishness doesn't reflect these things. We have this kind of stereotypical idea of what it is to be Irish. And it's not who I am. But I'm still Irish, so I feel like quite often my identity is ignored or denied, when my Irishness is every bit as valid.
>
> I was doing a talk one night in a Protestant church hall, and a woman came up to me after. She was telling me that her dad was in the Orange and he was raging that she was here. But she said, 'thanks so much for saying that. I feel Irish and I want a united Ireland, not for the politics, but just so I could feel that I belonged somewhere'.
>
> I thought she really articulated something there. That feeling of Protestants being somehow cut off from an Irish identity here.
>
> I think the United Irish history, that's such an important thing that has been forgotten, and hidden, and cast aside. I'm a Presbyterian. My great granny is buried at Saintfield. I remember doing a 1798 tour in Saintfield with a group from West Belfast. You know, I am a Presbyterian and yet here I was with Catholic people learning my own history. I never knew it before. So that gave me a new pride in being a Presbyterian. And it gave me a sense of belonging.

As I listen to Linda, I feel I am tripping over people's ghost limbs. How many of us have been carrying all this around? Loving all that is good about English radicalism, but feeling disconnected from our Irishness. Feeling that we are alone in our difference.

Linda, though, has gone further than most of us. She has been path-finding. Showing others how to reconnect to our heritage, to restore belonging. Ploughing furrows for the rest of us to walk in.

* * *

Linda married Brian Ervine in the 2000s. Brian became the leader of the loyalist Progressive Unionist Party in 2010 after the death of his brother, the late David Ervine. Although Brian and Linda's politics often differ, the pointlessness of sectarianism, and a love for class-based politics, is where their minds meet. They also both believe in the transformative potential of education. They met while teaching at the same school.

> My background is that I had no education. I never really went to school. I was very intimidated by middle-class people. When I did adult education, and then the PGCE at Queen's University Belfast, I was so terrified. It was so out of my comfort zone. I had no confidence at all.
>
> When I went to Castlereagh College, there was an older man in the class who told us quite often that he had a degree in science. One day the teacher asked me to show him how to embed quotes in a text. The science man was horrified. The likes of me. He saw me as the cleaner, because I was so working class. A few years later, I was so excited to get to Queen's. And I saw him again. He thought I was cleaning, and asked, 'what are you doing here?' I said, 'I done my A levels', because that was just how I spoke, 'and I'm here to do my PGCE'. He turned to his friend and said, 'Good Lord, they'd let anybody in here now'.
>
> But here's the sad thing. I thought he was right. Because I felt so valueless. See the first six months I was at Queen's, if somebody had said to me, 'away you home love, there's been a mistake,' I'd have toddled off home.
>
> I used to do any qualifications going. There was one ICT training course I did, and I had to take a teaching practice session at the college. I put stuff into the printer and some of it came out white, and some of it was yellow. So I said to the class, 'if you have a look at the yella sheet'. And this one said, 'yella? what's yella?' And I remember just feeling awful. Because I never grew up speaking any other way. Today I know that this is my vernacular. It's just how I speak. If you don't like it, that's your issue. But I didn't understand that then. All I felt was inferior.
>
> I was following this journey of education. I wanted to change my life so

> much. I had been a parent from 16 and I was in my mid-thirties. All I had known was menial jobs, parenthood, no money, unemployment, struggle and violence. It was a mess, and all of a sudden there was this shining light.

And it was a light that Linda fixed her eye on. But, just like her later journey with the Irish language, gaining an education was bittersweet. With depth of understanding, came an outsider status.

> A Scottish working class poet came over and read a poem, which I related to later. It was about how education is a journey that you go on. But it's like going to another country, and it's unfamiliar and frightening. And then you settle, and you make it part of your life. But when you try to go back, you discover that you are an alien in your own country. All of a sudden your own people treat you differently, because you are not one of them anymore.
>
> I noticed that first of all in the chippy, because I was still working in the chippy when I was at Queen's. All of a sudden I had different interests and experiences that the people I worked with couldn't really relate to it. And that made me different. You make people feel uneasy, because they feel that you're looking down on them. And you're not. But they don't see that. And all of a sudden your world becomes different. Your conversations become different. You find something, but you lose something as well. I will always be who I am; I'm working class. But I have moved into another world as well.
>
> And the same thing has happened with the Irish. Because I am often looked on with suspicion by my own community. People are often very threatened by something that they can't relate to.

I think this echoes how a lot of alternative Protestants feel when they explore a new politics. That you lose the easy familiarity and sense of belonging to your community.

But, as Linda says, with Irish as with education, you gain so much.

> I found learning Irish changed the way I felt about my English. It's all these things I'd say, like 'we bes here', because that's what you grew up saying. And all of a sudden you have an understanding of youse and youssuns, which comes from the Irish having a plural 'you'. It was a lovely link for me. Your grammar is not bad grammar. It has a history and a heritage and a meaning and a link back to the past.

THE GHOST LIMB

I think about all of us who have found Irish speakers in our working class Protestant (and Catholic) families. How the attempt to erase local speech ended up being internalised by people as an inner voice of failure. That what they were saying was wrong, instead of an authentic way to speak English on this island. Once again, I'm struck by the knowledge unlocked by the Irish language. Its restorative power.

***

Turas is Irish for journey, and is a hub for Irish language and culture in east Belfast. Based on the Lower Newtownards Road, 65 per cent of its learners are Protestants. It has given many of us a way to reconnect with our heritage that we couldn't imagine before.

Linda tells me about Turas' origin story. It's a project that grew from the seeds of cross-community encounter, friendship and curiosity. Linda has a strong personal religious faith, so she talks about the journey in terms of providence, as something that God meant to be.

> I didn't go out to find the Irish language. It came to me. I believe in providence. It was just a series of events. I was teaching at Ashfield Girls' School for nine years. The Irish popped up. My Principal had agreed to do an event with Comhairle na Gaelscolaiochta [the body that promotes Irish-medium education in Northern Ireland] and I said, I'd be happy to do it. That was the first mention of it. Then a wee girl in my year eight, her granda, who was very loyalist, was learning Irish. I thought that was interesting. I didn't do anything about it, but it was almost like I wasn't going to be allowed to avoid it, you know?
>
> So the next thing that happened, I joined a cross-community women's group. We went back and forth between the East Belfast Mission and the Short Strand Community Centre. We did all sorts, a poetry book one week, a wee weekend away, it was just good craic and good company. Then they said, 'do you want to do a six week taster course in the Irish language?' And I thought it might be interesting, and went with my friend.
>
> The teacher turned out to be Máirín Hurndall, a Protestant Irish speaker. She told me there was going to be a dianchúrsa, an intensive Irish language course, at An Droichead. We went, and it was such good fun. I think it stuck out that we were Prods. Because the teacher, Áine Máire, came up to us at

the break just to tell us how welcome we were and that there were all types of people learning Irish.

The way Linda tells the next bit makes me laugh. Áine said to Linda, 'We even have a man who is a member of the Progressive Unionist Party'. To which Linda replied:

Well my husband is the leader of the Progressive Unionist Party!
And that was the start of it.

I just loved it. I was busy in work. Brian was the leader of the Progressive Unionist Party at the time. Life was stressful. The Irish classes were like a wee oasis. We went to things at Cultúrlann, to Donegal, the summer school up at McCracken, which used to be in the Presbyterian church – it was like a massive holiday camp. It opened up all kinds of worlds I didn't know existed. That was the lovely social side of it. I never felt so welcome. Just the pure enjoyment of it. Going home every week with new words to learn, something to get your head around. I just loved it.

And then people kept saying to me, 'did you ever read this, did you know about that?' And then I started reading these books about Presbyterians, and making all these connections between Protestants and the Irish language. And just the complete shock of it.

I know I don't come from a sectarian background, but there was still a part of me that thought I was maybe doing something wrong by learning Irish. It's just a wee hump that a lot of Prods have to get over, including myself. But there was just something in me. It was just a feeling. I knew I had to go further with it.

That 'wee hump'. Wanting to learn Irish, but feeling that it might be wrong. That's the ghost limb. Nevertheless, Linda persisted.

Not long after this, she found herself forming a small voluntary class which met in the East Belfast Mission. She talks about serendipitous meetings and connections with people, where all the dots started to join. She got a little bit of funding from Foras na Gaeilge. Matthew Caughey who had been teaching Irish in Ashfield Girls school came to help out. 'Just the way it all happened', Linda says, 'it feels like it was meant to be'.

Gordon McCoy (2019) has written a short book on the history of the Irish language in east Belfast. It starts with early Irish speakers building raths in the Castlereagh hills between 600–900. Along the way, there are Gaeilgeoirí who are unionists, soldiers, clerics, Orange Grand Masters. It takes in Naíscoil Mhic Airt being set up in the Short Strand in 1984.

There is one page at the very end of McCoy's book which talks about Turas. It's a lovely way to look at it. That Turas is not a big change for east Belfast. It is simply a link in a very long chain of Irish language in this part of the city.

I've been weaving in and out of Turas for many years now. It's a place that feels like Dissenter HQ. Where minds and hearts are open. Somewhere where I am at home, despite my terrible Irish. Because it's so much more than a language hub. Everyone in Turas' orbit is looking to the future, building bridges. They are living lives that manifest the change they want to see in our society.

Maybe we will always be a small voice within the wider Protestant community. Maybe it's enough that somewhere like Turas exists and its doors are open. Maybe you just need a critical mass of people at any given time to provide hope. Or maybe, our stories will grow beyond these walls.

Linda says:

> When we started Turas, there was never a plan. But when people have come here over the years, they've found something. I'm thinking especially about the Protestants. There was nobody voicing how they felt or what they thought. There isn't really a platform for people like us. They didn't really fit anywhere. You couldn't really voice it during the Troubles, but now you can.
>
> We're birds of a feather here. There are so many positive people. We seem to attract a certain type of person. And I want this to grow over the years, just to make space for people. Not for people to be articulating what I say, but for people to be using this as a jumping off point for their thinking. I love the way that a broader Protestant identity, and the fluidity within it, has grown here. The idea that you don't have to stay stuck in that box.
>
> And at times it is a hard thing to carry. And I felt that this weekend, you know, getting attacked again over the naíscoil. But what else can you do? You can't just go along with the way things are. You just have to keep engaging. Keep doing what you're doing.
>
> I know that what we do here doesn't represent a majority. But it does resonate with many people, who feel a similar thing. That is such a powerful thought. It also shows you how things can change. How one person can

make a difference. And what would happen if we all spoke up? What a different world it would be.

* * *

Naíscoil na Seolta finally opens its doors in October 2021. We have to change location at the last minute. The campaign by disaffected loyalists was troubling us. Posters appeared across the Braniel estate, with an image of Linda photoshopped beside Michelle O'Neill and John Finucane from Sinn Féin. Threats start to flow in. The PSNI tell Linda to up her security. She, Brian and other loyalist Irish learners involved with Turas and the naíscoil met with the people behind the campaign to explain that the plan was to rent just one mobile classroom for a year or two. To put a human face on the idea of the nursery. But they were not for stopping.

As we were wondering what to do, the first protests started. Five people turned up with placards outside the local shop. Two were from outside the area. It was a tiny handful of people, in comparison with the flood of support. But the memory of loyalist protesters at Holy Cross in 2001 kept us awake at night.[28] We felt we couldn't take the risk with two and three-year-olds.

In the looping way that things happen, the naíscoil actually moved into my childhood church, Christian Fellowship Church on east Belfast's Holywood Road. It's a non-denominational church that is quite comfortable with its Irishness. Once the location changed, the protesters melted away. Maybe they felt like they won the day. The rest of us were just buoyed by the support, which ran deep and wide. Many unionist politicians condemned the threats. The donations that came in the wake of the intimidation allowed us to buy multicultural toys and dressing up clothes.

And now all these little sails are learning Irish words for the world around them in east Belfast, in a way that stretches back thousands of years. Tiny people who are new links in a long chain. Stepping through new portals that Linda and others have made appear. Into a deeper understanding of our heritage, and deeper relationships across traditional divides.

---

[28] Holy Cross is a Catholic primary school for girls in Ardoyne in north Belfast. It is situated in an area that used to be religiously mixed, but became segregated during the Troubles, leaving the school in a Protestant area. In 2001, Holy Cross was picketed by hundreds of loyalist protesters, shouting abuse and throwing stones, bottles, golf balls, urine, excrement and a blast bomb at Catholic children and their parents as they walked to school. See Cadwallader 2004; *Belfast Telegraph* September 2021.

12

A Bridge To Scotland

When I was a teenager, I had a little lilac cassette player from Argos. It was the early 1990s, the age of mix tapes. I recorded songs from Irish language radio onto scratchy tapes. They felt like they had something to do with me, but I wasn't sure what.

One song I'd keep coming back to was, what I know now is called, 'Dónal agus Mórag'. I played these cassettes for 20 years. They were like fragments of code. I transferred them into each successive car like little relics. I'd sometimes hear scraps on Raidió Fáilte. When the first notes would strike up on the car radio, my children would shout, 'that's your song!'

But it still made no sense. What to even enter as a Google search term was beyond me. This seems crazy now. 'Agus' is simply Irish for 'and'. The tiniest, most humble, of building blocks. But it took for me to start Irish language classes for the penny to drop. The next time the song came on Raidió Fáilte, I picked out enough words to google it when I got home.

That night I played 'Dónal agus Mórag' twenty times on a loop on Spotify, swinging my kids giddily around the living room in a badly executed céilí. I still had no idea what the song was about. The knowledge, when it came, took me somewhere I didn't expect.

Dónal agus Mórag got married in Rathlin island, off the coast of Antrim, probably in the 19th century. The song is about their epic, gout-inducing wedding. Early verses had been collected by Mary Campbell and others from Rathlin (Campbell 1951: 89 & 128) and Neil McCurdy, a piper and stonemason probably brought the fragments to Donegal (Ó Cléireacháin 2015: 143). The modern song, as I heard on the radio, is by the band Altan.

Sometimes I think of the other people who have walked around with these song fragments too. Filling in the gaps.

The song helps me connect some dots. An Sruth na Maoile – the Straits of Moyle – is a meeting point between Ireland and Scotland. On a clear day, you can see Islay, Jura and Rathlin from Donegal and Antrim. From Islay you can see Rathlin and the Antrim Hills. Some days it almost seems like one land mass.

The language spoken in Rathlin was a meeting point too. A transitional dialect between Irish and Scottish Gàidhlig, containing features of each.[29] A bit of Manx too. Many of the songs from Rathlin have Scottish origins, some dating back to the 1500s (Nic Lochlainn). Stuart Eydmann (2018) talks about the flow of people between regions. Fishing, seasonal employment, soldiers, travellers, Argyll islanders visiting Ballycastle's Lammas Fair. Cultures tangling, layer upon layer. A linguistic bridge between islands.

* * *

The deeper my journey with the Irish language, the more it circled me back not just to Scots Gàidhlig, but also to Ulster Scots. In fact, I realise that I actually understand more Ulster Scots than Irish. I begin to see that these linguistic traditions and cultures cannot be neatly picked apart. Each is embedded in the other.

Linda Ervine says:

> It took me a while to get a handle on it. It was actually Irish speakers who encouraged me to look into it. Aodán Mac Póilin [an Irish speaker and author] was really into Ulster Scots. He loved that heritage. Gordon McCoy did a project on the Languages of Ulster, which looks at how Scots and Ulster Scots are influenced by Irish, and vice versa, and how they're all influenced by other languages. I find these overlaps really lovely and fascinating.
>
> I do a lot of work with Liam Logan, who speaks Ulster Scots. We did a thing for NVTV [a community TV channel] where we sit back to back. We start by saying that this is how a lot of people think about Irish and Ulster Scots. Things like 'dislike, distrust'. And then we talk about all the connections and relationships between the languages. So Liam, a Catholic Ulster Scots speaker, and me, a Prod speaking Irish. We make a point of travelling to things together, so people realise that we are friends and not in any way in opposition to each other.

---

[29] https://languagevolcano.wordpress.com/tag/east-ulster-gaelic/

You can see this synergy in *The Hamely Tongue* – a documentary about Ulster Scots made by Irish language activist, Deaglán Ó Mocháin.[30] In the film, presenter Seimí Mac Aindreasa sits in on a traditional music session, swaree, being led by Willie Drennan in an Orange Hall. 'Where exactly am I?' Seimí asks. 'Closing my eyes, I could be in a parish hall in Donegal in my youth, absorbing my own culture.' He travels to Dunloy, where Irish and Ulster Scots influences sit side by side. Both 'Fair Fae Ye' and 'Fáilte'[31] are written on stones in the village. It is moving to watch this journey of thought. The film ends with him watching a sham battle, where the two opposing sides walk off together. Seimí ends by saying, 'step by step, I too leave this false battle behind'.

James Fenton, Antrim collector and poet, gets to the heart of it. He says that Ulster Scots is a language of the people:

> Yins that are against it, would try to argue that it's an invention for Protestants. And yins that are for it, would maybe try to give the impression that it's their tongue and naebodie else's. Both views are nonsense, it's rubbish. It's oor tongue. And by oor, I mean us al.[32]

* * *

I first heard of Ulster Scots around the time of the 1998 Agreement. My first reflex was to reject the term. I'd fallen into the trap that Fenton describes, thinking that it was a political concoction, invented to even things up with Irish, used to claim that Ulster Protestants are a separate tribe. At times, Ulster Scots does take these forms. But ethnic stories of peoplehood are not what I am looking for.

As I wander around the landscape of Antrim and Down, I realise I'd been tuning into the surface politics of Ulster Scots without exploring its depth. As a city creature, I'd lost my natural connection with the people who speak it. My recoil did not do justice to how many of my neighbours saw the world. Wesley Hutchinson (2018), writing about the Ulster Scots imagination, encouraged me to think instead about its rootedness and expansiveness. Moss and mountain, farm and factory, church and community.

The cogs finally start to turn. I pick up a booklet in North Down museum

---

[30] 'The Hamely Tongue – Cultúr Ceilte', TG4, 2010.

[31] Ulster Scots and Gaeilge respectively for 'welcome'.

[32] Fenton, James. 'Iver Hantin Echas – Exploring the Ulster-Scots Tongue', BBC 2, January 2006.

that contains an Ulster Scots language test, asking if the reader knew these 'hunner words'?[33]

The hunner words are lovely. All eejits and oxters and things that are footery. Blethering and guldering. Being scunnered because you're a mingin slabber who boked when you were steamin. Words that were brought to Ulster by many of the early Planters and migrants, with the broad accents and everyday turn of phrase of lowland Scots. Words that make me feel rooted to this piece of our island. Ordinary people words. Words that reflect our black humour and grit.[34]

They are also words that have been blattered out of people. Because many of the new settlers in Ireland were far from the elite. While some of the new planted families and their friends were wealthy, Stewart of Donaghadee described other newcomers from Scotland and England in the early 1600s as 'the scum of both nations, who, for debt, or breaking and fleeing from justice, or seeking shelter, came hither' (Stevenson 1920: 45).

Over time, Ulster Scots became bound up in class politics. In 1860, David Patterson, a teacher at the Ulster Institution for the Deaf, Dumb and Blind, published a book *The Provincialisms of Belfast and the Surrounding Districts Pointed Out and Corrected*. Patterson lists all of our local 'mistakes', our corruption of English, improper sounds and spoiled words. He would like us to say child instead of chile, yon not thon. Words like skelfs and farls are only used, Patterson says, by the 'low and vulgar'.

I am annoyed at Patterson. A broad Ulster Scots speaker talks to me about her work voice and her home voice, how she often has to switch quickly between the two. There's a snobbery about Ulster Scots that has not gone away. I come to see these words as connected to a local independence of mind, a refusal to be told what to do by our 'betters'.

As I allow my mind to open and soften, the more I find myself drawn to these sounds. They remind me of long County Down walks with my grandma and granda, naming the sheughs and the slaters. I start using them in my own speech. The words feel good. At first, it's the simple joy of the sounds. The fact that a 'slater' feels more natural to say than 'woodlouse'. But as I walk

---

[33] 'Hunner': Ulster Scots for 'one hundred'.

[34] These are Ulster Scots words from my own everyday speech. Eejits – idiots; oxters – armpits; footery – fiddly; blethering – talking nonsense; guldering – shouting; scunnered – embarrassed; mingin – gross; slabber – messer; boked – vomited; steamin – drunk.

around 1798 Dreamtime, I realise I have found something else too. Many of the voices reaching out through time are speaking in Ulster Scots.

* * *

While the genteel United Irishmen wrote political pamphlets in standard English, Ulster Scots was the vernacular of most of the northern United Irishmen. It is the language in which a lot of the history of the northern rebellion was recorded and its folklore written. Many ordinary United Irishmen wrote poetry in Ulster Scots. They were drawing on the tradition of Rabbie Burns, who despite having both conservative and radical themes in his work, inspired people in Ulster with his broad Scotch poems that spoke about everyday people and the things they did.

The BBC's 'Narrow Sea' radio documentary paints an image of the weaver poets propping Rabbie Burns books against their looms, reading while the bobbin spun back and forth, soon becoming inspired to record their own experiences.[35] Weaver poet, Samuel Thompson, published some of these poems in the *Northern Star* and was sympathetic to the United Irishmen. James Orr, the Bard of Ballycarry, and James Campbell of Larne participated in the rebellion.

In terms of what motivated some of the Ulster Scots poets to get involved in the United Irishmen, Carol Baraniuk (2021) pulls out James Orr's poem 'To the Potatoe'. It shows the social radicalism of some of the weavers' work at the time. Orr's poem, she says, 'deplores the condition of the rural poor who existed on a basic, starvation diet, conscious of the ever-present threat of eviction from their rented cottages'. Baraniuk sees the poem as a call for non-violent political action.

> What wad poor *deels* on bogs an' *braes*, [devils, hills]
> Whase dear *cot-tacks* nae meal can raise; [cottage lease]
> Wha ne'er *tase* butter, beef or cheese, [taste]
>   Nor pit new *clais* on; [clothes]
> While a' they mak' can har'ly please
>   Some *rack-rent messon*. [rack-renting upstart]
> (Orr 1936: 56-9)

---

[35] 'The Narrow Sea', episode 46, 'The Rhyming Weavers', written by Jonathan Bardon, BBC Radio Ulster.

I meet modern Ulster Scots poet, Alan Millar, on a United Irishmen tour. Alan reads a poem of his own, *Whar is Campbell?*, where he searches in vain for Ulster Scots poet and 1798 supporter James Campbell's grave (Millar: 2018). Alan imagines himself centuries ago, having a conversation with Campbell over a drink. I am struck to find others exploring the Dreamtime in a similar way to myself. Asking slightly different questions. Finding slightly different answers. But all of us connected by the invisible pull of these histories.

One day, I tweet complaining that not many northern Protestants are taught about 1798 in schools, and meet a wave of opposition. No Protestants I know were taught United Irish history in any detail. Yet, online, I meet other Protestants who have studied it. They are irked at me for suggesting otherwise. I understand why, given how important this history is to many Protestants, including many unionists. I meet Ulster Scots speakers who have written 1798 materials for the local curriculum. Dedicated teachers who teach the topic because they love it. I discover that the Ulster-Scots Agency has designed teaching materials on the 1798 rebellion for Key Stage 3 pupils.[36]

Beiner (2018: 588-93) documents how 1798 came to be included in the revival of Ulster Scots from the 1990s, including the collection of Ulster Scots place-names for rebellion sites, multiple newspaper articles and booklets, music and concerts, films and documentaries, festivals, tours and re-enactments. Beiner (2018: 591) says that '[at] least some advocates of Ulster-Scots came to consider themselves torch-bearers of a 'third tradition', standing outside the standard dichotomy between the Irish nationalists who identified with Gaelic culture and the Ulster unionists who identify with British-English culture'. I begin to realise how much heavy lifting Ulster Scots speakers are doing for the memory of 1798 amongst Protestants.

Once I start to listen to people who love Ulster Scots, I hear a love of the local. A thran independence. A dissent from, and loyalty to, a home place that I relate to. A tradition that comes from the ground up. Whose songs and poetry hold the dreams of ordinary people. Ulster Scots has more than its share of radical thinking. A direct link with 1798. Also with American independence, as waves of exiles flowed across the Atlantic and ideas cross-pollinated. I think that perhaps Ulster Scots is another key which could help Protestants

---

[36] *Climb The Liberty Tree: An Exploration of the Ulster-Scots Role in the United Irishman's Rebellion on 1798.*

unlock an alternative history, and an alternative story of belonging, for those that want it.

* * *

I worked my way backwards to all these realisations in the only way I knew how, from Irish to Gàidhlig to Ulster Scots. Ending up loving these words that my grandparents taught me, but that I had come to reject. 'Dónal agus Mórag' was the first shaky step in building that bridge.

I would love a physical bridge to Scotland, in a world where resources were not so limited. I daydream about taking a notion at lunchtime, packing the car and arriving at my sister's house in Glasgow for tea.

But we have a different kind of bridge already. Family, friends, words and imagination. I know my ancestors walked the same Glasgow streets as my sister, at Divinity School, rearing kids, attending Calvinist Bible halls. Other friends' forebears came from the Highlands and islands, and their hearts are restless for the connection.

I tick the Ulster Scots box for the first time in the 2021 census. I seek out old Ulster Scots books and 21st century TikToks. I read *Shuggie Bain*, the 2020 Booker Prize winner, with searing Scots dialogue about working class life in Glasgow in Thatcher's Britain. I watch Mark Thompson and Ruth Sanderson present *Hame* on BBC Ulster, loving the thrill of recognition of an old gospel song. I roar laughing in the local pub as a neighbour recites an Ulster Scots story poem about an errant goat. There is craic to be had. Late at night, I watch YouTube videos of people reading the Psalms in Scots and they soothe me.

It dawns on me that Ulster Scots is a bridge to the future, as well as the past. Ulster Scots is a tongue that is alive and modern. It connects modern Ireland to modern Scotland. Watching Ulster Scots programming on BBC Ulster at the same time as Frankie Boyle's BBC 'Tour of Scotland' one night, I am struck at the differences. I love both. But our local heritage can often feel like preservation against the odds. While Boyle's documentaries are a feverish dissection of real time cultural change. Both feel important. And, I realise, they are not separate things. There is joy to be found in the places they overlap.

I'm drawn to how modern Scotland imagines itself too. My friend Stephen Baker often reminds me of Canadian poet Denis Lee's words, engraved on the Scottish Assembly Building: 'Work as if you live in the early days of a better nation'. This is what I want for us here too.

For most of my adult life, Scotland has pulled towards left of centre politics. From healthcare to welfare to university tuition fees to renewables, where Scotland has devolved authority, it often makes more forward thinking decisions than other parts of these islands. It is modelling inclusive nationalism, with civic not ethnic ideals at the core. The Scottish government deliberately reached out to EU citizens after Brexit, saying they hoped they would stay. In May 2021, neighbours of Glasgow asylum seekers blocked a street to prevent their detention, chanting 'these are our neighbours, let them go'. At its best, Scotland models a future-facing fictive kinship – the United Irishmen's magic key. Scotland struggles with sectarianism too. The alcohol-soaked, drug-numbed legacy of poverty and trauma. But I feel we have much to learn from modern Scotland.

I cannot write more, because I feel like a pilgrim embarking. Someone who has newly stepped into the Ulster Scots Dreamtime, stumbling around, trying to make sense of it. I have spent time with the things that come most easily to me, that resonate politically. Yet I know there is more.

There's an Ulster Scots writer in Larne whose work pulls me in, Angeline King. I drop her a line to see if she could help me understand how she moves through the Ulster Scots world. She says yes. And so, I keep walking.

13

Larne Language

Angeline King's Larne is not what I expect. I fall under its spell. A generous, multilayered mini-verse. Sea swept and community powered.

Driving into the town on a sunny March morning, I do the thing that I would learn Angeline hates. I take photos of the protest signs – 'Ulster Betrayed by Boris'; 'EU Hands off Ulster'; 'Ulster Says No to the Sea Border'. It's not long after Brexit, and the 'sea border' Protocol – with customs checks at Larne – is causing a lot of political disturbance.

But that's only one layer of Larne. Angeline shows me many, many more. Vikings, Celts, Irish dancing loyalists, Protestants blended with Catholics, Ulster Scots blended with Ulster English and Ulster Irish. And I leave understanding why the caricature of her home place is such a source of frustration.

In the Belfast Entries, Leo Boyd wrote over and over, 'there is a city within your city'. I wondered if Angeline would show me a hidden Larne within Larne. But I left thinking that Angeline's Larne just is Larne. And that it's the rest of us who have superimposed a narrative on it from the outside.

This is similar, I think, to how so many of us have superimposed a narrative onto Ulster Scots. In Angeline's world, Ulster Scots is not about politics. It is a language of family, place, earth and sea. Irish language is embedded within it, not in opposition to it. A humble, yet radical, proposition.

Come to Larne. It will make sense in a minute.

***

Angeline King is a novelist from Larne. She left a ten-year high-flying career in IT and started writing professionally in 2014. She loves languages, has a degree in French, speaks fluent Dutch and is an Irish learner. She is known for her novels, poems and work in Ulster Scots.

Angeline is writer in residence at the University of Ulster at the time of writing. She teaches a course, 'New Ulster Scots', where writers – as it happens mostly women – are creating new work about current events, sometimes writing in Ulster Scots for the first time.

It's fair to say that Angeline is not embedded in the traditional Ulster Scots movement in Northern Ireland, which has a tendency to be rather male and close knit. Rather, she works alongside it, sometimes overlapping. But mainly, she does her own thing. She's inspired by writing in the voices, and about the characters, she grew up with. She calls these voices 'Larne language'.

Angeline never went out of her way to learn Ulster Scots; it's just the way her family speaks. She didn't tick the Ulster Scots speaker box in the 2011 census, because back then she didn't know that was the name for it. At the time she was speaking 'business English' for work every day.

But as Angeline settled into being a writer, and without labelling it, she found herself naturally drawn to Larne language. After writing a few novels in standard English, including her debut novel *Snugville Street* (2015), she decided to play around with something light-hearted:

> I didn't sort of sit down one day and say, I'm going to write in Ulster Scots. I just dashed off a wee blog. I told this story about a wee girl who went to school, and the teacher kept correcting her when she was speaking.
>
> So, she would say, 'Miss, I cannae spell that'. And the teacher would say, 'you mean you can't', and she would say 'aye', and the teacher would say 'you mean yes,' and she would say 'uhum'.
>
> And it would have a silencing effect, that 'uhum'. And that's what happens to Ulster Scots speakers when they go to school. We didn't know we were speaking Ulster Scots. We had no idea. Never heard of it before. We never said, 'hey, we speak a funny dialect'. We just got on with it. You went to school, you got corrected. You learned to speak properly.
>
> Probably, in the back of your head, you're thinking to yourself, 'I speak really bad English'. But it would be very far at the back of your head. It wasn't a conscious thing at all. I just suddenly became aware that I was being corrected right through my life.
>
> So that wee blog was just a bit of fun. And my goodness, it went around Larne. It went round everywhere. Everyone was laughing. It was really good craic.

More books started to sell locally. People were relating and responding to seeing the way they spoke, and their experiences, written down. So Angeline wrote another blog in Larne language, called *The Band Stick* (2017). This was a short story about the Twelfth of July. Angeline's description of how it came about gives us glimpses into her Larne where culture and language are mingled and cross traditional divides:

> In my street, there were lots of mixed marriages. But the culture was probably more Protestant in that the kids with the band sticks would have been more prominent. So the little Catholic boys would sit and do up their band sticks and everything with the Protestant kids. I remember my brother went over one day to give a Catholic neighbour a wee flag because he felt sorry for him not having one.
>
> So I stole all those little bits of my childhood, and put them in this story called *The Band Stick*. And I got loads of responses to it from people I didn't know. A lot of my readers would be just normal working class people. Like a cleaning lady came to my door one day and asked, 'can I buy your book?' I got an email from a loyalist community worker saying 'I just want to congratulate you'. And I thought that was brilliant. To have such a wide range of people reading an Irish female novelist's work.
>
> *The Band Stick* story really hit a nerve. I think people were looking for a positive cultural reference. Because I don't think a lot of people had seen the Twelfth culture written about positively before. Even if you look at *The Twelfth Day of July* by Joan Lingard (1995), the solution that the children come to together is to go to Bangor for the day and eat ice cream. So there's no solution whereby the Catholic and Protestant children stand together and watch the bands – which is actually what I lived. In the end, I published *The Band Stick* with another two stories in a book called *Children of Latharna* [the Irish for Larne] (2017).

This love of Ulster Scots and working class Protestant culture within a mixed community setting is a defining feature of Angeline's life, as well as her work. She gives an example:

> There's a guy in Larne, and he put a thing on Facebook just before the Twelfth to say, 'can anybody tell me what time the feeder parade starts up? Because I'm taking my wee girl down to see it'. He's Catholic. His wife is

> Protestant and he is very determined to bring up his children to know that culture so that they can respect it. And so that they can respect their friends.
>
> And right enough that day, I took my mum and dad to the Field[37] at Larne harbour. And there she was on the bouncy castle. She stayed the whole day.
>
> My stepdaughter is a Catholic as well. She was intrigued one year and really wanted to go. So we asked her mum if it would be ok, and she had no problem. We had a ball. It was so funny. My mum and dad thought it was great too. Her and dad are really into the band culture. It was the greatest compliment we could have given my mum.
>
> It was almost like my mum was putting on a show. She had brought a wee picnic and was giving out the sandwiches. She was so happy to share what it was like on the inside. My stepdaughter even ended up wearing a pair of those big Union Jack earrings. She must have got them at a stall. It was really funny.

I love this story of Angeline's. I've made similar trips with my own kids to the band parades. The Twelfth is not something I feel an affinity with. But, like the Larne dad, I want my kids to know and respect their neighbours, and understand their friends' lives. Even if we have different politics.

* * *

We're walking now along the Antrim Coast Road that goes all the way up to the Giant's Causeway. It's a clear day and you can see Scotland easily, the mainland as well as the islands. All the heads of land, Ballygally, Garron Point.

'Hello, how are you?' Angeline says to a woman we pass. 'That lady was instrumental in setting up the Gaelic class with me in the Methodist church', she says.

> She was one of the Methodist church committee members. I'm not a Methodist, but I just wanted to set up an Irish class and her minister wanted to set up an Irish class, so we did it together.
>
> Initially, I contacted Linda Ervine because I saw a thing about her in the newspaper. And I said to her 'I want to set up an Irish class in Larne. Could you help me?' She actually came down to Larne herself. We had a group of

---

[37] The Field is a shorthand term for the place (often a park or literally a field) where the Orange Order, the bands, their friends, family and spectators gather after the initial march on the 12th of July. Usually there is food and drink. Often there are speeches from clergy, politicians and senior Orangemen.

about 50 people interested. Most of that first group were Protestants who had never known Irish before.

We went to the Methodist church with a good core of 14 or 15 every week, but then more people came along who had learned Irish at school and they were a bit more advanced. And so we had two classes. A couple of people from Ballygally got together, and they started to organise themselves. So it all kept going.

Angeline speaks many European languages. She clearly has an ear for it. I suspect I know the answer to this question, but I ask it anyway:

So was Irish just another language for you, because you love languages, or was there another reason?

She laughs at me.

Of course there's another reason. I had a character in *Snugville Street* who wanted to learn Irish, and that speaks for me as well. And then when I started to go into the Ulster Scots world, learning Irish became even more important, because I didn't want to be pigeon-holed.

But it's almost taken on its own journey. Irish is even more important to Ulster Scots than I realised. I'm hearing pronunciations in Irish class, and I'm hearing words all the time, that are in Ulster Scots, and I've started to see the connection. I can see the journey, it's all starting to come together. So the Irish class has actually been a really important step for my Ulster Scots.

To me Ulster Scots is Irish and Scots and English all mixed up. It's a bringing together. That's what Irish means to me. I don't see Irishness as just attached to republicanism. I see it as an identity. There's Viking blood in there, there's Norman blood in there. I think if you went to my Covenanter side of the family in Ballymena around 1845, and asked what nationality you are, they'd just have said Irish. What else would they have said? They wouldn't have known what Ulster Scots was at that stage.

It's only recently I've started to understand the difference between Ulster English and Ulster Scots. Ulster English is basically English with lots of Scots words and Gaelic sounds, spoken in an Ulster accent. You have expressions, like the 'scraich of dawn', and 'scraich' is a Scots word. And also Irish grammar, like when you say, 'I have a pen on me'. So that's Ulster English, that combination.

When you look at it this way, it makes sense. Languages mingled in this corner of Ireland They did not have cordons thrown around them. They evolved together, each embedded in, and part of, the other.

* * *

The first time I came into contact with Angeline was through her book, *Irish Dancing: The Festival Story* (2018). My own Protestant granny had been a champion Irish festival dancer in Newry. There was a huge glass cabinet in her good room, which contained countless medals. I still have Irish dancing music books handed down through my family from the time of the Gaelic League.

As we walk by the sea front, Angeline points to a tall building behind us.

> That's the Chaine Memorial tower. That's across from where the Irish dancing festival used to be. Now it's in the Orange Hall. You'd have had up to 2,800 kids come each year in its heyday, mostly girls but some boys as well. It was just a beautiful sight to see all the dancers. This was one of the oldest Irish dancing festivals. It started in 1928. Ballymena is important as well; its Irish dancing festival started in 1929.

The book came from Angeline's desire to understand why Irish dancing was so important in certain Protestant areas in the North, and the huge role it played in bringing Protestant and Catholic children together. Angeline had been Irish dancing since she was small, and remembers attending classes with a Protestant school friend and their Catholic next-door neighbour.

> For that period of one-and-a-half hours on a Saturday morning, these two next door neighbours, who were in different schools because of their religion, were in the same school. I think that's important.

Something that struck me when the book came out was the story of Juliane Mitchell, who did Irish dancing here from the age of 6 to 18. Juliane is the daughter of Billy Mitchell. Billy was jailed for paramilitary activity in 1975, and later became a progressive loyalist in the mould of David Ervine. I had befriended Billy in the early 2000s while doing academic work with the UVF/RHC about the peace process. Billy had written Juliane a letter from prison, where he encourages her to keep at the dancing. Angeline's book tells stories about how loyalist paramilitaries made trophies for the Carrickfergus Festival in prison (King 2018: 260-2).

Angeline also singles out the Irish dancing teachers, whose dedication kept the tradition alive, uniting children across communities throughout the worst years of the Troubles. Even when the roads were blockaded during the United Unionist Action Council Strike in 1977, the teachers were determined to keep the festival running.[38] Two thousand, two hundred people attended that year. The Festival thriving despite – or possibly as a refuge from – the violence.

*　*　*

By now, you've seen Angeline's Larne from a few angles. The generous mixing and meldedness of it all. But there's something left to see. And that's the way that a group of local people, including Angeline, have sought to transform public space in the town. They set up a group called Larne Regeneration Generation in 2015 to promote the things they loved about their town.

> Larne has this reputation for only being a loyalist town. It's just not true, and it's frustrating to have that stereotype.
>
> We've been putting up murals of cross-community heroes. We put up Richard Hayward in the town centre. He was a travel writer and a folklorist and broadcaster and one of the first people in Ireland to create films and act in them as well.

There's a mural of Ulster Scots traditional dress by Geraldine Conlon, a fashion designer. Another mural is about the McNeill hotel, which was one of the big hotels on the main street. Lots of the street art nods to Larne's once thriving tourist industry.

> There's also a mural about a battle between Vikings and the native Irish in the 1000s off the Main Street. The Gaels won. We didn't set out to purposely depict that, it's just a story about the town's past. And one day I was walking along, and it suddenly occurred to me that we'd put a Gaelic hero, King Conor, on a wall.

We walk past the Catholic school in the middle of the town. 'People assume that Larne wouldn't have this', Angeline says. 'But there it is.'

---

[38] The 1977 strike of the United Unionist Action Council was led by Rev Ian Paisley and supported by the UDA and Ulster Workers Council to protest against an alleged lack of security and to demand a return to unionist majority-rule government at Stormont.

> Three of my [Catholic] husband's sisters are all married to Protestants and some of their kids go there, some of them go to another Catholic school, some of them go to the Protestant school. Larne High school is all mixed now too.

Angeline walks me around the Factory area of Larne, where a lot of her novel *Dusty Bluebells* (2020) is set. There was a linen mill there. A high stone wall ran between the kitchen houses where the workers lived, and the big houses where the wealthy people lived. The wall loosely inspired the book.

> When we were kids, we were able just to run up to the shore and be at the park in two minutes. I lived right here until the age of six.

There's something so rooted about Angeline's sense of identity and place. A sure footedness that I have sometimes struggled to find myself. Angeline says she's always felt she lived in a shared place, and a both place. She was brought up with folklore, traditional music and dancing. She says, 'there was never in my life a barrier to jigs and reels on a Saturday morning at the Andrews' School of Irish Dancing'. None of these cultural worlds were off limits. Just part of her everyday life.

Angeline points out her aunt's house, where she spent a lot of her time growing up. 'My aunt just filled me full of stories, you know. It was almost like a storyteller's world.'

We're walking now through one of the most loyalist areas of Larne. The sea border graffiti is up on the walls beside the old Brown's Irish Linen factory. The Rangers Club is here. Angeline tells me that 'a beautiful arch' goes over the street every 12th July.

It's almost time for school pickup, so we can't linger. But Angeline tells me two things. That this is one of the least affluent areas in the whole of the UK. And that her daughter loves playing here.

* * *

'Totally do it', Angeline says as I take out my chalk. 'Do a nice one there overlooking where the first shots of rebellion were fired.' I scrawl 1798 on the footpath, looking nervously over my shoulder. Angeline is laughing. I'd say she wouldn't be averse to making the odd chalk mark herself.

1798 is not a date that Angeline particularly identifies with. As she often repeats, she is not a very political person. We will drag her along to some local 1798 tours later in the year. She will read Ulster Scots poems, helping us make connections between place and language.

When I read Angeline's novel *Dusty Bluebells*, I tell her it was the first feminist book I'd read in Ulster Scots. But that's not necessarily the way she sees it. For her, the characters were strong women just getting on with their lives. Holding things together. Because that's her experience of what women do.

And I love this about Angeline, and Angeline's Larne. They are both full of generous understatement. Everything she writes is a celebration of the twistiness of place. The fusion of cultures and languages. A love for our differences as well as our common human experiences. Hers is a spirit that has no need of a label. No ghost limb here. But plenty of inspiration for its healing.

Faith

The religious traditions of Dissent and Christian socialism have had a strong influence on politics in Ireland, from early Christian times through 1798 to the present. This section explores some of the ways faith manifests itself in alternative Protestant politics today. Ian and Pamela Mitchell chart their journey of anti-sectarian politics through the charismatic movement during the Troubles to modern day Quakerism. Lisa Rea-Currie talks about Celtic Christianity and Christian socialism. I explore the tradition, and current forms, of Presbyterian Dissent with Rev. Cheryl Meban. And Baptist Rev. Karen Sethuraman gives us insight into her world of peace-building and radical reconciliation.

14

Counter-cultural Christians

One of the first things my mum taught me about grocery shopping was never to buy South African fruit. I would watch her in Wellworths, eyeing up the apples for ripeness and closely checking the origin stickers. I didn't know at the time that this was part of a global boycott to protest apartheid. Some of the earliest songs we learned to sing were 'Free Nelson Mandela' and 'Biko', about black south African anti-apartheid activists and socialists. We'd blast them out on car journeys, singing at the top of our voices.

There were other things in our house that seemed different from my friends. Amnesty International magazines would arrive monthly. For a long time, so did material from the Campaign for Nuclear Disarmament (CND). I grew up listening to debates about pacifism and politics at the dinner table. While wider family members had a fondness for Israel and took pilgrimages to the Holy Land, my parents taught us about Palestine.

We had Irish passports all our lives. I'm not sure I've ever had a British one. There were flirtations with nationalist politics, certainly in the voting if only briefly in the joining. When remembrance day came around each year, if we wore poppies at all, they were white. A symbol of peace.

At the time I thought that I had a radical political upbringing, and that this was in a separate compartment from my religious upbringing, which seemed less radical altogether. It took me until adulthood to realise that they were two halves of the same whole.

* * *

My parents are Pamela and Ian Mitchell. I asked if they might tell their story in their own words. And here it is.

Pamela grew up in Newry. A Protestant family in a Catholic town. Her parents were fairly secular and not particularly unionist, despite Pamela having a UUP election agent grandfather. Maybe this was balanced out by her Irish dancing mother. The family had plenty of mixed marriages over the years. Friendships criss-crossed sectarian lines, even in the bad years of the Troubles. Pamela wasn't very aware of religious differences until she had a Catholic boyfriend, age 16, and her father passed on a message from someone in the town that if the relationship continued, the boy, Marty, would be in danger. Pamela was disgusted at this. And so, a lifetime of resistance to sectarianism began.

For Pamela, faith was a respite from a difficult home life. She became a born-again Christian in her teens and sought out the quiet, supportive spaces that religious gatherings provided her.

> I used to sneak out and go to 'The Jesus Place' in the Baptist Church. We had Protestants and Catholics there. They just put scraps of carpet and cushions on the floor in a side room of the church. That was all it was. I met some of my best friends there. We just talked a little about the Bible and hung out.

Ian's story is slightly different. A son of missionaries, Ian was brought up in the orbit of evangelicalism. There was a Brethren strain in the wider family, which perhaps explains their relatively apolitical outlook. His granny was an Orangewoman, but this wasn't a big feature of Ian's life.

Politically, Ian says:

> I made the switch when I was 16, in January 1969. The day I heard about Burntollet, that was me done with unionism in every way.

This is a reference to a People's Democracy civil rights march from Belfast to Derry. Roland Spottiswoode was at the march, and tells us more about it in chapter 18. Ian recalls the impact Burntollet made on him.

> I thought 'if we [Protestant unionists] can do this, then I don't want to be part of this thing. Ever'. I didn't know the term 'Protestant ascendancy' back then, but I did know that Prods got the good jobs, and there was a difference in the voting system. And that was me done with it.

Pamela and Ian met at Queen's University Belfast (QUB) in the mid 1970s. The Troubles were all around them. A Catholic friend of Ian's was shot dead by loyalists coming out of a Chinese takeaway on the Antrim Road in 1975. I grew up listening to, and then singing myself, the song Ian wrote for him. Their Protestant friend was killed by the IRA the following year in the Kingsmills massacre. They deplored all of these violences.

* * *

After QUB, and an early surprise pregnancy (me), Ian and Pamela bought a house and gravitated towards a new type of informal church. There were a few embryonic options at the time. Henry and Gerry Hull were leading the way in the Gilnahirk Fellowship. Ian and Pamela ended up following some university friends into the Bangor Fellowship.

The Bangor Fellowship looked different to the churches they had known before. At the time, it was putting on a musical roadshow called 'This My People' which was about bringing Ireland together. The solution it proposed was faith – it called on God to heal the land. In Ian's words:

> It was the first time I'd heard Christians saying 'we are part of the problem' and that was radical. It was strongly non-sectarian. That connected up with our politics.
>
> We were neither Catholic nor Protestant, that was the ethos. A line from those days, was when people asked, 'do you have any ex-Catholics in the Fellowship?' we'd say, 'yes, and we have lots of ex-Protestants too'. And that was compelling in the 1970s.

I vividly remember my parents filling in the 1991 census – the first time I'd been confronted with the fact that you have to complete boxes to explain your identity. For religion they wrote 'Christian'.[39] Ian and Pamela, along with many others, were making their point officially. Opting out of a binary they rejected.

Many of the fellowship groups became involved in charismatic renewal. This was a movement centred on the Holy Spirit, often involving speaking in tongues and healing. The term 'house church' became popular, which referred

---

[39] For the 1991 Census, the instruction was: Please state the Religion, Religious Denomination or Body to which the person belongs. The general term 'Protestant' should not be used alone and the denomination should be given as precisely as possible.

to the fact that many churches started as small organic meetings taking place in living rooms. One of my earliest childhood memories is trying to get to sleep while guitars played religious songs in the living room and voices drifted up through the floorboards.

Charismatic renewal was happening all over Ireland at the time, and of course far beyond. Mark Tierney (1975), a Catholic priest in Dublin, identified charismatic renewal as one of the fastest growing movements in the Catholic Church in the 1970s.

This inclusive orientation to faith was to shape Pamela and Ian's religious journey for many years. They were close friends with people in the Community of the King Church in Belfast, which was an evolution of the Gilnahirk Fellowship. In 1988, Community of the King grew larger when it merged with the Belfast Christian Family, a Catholic charismatic prayer group. Later, the Charis community would evolve out of this, and still exists today.

Gary McFadden from the Charis community was involved from the beginning. I met him in an Irish class recently, and was fascinated to piece things together. Gary describes how groups of Christians in Northern Ireland at the time 'heard the Lord's call to be an ecumenical witness as a community in a society riven by division' (McFadden 2007). In practice, this meant people sharing their lives across traditional community lines. Marrying one another. Having kids. Worshipping and praying together.

In a similar spirit, the Corrymeela community in Ballycastle was established by Ray Davey in 1965. Its aim was to create a place for people with different political and religious beliefs to build community together. It also looked beyond constitutional politics, providing a safe haven for LGBT Christians in the 1980s. Corrymeela is a space I have woven through often in the course of my own life. Many of my friends are members. Committed to faith as an act of reconciliation. A thread that now also runs through the Four Corners Festival.

Integration was at the heart of these movements. It was not lip service or a part-time project. It was a way of life. And all of this during, despite, maybe because of, the Troubles.

This way of living involved taking political risks. On the Unionist 'Day of Action', 3 March 1986, there was a general strike across Northern Ireland to demand an end to the Anglo-Irish Agreement.[40] Factories and shops closed. There were loyalist street barricades and riots. Most Protestants did not go to work. Children were not sent to school. Except on the Cregagh Road, a small boy from the Community of the King Church and I were sent in to Harding Memorial Primary School. We were the only ones there. The school was eerily silent. We coloured in all day. Our parents were doing something different politically. Registering their lack of support for the unionist consensus at the time.

It is important to say that these churches were often theologically conservative. As children brought up this movement, many of us have stories of religious trauma, as do our parents. There were times when being too female, too queer, too subversive in our myriad ways led to harsh judgement and curtailment. A lot of us made repeated religious conversions for the thought crimes that few teenagers could, or should, resist. At worst, it led to deeply harmful practices like gay conversion therapy.[41] Pádraig Ó Tuama's (forthcoming) poetry is a good insight into the scars that were left in many of us by these strictures.

But there was light with the dark. In a society deeply divided by violence, the movement authentically reached into both Catholic and Protestant communities in the North. It created space for encounters that wouldn't otherwise have happened. When I was teaching in QUB, I had a student in Sinn Féin, a similar age to myself, and we'd compare notes about our experiences of these same charismatic circles growing up. I would never have met him during the Troubles, outside of the church.

When I worked with former loyalist combatants in the mid 2000s, I became friends with a former UVF prisoner who had become born-again in prison, began to attend one of these churches and married a Catholic. This was not unusual.

Northern Ireland was becoming mono-cultured during the Troubles. People were being put out of their homes for being the wrong religion. Violence was

---

[40] The Anglo-Irish Agreement was a treaty between the UK and the Republic of Ireland in 1985. It gave the Irish government an advisory role in the affairs of Northern Ireland, while confirming that there would be no change to the constitutional status quo without the consent of the majority of people in Northern Ireland. Many unionists opposed the role it gave to the Irish government.

[41] See 'Conversion Controversy', BBC Northern Ireland, September 2020.

separating communities and lives were increasingly being lived apart from one another. What started as forced evictions often turned into segregation by choice, as people feared for their safety. Meanwhile, Pamela says:

> We were at meetings, hugging nuns.
>
> We knew that what we were doing just felt right. We did know that what we were doing wasn't the norm. But for us this felt like the normal way to live. And all the sectarian stuff was so abnormal.

Ian said they had a genuine belief at the time that this form of anti-sectarian Christianity was going to spread across the North of Ireland. Pamela says:

> We had a real vision that what we were doing, in our small way, if we kept doing it, that people would see that people are just people, and it would bring some form of healing.

But things didn't work out this way. Counter-cultural Christianity did not bring peace. Tidal waves of violence kept washing over Northern Ireland in these years. The spaces for radical political thought were contracting. It was probably all that could be done at this time to hold the fort. To refuse to allow sectarianism into their families and the small worlds and communities they were part of.

* * *

In the mid-1980s, the church that Ian and Pamela were part of took a different direction. A large building was bought on the Holywood Road in east Belfast. It became Christian Fellowship Church, or CFC.

By the late 1980s, the membership of the church was changing. Members joined from more conservative Protestant denominations. It was the age of Thatcher and Reagan. A lot of these churches were adopting business growth models. While there was still an informality in how things were done, the church began to move away from its counter-cultural hippy roots and became respectable.

Ian and Pamela describe their discomfort with the changes. While Ian was one of the initial leadership team, he slowly began to grow uneasy with what he perceived as being some of the unintended consequences of the church's growth model. He felt a huge mortgage would change the character of the church. Which of course it did. But yet, he signed up as a guarantor for the new building. He was locked in at this point, committed to making it work.

Within the structure of the wider church, Ian and Pamela had always run their own home groups. These groups were somewhat DIY in their ethos. Often attracting people from the fringes and left field. Pamela says:

> We didn't feel it was about preaching to people. We were just there for them. Sometimes praying with them. And somehow our home group got bigger and bigger. At one point, it became so big that we had to hire a leisure centre.

In 1987, they decided to start a church plant in Banbridge – a smaller satellite of CFC – partly in the hope that they could establish something less formal outside the main Belfast church. A low-key sign on the outside of the new church said simply, 'Number Nine'. A hint of American storefront church in its vibe.

Very soon, Number Nine filled up with people on the fringes. There were drinkers and drifters, as well as the more respectable Protestants that the CFC brand now attracted. It was a difficult balance to hold. Some people objected to the church band being scruffy and hungover. Ian had no problem with this. 'I said to them, 'are you telling me that sinners couldn't lead other sinners in worship?' Pamela was becoming increasingly frustrated at the pace at which leadership roles were opening up to women in the church.

During these years, Ian and Pamela describe how they increasingly felt like outsiders. Their left-wing ideas and their alternative politics seemed to not fit in anymore. Ian says:

> I still longed for the radicality of how it had been, prioritising community over religion, relationships over structure. Plus I think we wanted more freedom to express our left-wing politics through our faith. While we were singing 'Free Nelson Mandela', I wondered if others in the church felt he should still be in jail.

In 1992, Ian and Pamela left Number Nine. They attended a Presbyterian Church for a while. They were on the periphery of the post-evangelical emerging church scene in the 2000s.[42] Along with some friends from their

---

[42] Post-evangelicalism/the Emerging Church Movement developed in the late 20th century as a response to traditional forms of evangelicalism. It takes postmodernism as a starting point and emphasises the deconstruction of Christian faith and community. It has been popular in Northern Ireland. See Ganiel and Marti 2014.

church days, they formed a book group which has met in their houses for the last 15 years. They occasionally read theological books, and just as often do not. And in 2018, they found another religious home.

* * *

Ian and Pamela have been attending Quaker meetings in Belfast for five years now. Ian says:

> Joining the Quakers was the end of a long journey. I'd been going to some post-evangelical events, and it just wasn't working for me. I just wanted to find something older and a bit more durable. But still radical. Somewhere with a political edge to it as well as a more nuanced approach to faith. It's something we'd been thinking about for a long time.
>
> The first week I went, someone did a reading and said she was going to substitute the word 'God' with 'goodness' because she wasn't really comfortable using the word 'God'. 'There's scope to think of God as a metaphor', I thought; 'This is something I could get behind'.
>
> Love is a counter-intuitive thing. So is kindness. I think the idea of the survival of the fittest has to have a counterpoint in the world. And I find that counter-point opens up a bit for me in silent worship. I think that's what I've always believed. I just didn't have anywhere to belong to and express that.

Pamela adds some political context.

> We started researching Quakerism. They have a few bedrocks of their faith – they call them testimonies – simplicity, truth, integrity and peace. That's it. And I thought this is how we've been trying to live. You know we've always been pacifists. So that appealed to me too.
>
> During a meeting, we sit in silence. People just interject with a few sentences when they feel it would add to the group reflection. The first time I went, a woman in her seventies stood up and said she was going to Scotland the next day to join an anti-nuclear protest. She also went to the Quaker protest outside the last arms fair in London. They just sat down on the zebra crossing to meditate and worship, until the police removed them. Another guy was protesting against Capita (a much-criticised private provider of social services) outside the Department for Work and Pensions. I was able to stand up one week and ask people to write to the government

on behalf of Nazanin Zaghari-Ratcliffe [a British-Iranian woman imprisoned for six years in Iran]. I really appreciated that.

Ian is currently enrolled on a course on Quaker peace-making. He tells me that during the Holy Cross protests of 2001-02, when loyalists aggressively picketed Catholic children on their way to a Belfast primary school, that Quakers were there many mornings, talking to people, mediating. This is a pacifism that does not sit at home, or on the fence.

* * *

This is just a small window into the many different directions that counter-cultural Christianity in Northern Ireland has travelled. The myriad ways in which people from Protestant backgrounds tried to carve out anti-sectarian spaces in a deeply divided society.

Some of the people on this journey landed in more theologically conservative places, but retained their anti-sectarian grit. When Naíscoil na Seolta, east Belfast's first integrated Irish language nursery school was experiencing intimidation and needed a home, my childhood church, Christian Fellowship Church, stepped in and offered us their building. The church welcomed the naíscoil with open arms. They said that their ministry was reconciliation. The pastor signed up for Irish class.

This underlines to me that anti-sectarian politics can happen in all kinds of religious spaces. The United Irishmen had just as many religious conservatives as they had liberals. These things challenge stereotypes in interesting ways.

Other counter-cultural Christians stuck to the looseness of the early days, whether in their private lives or in wider communities. Some moved to England, Scotland or further afield, where they could develop their faith outside of the constraints of northern divisions. Some left the church altogether. Some explored Celtic Christianity. And some eventually found homes in mainstream denominations.

Faith that emphasises anti-sectarianism has not always been the mainstream in Northern Ireland. But it's where my parents tried to craft a counter-cultural life during the conflict. It's where I learned my politics.

Pamela says:

> When we were younger we had that zeal. We thought we were going to bring everyone with us. Now we've realised that all we can be is ourselves.

We may be a minority, and we're happy with that.
But we are also realising that we're part of a whole long thread of people.
There have always been people like us.

And she is right. There always have been people in the North who have lived lives of radical Dissenting faith. And there are many who walk in these furrows today. You just have to know where to look for them.

15

The Abbey

'Any normal people would meet in the town square', Lisa's husband Jonny says to her. 'Why are you meeting in a graveyard?'

But Lisa and I know. We don't even have to discuss the spot we want to go to. Just magnetically pulled, like we always are, to the crumbly walls of Movilla Abbey in Newtownards.

It's St Patrick's Day 2021 and the spring sun is shining. We're drinking coffee and eating squashed fly biscuits. Propped up against the Abbey walls, in the place St Finian and St Colmcille walked 1500 years ago. Movilla was a meeting place for the United Irishmen before the 1798 rebellion in Newtownards. United Irishman Archibald Warwick is buried about five metres west from where we sit. Lisa's great-great-grandfather Rea is buried six metres south west.

Layer upon layer upon layer.

'It's a thin place', Lisa says.

> It's an in-between place for me. A place where I can let my imagination go wild. Telling myself stories about the United Irishmen, and the saints, and my own ancestors, and just kind of live there in my imagination for a while. And then just over the wall, is the church where I work and live my life. And down the road, there's the town, which I have quite a complicated relationship with, because of feeling a bit different. But here is an imagination place.

Lisa Rea Currie is a close friend. She lives with me in the Dreamtime. Conversations between Lisa and I bounce seamlessly between centuries. We spend a lot of time in communion with the people buried around us at Movilla. Some of them feel like part of our present tense.

As people who feel culturally Irish, both Lisa and I struggle sometimes to feel at home in the unionist areas where we live. Imaginatively travelling through time and connecting our lives with fellow pilgrims helps ease the ghost limb. There's something about being in the physical space of Movilla Abbey that softens our dislocation.

And this is why we have to be here, not the town square. I want to ask Lisa about what Movilla means to her, and, with her help, tell a story about place, faith and heritage.

* * *

Lisa grew up in Ballybeen, a housing estate outside Dundonald which is often described as loyalist. She passed her 11+ and went to a grammar school, but being working class is still a strong part of her identity. Working now in heritage, she is also an Anglican Diocesan Reader in Movilla Abbey Church – a mixed Anglican and Methodist congregation, overlooking Movilla Abbey itself.

While having this fairly traditional package of Protestant identity markers, Lisa feels quite culturally Irish.

Lisa liked to read poetry in school, connecting with Séamus Heaney's celebration of landscape. And relating to Louis McNiece's sense of awkward belonging with 'one foot here, and one foot out'.

> Reading this poetry was definitely when I started to realise that I really, really loved where I lived. Like the actual land of where I lived. I also realised my sense of place didn't necessarily fit with other people who were from my background. I definitely started to explore other ways of being. Politically and culturally. But I lacked paths.

It was socially difficult for many Protestants to show they were interested in Irish culture in the 1990s. It was the tail end of the Troubles. Lisa says her friends at school and people at her church youth group had begun to notice that something was different about her. She remembers going to a church residential in the 1990s, where someone suggested as a prank that she should dye her hair green and drink green milk. This was a strange way of being singled out as different. Being identified as Irish, and as a Lundy. Which was not always safe or comfortable when you live in Ballybeen.

Lisa went to Scotland for university, and was able to relax a little and explore these feelings from a slightly different angle. She did an undergraduate dissertation on Ulster Scots poetry, still grappling with ideas of language, place and identity.

> Ulster Scots was definitely me searching for another layer of identity. I did find that to an extent in the weaver poets. You get a pure celebration of landscape in the weavers' poetry, like James Orr from Ballycarry. That space was there.

But it was 2002. Not long after the 1998 Agreement. A time when Ulster Scots was very politicised. Things are a bit different now.

> It was a hard time to be doing it. I would've loved to have been doing it 15 years later, with the wealth of information that's out there now, and the fact that Ulster Scots has probably moved away from the political sphere to a more cultural sphere. But, for me, it was all about place and landscape and being connected and feeling rooted.

Ulster Scots, for Lisa, was a way to ease the ghost limb. Something that felt authentic to the Ards Peninsula where she grew up in her early years. Authentic to the language of the shipyard poets in east Belfast, where she works now.

In recent years, Lisa discovers an Irish-speaking great-granny. We begin an Irish class together. She finds ancestors from the massive O'Neill/Uí Néill clan. She finds Savage ancestry too – the family which founded the Dominican Priory in Newtownards in 1244 (Hayward 2015: 72). Once she pulls these threads, Lisa begins to find lots of ways that her story intersects with the arc of Irish history. But she had already found a deeper way to connect herself with the place she loved. And that was faith.

* * *

When Lisa came back to Northern Ireland, her family moved to Newtownards and joined Movilla Abbey Church. The Church strongly recognises the heritage of Movilla's geography. Founded in the 6th century by St Finian, the Abbey was one of the most important monasteries in Ulster. Pagans had previously worshipped a sacred tree on the site, and the name Movilla comes from the Irish magh bile, which means plain of the ancient tree.

The ruins still standing today are from a medieval Augustinian abbey. Mesolithic and Neolithic artefacts have been found here, beads, gold and coloured glass, suggesting it was an early Christian jewellery and bead-making workshop. There are signs of bronze and iron-working. Stories in every layer of the soil.[43]

The modern Movilla Abbey Church was formed in 1980, when new houses were built in the area. Their idea was to take the church to the people, rather than vice versa. And the founders always recognised the Celtic spirituality of the place. 'That's what drew me to it', Lisa says, 'as well as being a less restrictive kind of faith'.

Before moving to Newtownards, Lisa and her family had been going to more traditional evangelical churches. But she felt called to study the Bible, and did not feel that the churches they attended had much space for women in leadership.

> For me, it was also connected with wider communities, and a wider church family. Being truly connected to the community that you're situated in.
>
> So we tried Movilla, and within six months I was on select vestry. Not long after, I said to my minister that I felt like God was asking me to study more, and he said, 'okay, I'm going to sign you up for Diocesan Reader training. And it starts next week'.
>
> It was two and a half years. And it took a lot out of me. There were bigger issues in the church around culture wars, sexuality and inclusion. And even though I knew where I stood on those, sometimes I'd freak out about whether I would have to do battle about the things I believe in, when I don't want to be in battle.
>
> But then I kind of kept coming back to the fact that it's not the church in the worldwide sense that I had to engage with. It's actually just this building here. And these people that go here. And the families and the community that's in it. And that's what I feel connected to.

Like many others, Lisa was looking for a faith tradition that had deep roots.

> It's all about having an apostolic tradition back to Patrick. Coming from a more evangelical tradition in Northern Ireland, everything's a breakaway

---

[43] https://andculture.org.uk/movilla-cemetery

of something else. Everybody is always reimagining that their way is the right way of doing it.

But how can you ignore the fact that there's been nearly 2000 years of Christian tradition on this island? How can we just ignore everything that happened pre-Reformation? It just seemed to me that there was such a wealth of tradition and learning there, and evangelicalism was completely ignoring it.

I also love Celtic Christianity's connection with place.

We talked earlier about thin places. And that was a real tradition in Celtic Christianity. It was probably something to do with how Movilla ended up here in its first iteration.

A thin place is where pre-Christian Celtic people believed that there was the thinnest space between this world and the spiritual world. And they would often have sites of worship there.

Celtic Christianity is interesting, because in its early version, it didn't sort of come in and tell people 'you are doing everything wrong'. It was more 'I really like what you've done here. We can see that you have found a space where you feel connected to God. We think that God is something slightly different than what you've got. But we think that you are talking to God. We recognise this place is a holy place, because you have recognised that it is a holy place.'

It started with where people were at, and offered ways of broadening their worlds. I think that in the last few years, more people have been reading Celtic Christianity as a more holistic kind of approach to faith. Going on a journey with people, rather than using faith as a tool of colonisation or oppression, or going in and burning the whole thing down.

If you look at sites, like here at Movilla, and Nendrum monastery especially – those were places where there would have been pre-Christian worship. And so it was really kind of working alongside people and serving them.

Reflecting on how early Celtic Christians might have approached life in Movilla is not just about looking to the past. It's about finding ways to live in the present and the future. How to relate to others on this part of the island. Some of the traditions of Celtic Christianity, as Lisa sees it, represent quite revolutionary ways of living. Communal, inclusive, earthed.

Lisa is wearing a black Mary's Magnificat t-shirt today at Movilla. Mary is standing on a skull and a snake with her fist raised high. Text loops around the image:

> Cast down the mighty
> Send the rich away
> Fill the hungry
> Lift the lowly

It's from Luke chapter 1: 46-55.

The t-shirt was delivered with a print, which says 'This little light of mine… is for burning down prisons'. 'This little light of mine' is an old children's gospel song.

I've been noticing multiple references to Mary's Magnificat recently. The t-shirt art, produced by an American, Ben Wildflower, keeps showing up in my social media timelines. Mostly posted by Christian socialists and feminists. I'd never heard of Mary's Magnificat before.

> It's a well-kept secret among Protestants. It's a Mary thing. Also I think because it's about disrupting power structures. There are quite a few parts of the Bible that are about God reallocating power. It's social justice.

As a Diocesan Reader, Lisa often leads prayers and sermons at church. She tells me there's a liturgical calendar that Anglicans follow, and every three years, on the second Sunday in Lent, it's Mary's Magnificat. 'Sometimes people skip it because it's a bit too Maryish,' she says. 'But I love it.'

Lisa has brought some Anglican rosary beads for me to see, after I was surprised to hear such objects existed. Lisa uses them sometimes for contemplative prayer. Holding something physical helps her feel connected and rooted in the moment. I slowly roll the rosary beads through my hands. It's soothing. I imagine the bead-making workshop here a thousand years ago. I wonder how they felt as they rolled the beads through their own hands.

The Apostle's Creed, said regularly in Anglican liturgy, reads: 'I believe in the Holy Spirit, the holy catholic church, the communion of saints…'. I find Lisa's faith compelling and counter-cultural in the context of Northern Ireland. A Protestant tradition which sees itself as catholic with a small 'c'. The inherent sense of social justice the liturgy contains, for those who want it.

THE ABBEY

How it draws on early Christian ways of being on this island. A faith that crosses all kinds of boundaries and is not afraid to challenge power. Rooted in place and time.

* * *

The first time Lisa and I visited Movilla Abbey together, our kids were small. We sat down in the grass beside the Abbey ruins, kids running around, everyone taking turns to pretend that they were St Finian and St Colmcille.

We have learned so much about the Abbey since then. We have crawled on our hands and knees to find the holy well. We have taken guided tours, and imagined our own tour. We have found Mary Ann McCracken's friend. We have run our fingers over the Celtic crosses on the early Christian coffin lids embedded in the old wall. We have puzzled over the Old Irish inscription on one of the slabs – 'Or Do Dertrend'. We have noted with sorrow their removal for conservation, and campaigned for their return. We have chalked '1798' on Movilla's walls. The Abbey continues to provide solace, mystery and space for imagination.

Today, Lisa and I are both tired. This St Patrick's Day marks one year of COVID-19 lockdowns. We've been homeschooling since Christmas while trying to work. We lie in the sun, quiet and child-free, and let our minds and conversation wander.

Of course we drift back to St Finian and St Colmcille. Loving the idea that they maybe lay in this same patch of sun too.

> I'm not sure how they would have felt about a woman being involved in church. But I think in that time there was definitely more space for women to be faith leaders. It might've been in their separate communities, but there was definitely a space for it.
>
> I think there might not be much difference between what they believed then and what we believe now. And I think that's quite nice. Connecting with these people 1400, 1500 years ago. And the timeless nature of God. It's not just something that was just made up recently. This is a long, long tradition of people believing similar things, in the same place.

Later, Lisa and I discover that some of the early Christian coffin slabs at Movilla were made in celebration of important women (Patterson 1879:

273-6). At least two of them had the female symbol of shears.[44] Similar female slabs were found in Holywood and Downpatrick. Perhaps they were abbesses, or benefactors, like Affreca in Greyabbey. A neighbour who has studied old and middle Irish believes that 'Or Do Dertrend' might translate to 'Pray for Deirdre'. Who is Deirdre? These questions open up new journeys of thought. Earthed ever deeper in this thin place that never stops giving.

I think to myself that Lisa and I will spend many more years in Movilla Abbey, imagining our lives and burrowing into our understanding of place. Recovering our histories and restoring our relationships with our heritage, our communities and our selves.

---

[44] The symbol of shears, or scissors, was often used on coffin slabs across these islands to denote women. The shears on the slabs from Movilla are placed beside flower petals on one slab and leaves on another. I have heard local historians at tours of Movilla wonder if the petals and leaves may relate to a woman's children, although this remains an open question.

16

The Father and Mother

Rev. Cheryl Meban and I walk the grounds of Malone House in the late spring sun with her two little dogs, Tristan and Goldie. Cheryl is Presbyterian chaplain at Ulster University. She grew up in south Belfast, just beside Malone House, and thinks of its vast meadows and woods as her back garden. It's where she learned to ride a bike. It's where she shredded her skirt falling off a skateboard while lashing downhill. For someone who feels like she is not truly 'from here', as in Northern Ireland, this place feels like home.

Cheryl frequently pauses the conversation to point out a robin or thrush. To show me where she saw frogs, heard a woodpecker, spied a kingfisher. Often to locate an adventurous dog.

I don't know if it was this goodness of nature that makes spending time with Cheryl feel like rubbing my temples. I think it's also because she tells me stories from the Bible that reach outwards. Stories where my doubting soul is not damned at the end. As a child of the church, listening to these Bible stories makes me feel like a girl again. But this time, the stories are about girls and women. And the heart of them, as with all of Cheryl's stories, is inclusion.

I want to speak to Cheryl because I love her voice, and the ideas she puts into the world. I'm also interested in her work in the Presbyterian Church in Ireland (PCI), the faith tradition which so many of the United Irishmen came from. Although the PCI is currently in a conservative phase, it has always been an internally diverse Church, where radicalism and conservatism, religion and politics, bounce off one another in interesting ways. To my mind, Cheryl channels the spirit of historical Presbyterianism in very modern ways. I see her quiet dissent as forged from the grit and hunger for justice within this faith tradition.

But these are just stories I tell myself. It is far too much to ask Cheryl to speak on behalf of a whole tradition. When I ask her if she sees herself as carrying a torch for the spirit of radical Presbyterianism, she answers with a firm 'no'. Cheryl says that all she can be is herself, as she feels called to be, in this time and place. That nothing more can be asked of a person.

* * *

Independence of thought is a big theme in Cheryl's stories.

> My mum is an English Baptist. Dad was from the Dublin Plymouth Brethren. His parents had come from Glasgow in 1933; they were Rangers supporters. Dad was born on 12th July and they called him Victor.

Victor was a free-thinker, and took his own approach to developing his ministry. He went to Bible College in England and studied theology, which was not the done thing in the Brethren, who preferred to keep things in-house.

> My mum, Faith, had her own mind as well. She did her Bachelor of Divinity when I went to primary school.
>
> By this time, dad was the Principal of Belfast Bible College, which was interdenominational.[45] Dad's role at the Bible College meant that mum didn't feel free to air her own views on theology. She witnessed theology that was supposed to be about 'grace' used as a weapon, and decided to embody, rather than speak, her faith.
>
> When I was still a child, we ended up moving to Lowe Memorial Presbyterian, where Alan Flavelle was. It had lots of people from Baptist, charismatic, Brethren churches coming, because Alan was preaching a broad evangelical Biblical message. So that was my experience then of Presbyterianism. That there was room for all sorts of people reading the Bible with integrity.

Coming from Dublin and England, Cheryl's parents didn't overly relate to local unionist and loyalist traditions. Cheryl gestures past a meadow:

> Our house was over there, and the Field in Edenderry is over there. The Twelfth every year was spent listening to drums, which to dad, who grew

---

[45] Not to be confused with Union Theological College, which is Presbyterian.

> up in Dublin with Catholic friends, felt like an insult. It felt like, 'we beat you, don't forget it'.
>
> Mum and dad couldn't really identify with anything joyous about the Twelfth celebrations. We were allowed to come down to watch the bands. But we knew that it wasn't the culture of our family.

This is an important insight into Cheryl's relationship with this place. She says, 'if I write a biography, it'll be called, "I was only born here". It means I don't really belong.'

Someone stops to pet Tristan, one of the dogs. 'He's a shih tzu chihuahua, puppy farm mix', Cheryl tells the passerby. 'You can put that in the book', she says to me. 'Maybe that's what I feel like.'

* * *

Cheryl is one of a handful of female Presbyterian ministers in Ireland (out of 326 at the time of writing).[46] When Cheryl talks about her faith, she often talks about women and girls. These aren't stories I am used to hearing. I like listening to them.

> From a small child in the Brethren, and at Every Girls' Rally,[47] I wanted to be a missionary. Last week, I re-read Gladys Aylward's biography, *The Little Woman*. She wanted to be a missionary to China, but was told she wasn't suitable. So she worked and saved up the money. She couldn't afford the boat, so she took a train to China and arrived into a war-zone. She was totally on her own in this place, and ended up adopting abused children, rescuing wives who were effectively slaves.
>
> So that kind of story of women missionaries – who just did what they felt they had to do, and be who they had to be, no matter what the powers that be said about them, and whether they were accepted or not – I suppose that was put into my system very young.

A few weeks before we met, Cheryl had written a 'Thought for the Day' on BBC Radio Ulster, where she had spoken powerfully about violence against women. A Metropolitan police officer had been arrested for murdering Sarah

---

[46] https://www.presbyterianireland.org/

[47] Every Girl's Rally is an international Christian youth movement, which runs in many local churches.

Everard, a 33-year-old marketing executive in London. Cheryl talked about the lack of safety so many of us feel as we walk through the world. Cheryl frequently uses her platform to give voice to women, in the Bible, and in the present. She talks about Acts 2, where 'women, girls, their voices are part of the spirit's voice'.

This has not always been comfortable for her in a church which currently leans conservative. Cheryl recalls doing another broadcast where she prayed to 'the Father and Mother'. Even though she used masculine language in the rest of the prayer, she received a torrent of abuse. Glenn Jordan, a Presbyterian, writer, thinker and friend of ours who died in 2020, quietly engaged with people online, defending Cheryl. 'That really meant a lot to have somebody who was willing to speak up.'

We're walking by the River Lagan now, talking about how churches change and evolve. Not all members will agree with all of the Presbyterian Church's teachings in any given moment. Currently, the PCI is deeply divided over its relationship to LGBTQ+ people. The General Assembly in 2018 decided to withhold full membership from anyone in a same-sex relationship, that LGBTQ+ people could not take communion, and that the Church would not baptise their children.

This led to turmoil amongst the membership. A prominent Presbyterian family, Lesley and Tony McAuley, very publicly left the Church. Their daughter is gay. They felt the Church was treating LGBTQ+ people like 'second class citizens' (*Belfast Telegraph* June 2018). An elder in a Presbyterian Church in Dublin, Steven Smyrl, who was married to his same-sex partner of 20 years, was stood down by the Church, despite the support of his local congregation (*Irish Times* February 2021).

Cheryl was due to speak at Mid-Ulster Pride in 2020. The event was cancelled due to COVID-19, but Cheryl's billing caused some controversy (*Belfast Telegraph*, January 2020).

> I spoke to Tyrone Presbytery about it, and brought two others who supported me. I didn't have to, but I just felt it was important to have that conversation. They weren't happy about me doing the Cookstown event. But I wanted to say that people need us not to be their enemy. Diversity is the way that God is actually building a church.
>
> Hopefully, we can hold that space open for people. It's like keeping your

toe in the door. If the door gets jammed shut, it's very hard to get open again. But if you can just keep your foot there, there's always a little bit of air and a little bit of an opportunity for conversation. A door can't be locked until it's jammed shut. I suppose in 2018 some PCI people tried to slam the door shut. And I just don't accept that this is the case.

We sit down on a park bench, watching the tiny dogs lug huge sticks across the meadow. Cheryl tells me about the book Glenn Jordan wrote with another friend of ours, Pádraig Ó Tuama, about the story of Ruth (Ó Tuama and Jordan 2021). I try to follow along with my non-theological mind. Cheryl is telling me that the Book of Ruth is about how religious laws were changed in favour of kindness.

> I love it because it interprets the law in order to do what is kind. Our commitment is to ensure people's wellbeing. And ensuring their wellbeing fulfils the law of God. That gives us a lot of freedom to say, 'actually, what we're doing here is trapping us in a system that is no longer fit for purpose. Let's fix it. Let's change it. Let's make sure that we're doing right by the people that are being marginalised, rather than excluding them to make ourselves feel good about fulfilling the letter of the law.'
>
> In the current culture, there's a whole generation of young people who assume inclusion. And they are feeling hurt and marginalised. That's not good for anybody.
>
> Gladys Aylward, the missionary in China, her story is very powerful for me in terms of questioning the structures of Presbyterianism. I love that she just got on with being herself, and the gospel happened. I know how important our structures are – they were designed to be democratic and republican – and I am more than willing to work within them. And I do. But I will also not give them more than their due. Because they are human structures. They are not the only way that God does ministry.

I think of a letter I saw in the *Irish Times* by Stephen Murray, a Cork Presbyterian. In it he said:

> To be a Presbyterian is to be a dissenter [...] There is no Presbyterian doctrine, *per se*, on any topic; there is the will of the majority as expressed at its General Assembly every June [...] The will of the majority will change, modify and ameliorate, given time, as it always does, and Scriptural

doctrines of love and respect will overshadow the narrow condemnation of male homosexuality in the Bible.[48]

Dr. Bill Addley, a former lecturer on Practical Theology, spoke at the 2019 General Assembly about internal dissent as a regular and recurring feature of Presbyterianism as it works through the issues of the day. John Dunlop, a former Moderator of the Presbyterian Church said something similar: 'I think you can be a dissenter without being a deserter' (Meban 2019: 36-7).

And this modern dissent has come to be the space that Cheryl inhabits.

* * *

Being true to our culture, Cheryl and I share a fifteen, the most famous of all the Protestant traybakes, at the Lock Keepers Inn. As Tristan the dog tries to lick desiccated coconut from the picnic table, Cheryl and I talk about the politics of Dissent in Ireland:

> Obviously our specific context [in Northern Ireland] has co-opted us into the power structures of the British Empire. This is why Ulster Protestants in the Union are caught. Because they have the Presbyterian dissidence that says, 'we're different, and we don't do things the same as you, and we want our right to be distinct'. But, probably as a hangover from 1798 really, most Presbyterians became Orange, opting into that empire.
>
> Some of the nastiness that happened, the way that some Presbyterians were lumped in with other Protestants and burned in barns during the 1798 rebellion, that pushed people into feeling that they weren't safe in trusting their Catholic neighbours, and they would be safer giving loyalty to the Crown and to being Protestant. So Presbyterians became Protestant, you know? But Presbyterians weren't Protestants until then, they were Dissenters.
>
> You look at Union College, the Presbyterian theological school in Belfast, and it proudly proclaims inside: 'The Parliament of Northern Ireland held its first fourteen sessions in this College, September 1921 to July 1932'.[49] So there's this kind of, 'it's ours, it belongs to us, we are supporting it and making it happen'. A Protestant land for Protestant people. That was kind

---

[48] 'Presbyterians – a tradition of dissent', letter to *Irish Times*, 26 June 2017.
[49] https://www.presbyterianireland.org/

of the offer at the creation of Northern Ireland. It was to let Presbyterians become 'the people'. To have their own place, but at the cost of a large Catholic minority, who were never going to have a chance to be in power.

Cheryl's description of this historical moment helps me process how the thran independence of the current Presbyterian tradition can sit so comfortably within the wider Union. I think about how many Dissenters disremembered 1798 by force, but also often by choice. Sticks and carrots. The suppression of the rebellion, and later partition, gave Presbyterians a pathway to be 'the people'. That tension has sat uneasily ever since.

But Presbyterianism continues to offer alternative frameworks for understanding society in Northern Ireland for those who seek it. It is part of many Protestants' understanding of faith, not to get too attached to human structures. Because the Kingdom of God is in heaven, not on earth. This has a way of cutting through traditional political analyses. Cheryl says:

> It's partly the Brethren thing, that you're brought up to believe that you're made for heaven. And also the evangelical thing, that we're citizens of God's Kingdom. You don't belong here. That's life-giving in a way, because it sets you free to pray for the place that you're in. Whatever the political structure is – British or Irish – I don't personally mind. Every structure by its nature marginalises people. What I care about is whether the heart that inhabits them is generous, and will make them work for good.

And this, I think, might be the thread I have been trying to pick up all along. The fact that having a deeper set of values – in this case, based in faith – can be socially and politically transformative in a place like Northern Ireland. It is radical to prioritise heart over dogma.

As Cheryl talks about what she loves about the Church, I hear even more examples of this. Cheryl mentions the peace agents that used to operate in the Presbyterian Church. These were groups of people whose job was to build relationships, often sharing prayer and Bible studies with Catholics during the Troubles (Ganiel and Yohanes 2019). It was always work that was done on the interfaces of communities, and in the margins of the PCI. But it was hugely important.

Today, it's the global church that excites Cheryl. She worked on the World Communion of Reformed Churches Executive Committee for seven years.

> The PCI was one of the founding members of the World Communion of Reformed Churches, which holds most of the reformed minority churches globally. Most of them are in the global south – marginalised from power, and suffering from injustice. So they're asking questions about the financial architecture of the world. They're asking questions about climate change. They're thinking about equality, gender equality, disability. How we include people.

Cheryl is proud that the Church has continued its role in world development. In Beirut, convening PCI's Mission Overseas, Cheryl worked with the Church as they dealt with extreme violence and the arrival of many refugees to Lebanon.

> I was so impressed with how they got their partners together. They had the Maronites, the Orthodox, maybe Quakers, they had Christian Aid, the Red Cross. They had the first woman who was ordained in the National Evangelical Synod of Syria and Lebanon. The second is now the President of the WCRC, giving global leadership from a place of suffering.

My own most recent personal interaction with the PCI was fighting for asylum for friends from Eritrea who attended a Belfast congregation. The Church provided financial support and loved them like family. The minister flew to London with them for meetings and hearings. The case lasted six years, and the congregation did not stop until our friends' case was won.

All this is to say that although it is currently undergoing a conservative turn, the PCI continues to work for social justice in interesting ways. It is, in some contexts, still willing to ask difficult political questions. It can offer alternative frameworks of ethics and meaning. But it's also interesting to me that the radical inclusion that has always been a theme of Cheryl's life, is primarily something she can identify globally, but only in some times and places in present-day Northern Ireland.

* * *

Hearing Cheryl's story reminds me of Glenn Jordan's book title about northern evangelicals, *Not Of This World* (2001). This comes from the Biblical idea that Christians live in the here and now, but have a higher purpose. It occurs to me that Cheryl might be in Northern Ireland, but not of it. And I wonder if the sense of being half insider, half outsider that Cheryl grew up with helps her maintain her vision. Many good things in life come from not feeling comfortable.

While Cheryl speaks only for herself, I cannot help but be moved hearing her voice ideas of inclusion and justice from a Presbyterian perspective. Modern religious Dissent takes many shapes and forms. Not everyone will work things through in the same way that Cheryl has. But her form of Presbyterian Dissent speaks to me. I imagine my favourite women Dissenters of the 1790s, and I cannot help but feel like Cheryl walks a similar path.

As we round the dogs up, and head back to the carpark, Cheryl says:

> I feel like a pebble in a river. The river is changed because you're there, and you're changed by the river. But I don't determine where I stand or how the river is shaped. I don't have to be able to decide that. It's what I still hope, that God has some sort of plan for goodness and redemption.

'I hope she does', I say, probably inappropriately, but feeling giddy with liberation after hearing all the stories about girls and women.

Cheryl laughs. 'I've never gotten used to female pronouns for God. But I use different words in different contexts, languages and cultures. I suppose if I can change them for other people I can change them for God.'

The recording is filled with birdsong.

17

Karen The Baptist

I meet Karen the Baptist at Forestside shopping centre in Belfast in late June. The nickname comes from a friend of hers in Sinn Féin. It makes me laugh. And it opens up all kinds of questions. How does a Baptist minister from east Belfast go about making republican friends, to the point where the banter is so relaxed and free-flowing? This is not a typical Northern Ireland story. There's been a journey here, and I want to ask Karen how this path opened up to her.

Both of us are a bit jittery this morning. Loyalist rallies are taking place weekly, with a hard undertone of violence. Both of us are putting our heads above the parapet to talk about the future of Ireland, Karen much more so than me, and feeling quite exposed. I'd had a notion that we could walk the streets where recent riots had happened. Karen had gone out those nights to help calm tensions. But today, we just want coffee and a quiet place to talk.

As we pull up some chairs in a private booth, Karen begins to tell me her story from the beginning. It's a story of deep religious and political change, radical reconciliation and healing.

* * *

Rev. Karen Sethuraman grew up on the streets of inner east Belfast. She had a fairly classic PUL blend of identities and experiences.

> I was raised in a Protestant evangelical home. I went to a little tiny Baptist church. I was raised by a single mum. When I grew up, the Twelfth was a big thing. We didn't need to worry about putting deck chairs out in the street, because my aunt had a bay window up in her bedroom. It was like the Queen's box. It was all I knew.
>
> I grew up in the Troubles. Fighting and throwing stones were just part of

life where I lived. I grew up chucked out onto the streets to play. You'd get a call at ten o'clock at night to get in.

We had street parties to celebrate the Royals. I was a massive supporter of the England football team as a little kid, and I had the England football shirts. And that was it. That was my bubble.

In many ways, the trajectory of Karen's life seemed set out for her. A life lived in the community of Protestant evangelicalism. But she had a questioning spirit. She loved listening to other people's stories, and found herself being changed in the process.

Something in my early teens was beginning to shift. I wouldn't say it was in any way political. It was a faith thing deep inside.

When I was younger, church bored me. But there was a fantastic youth group. It kept me out of trouble and I'm thankful for that. But something in my young mind started to ask questions. Somebody in the youth group came out as gay. And I started to think, 'why are you treating him like that? Does he really need to be put out?'

I also remember having to evangelise to Catholics. I was given leaflets to evangelise to them. And that was my only contact with Catholics. Because there weren't any, as far as I knew, at Orangefield High School. I just knew nothing else.

I started studying theology at the Bible College in Belfast, and started to realise there was another narrative. All of a sudden it was like somebody put new spectacles on. I had a great American lecturer who really struggled with the Northern Ireland context. And I think in a way he became a mentor to me. Because he taught me to think outside the box. And that's when everything started to really fall apart. And it was my faith journey that began to change my views. And somewhere in that, I think I really did find Jesus. And he was not the Jesus that I was taught.

The Baptist Church in Ireland is small, tight knit and pretty theologically conservative. As Karen continued to question the version of faith that she grew up with, it became difficult for her to live within the church's boundaries.

Karen started getting involved in peace and reconciliation, addiction clinics and all kinds of grassroots community work. She worked with loyalists, running various programmes in a community house. She loved it. She also began to develop friendships with Catholics, even though that fell outside the remit of her job.

I was told not to work with the Catholic clergy. But I was meeting secretly with a nun called Sister Ursula. I met her every Monday to pray.

The work I was doing led to friendships with people from all backgrounds. Hearing other people's stories began to shift things for me. Every time, it just wrecked me. I fell in love with people. And that's my Damascus road experience. The stories I was hearing were from people outside the world I had growing up. It broke my heart hearing that while I was at street parties, on the other side of Belfast, internment was happening. I was shocked at how much I'd been in a bubble and how I was not aware of it.

Changes were also happening in Karen's personal life. She met her future husband Karu – who is South Indian, born in Malaysia – through mutual friends while he was a student. She says:

The first time I brought Karu home to meet my mum, I pulled into Hyndford Street in east Belfast, right on the end wall was painted 'All Blacks Out'. Freshly painted that very night that I was bringing my boyfriend home. I don't think it was about me, but my mum was convinced it was, because I was the only one dating a person of colour.

Karen's mum was a DUP voter. But she was not very interested in politics. She just lived her life in east Belfast, knowing it was safer 'to stick to your own community'. But it was not in Karen's nature to do this.

I started to realise that my theology and my reality are not matching up here. I just realised that this is not who I am. A Protestant loyalist evangelical is not who I am.

I started to work in Downpatrick and I was pulled to the side, and told to stay in my own neighbourhood. I loved the role, loved the team, loved the staff, and it was a very vibrant church. But it was made clear to me that if I wanted to be a minister, it would have to be in England. I knew I had to leave. I had nowhere to go and nothing to do. But I wanted to do life with people. I just didn't fit.

I would say I'm an Anabaptist.[50] I believe that was what was happening to me at that time. I realised the church wasn't going to change. So I knew

---

[50] Anabaptists are a Protestant Dissenting tradition who believe in freedom of conscience, non-violence, and adult baptism.

> I had to step out. I remember facing the elders and saying, 'guys, I have changed. The very people that you're saying you don't want me to work with – it's who I am.'
>
> I didn't want to have that mission focus of building our church for the Kingdom. I wanted to just be present with people, and should they never want to know Jesus, that's fine with me. I wanted to do life in the streets. That's where I am called to be. And I don't need to have any title to do that.

Karen calls the next period of her life 'the wilderness years'. She is brave when she talks about it. But I know, from my own family, the total dislocation that happens when you leave an evangelical church. Karen says her family lost their sense of community: 'I never lost my faith, but I lost everything that made my whole life'.

People told Karen that she was unlikely to succeed in her calling, and that if she wanted to continue her work, it must be at least nine miles away from her former church. Rumours swirled around the town. People from the church did not want anything to do with Karen. She felt misrepresented and misunderstood.

After she and the church parted ways, Karen's family left to go on holiday.

> As I was standing in the airport, I got a call from a woman I'd got to know really well in Downpatrick. She phoned me from her rehab clinic. She'd heard that I'd left the church. She asked, 'are you setting up a place for people like me?' And I said to her, 'no, I'm going to set up a place for people like me, but you're welcome to come along'. And she said 'I'm with you'. And she probably saved my life that day.

That was the beginning of Karen's new life outside the Irish Baptist Church. But the trauma of leaving followed her around. She received threatening phone calls. Letters telling her that she would be a nobody.

Help, when it came, was from an unexpected place:

> I spent a number of years in this wilderness. And who came to my rescue? A local Sinn Féin councillor. He calls me Karen the Baptist. We had a really good friendship from working together in the community. He said that he'd heard what had happened with the church. And I was trying to be brave saying 'it's ok, I'm alright'. And he said to me 'just tell me what you need'. I think I'd created relationships in the years that I worked in the community, and people had my back.

> One time, I tried to do a certain community project for families affected by suicide. The families had contacted me and said 'we want to do this tree of lights at Christmas and we'd love you to speak at it'. The church contacted the group and said they would only do it if I pulled out. I said to the group that I would pull out. I could never match the resources that the church had. But everyone else stood with me. The charities and my friends in Sinn Féin. And I didn't pull out. They said to me, 'we are your community'. I don't share Sinn Féin's politics, but our common ground was making our communities better.

Although a couple of ministers from the churches later apologised to Karen, these experiences shaped her deeply. She could have melted away, perhaps like she was supposed to do. But Karen chose to stay. And to reinvent her sense of belonging and community.

Karen and her family loved life in South Down, but she eventually felt called to continue her work in Belfast. She helped set up various projects, including a peace and reconciliation hub and a space for LGBTQ+ people of faith who felt excluded from the church.

During this time, the phone rang. Karen was invited to become chaplain to Deirdre Hargey from Sinn Féin, who at that time was the Mayor of Belfast.

> I told my mum about the invitation, and explained to her that the Mayor was from Sinn Féin. There was a UVF flag on my mum's lamppost outside. And I wanted to explain, in case the news went public. She just looked at me and said 'you need to do this'. I think over the years she'd shifted her views when she saw the outpouring of love for her daughter from a community that was not our community.

Deirdre and Karen hadn't met at this point. Karen says they both laugh now at the awkwardness of their first meeting, Karen in her Reverend's dog collar, Deirdre not sure what to make of it. But they became friends. Karen loved Deirdre and her team. 'They were just for people'. The work brought her right into the heart of Belfast. 'Deirdre opened up her family and community to me. And I never once felt that she was only for her own community.'

> I remember my friends were laughing with me when I had to do the grace for the Mayor's installation dinner. They were asking if I was going to do a big 'pray for the Queen' speech. But I wrote a blessing for Belfast. That

common ground of wanting the best for our city.

One thing I love about my friendship with Deirdre, is that she comes from the very area that I was told to stay out of when I was growing up. I remember my family saying to me, 'you stay away from the Market [a Catholic part of inner Belfast]. Don't you dare ride your bike down there.'

The first Mother's Day after my mum passed away, there was a text on my phone from Deirdre, saying I've left something on your doorstep. This was in lockdown. She was Communities Minister in the Northern Ireland Assembly. And I ran out to the front door and caught her driving past. I couldn't believe that she'd taken the time to do that. She didn't tweet about it, just quietly she was there for me.

Somewhere in that we struck up a friendship that had a ripple effect. I think a trust developed. I was chaplain to Danny Baker from Sinn Féin after that when he was Mayor. To me, the chaplaincy was a massive thing. I just saw that as grace in action from a Sinn Féin Lord Mayor. It really blew me away because I was brought up to 'be careful of them, they have their own agenda'. But during my time as chaplain, I never felt like that. You can't put that on for a two-year term. That's not to say that anyone is perfect. But I just saw a grace in that for their unionist neighbours.

Karen was at the spring 2021 riots on the Springfield Road – the Catholic side of the wall – helping diffuse tensions on the streets. Her office is based on the road. While she was there to help keep the community safe, she describes being struck at how others, in turn, were trying to keep her safe.

I am very moved listening to Karen speak about these experiences. Something a lot of alternative Protestants can struggle with is defining themselves in relation to republicanism. An affinity for republican ideals can sit beside the trauma of the conflict. But Karen has gone deeper. She has opened up her life to friendship and encounter. And she has allowed those friendships to change her. She is modelling what peace can look like in her own life. This seems to me like a very good way to do things. So many blockages melt away through the simple act of friendship.

I wonder out loud if Karen ever worried about being seen as party political, and I loved the way she pushed back against this.

I've had people say to me, 'you're in their back pocket', you know? And I said, 'that's an insult to my intelligence, as if I'm not a woman to make up my own mind'. Some people see this through the lens of being used. But I see this through the lens of friendship. That is not political.

A few weeks before we met, Karen joined Ireland's Future, a civic society organisation which holds discussions around Irish unity. They had their first large public meeting at the Waterfront in 2018, which I attended. Although I recognised plenty of Protestants in the audience, Ireland's Future were criticised for not having unionists on the stage. They've been trying to address that since, holding a digital event, 'New Ireland: A Warm House for All', in February 2021, which Karen spoke at along with four others from unionist backgrounds. 40,000 people watched it (Dáil Éireann 2021: 4).

The day before we met, Karen represented Ireland's Future at the Irish government's Oireachtas Joint Committee for the Implementation of the Good Friday Agreement. She describes her motivation:

> I am a Neither. I am for the unheard. I am for the middle ground. I am for the people who want to be persuaded. It's the people who are happy to say, 'yeah, I'm a unionist or I'm a nationalist, but I'm not wrapped in a flag'. And that's the majority of people. I read out a report to the Committee of a hundred kids from across the communities here. Not one of those young people mentioned flags.
>
> I genuinely do not feel that my background is any way diminished just because somebody has lifted the future of the island onto the table. I'm convinced that most people want to be talking about healthcare, education and issues that affect their everyday living. Those are the things that really matter to people.

Karen had some ideas for the Committee about how the Republic of Ireland might approach their relationship with unionists.

> I wanted to tell the Committee that they need to hear the unionist people. If your starting place is, 'do you want a United Ireland?' you don't need to invite unionists – the answer's no. They won't come. So let's not waste any more time on that. The starting question should be: 'Come and tell us about your vision and hopes for remaining part of the UK. Build your case.' And I am willing to be persuaded. I am willing. I want my unionist friends to be able to be part of that.
>
> I'll try and do the work over the next number of years. I'll try to be part

of a vision and try to say let's join up with the South, let's see what a New Ireland could look like. But I am willing to be convinced by others. And at the end of the day, the people will answer that question. A Citizens' Assembly is my big thing. That would be a good place to start.

Ireland's Future were fantastic. They said this was exactly what they needed. I had the freedom to be whoever I wanted to be.

Karen's family and friends were supportive of her joining Ireland's Future too, despite coming from a wide range of perspectives.

My husband's family are South Indian. He was born in Malaysia and came here to study, then he got his British passport. So he feels connected to the UK in that way. One of my daughters loves everything Irish, and the other is more in the middle and likes Alliance. But they all said that I needed to do this.

And then I sat with my closest friend the night before I was meeting Ireland's Future. And he's a capital U unionist. And he said 'you've got to do this'. The same with my capital U unionist team member. And I think that's because they knew me. They knew my heart.

And that's how it works in Northern Ireland. Most of our families are kaleidoscopes of political opinion. And I think that's how alternative Protestants will change the debate about the future of Northern Ireland. Because while many of us may want to see constitutional change, our lives are full of unionists whom we love. Karen says,

My wider family have their Union Jacks out now. They are your hardcore loyalists. And if they think I don't care about them, then I may as well hang up my hat.

* * *

Alongside developing her work in Northern Ireland, Karen's religious journey continued. She had many friends and fellow travellers in the Baptist Union of Great Britain, which is a diverse place, with many congregations being more liberal than in Ireland. After an intense selection process, where Karen laid bare who she was and what she felt called to do, the Baptist Union of Great Britain accepted her for ordination. They said: 'No ifs or buts. We love your work and we're going to stand over it.' And that is how Karen the Baptist became an official Reverend. The only female Baptist minister on this island.

THE GHOST LIMB

I'm struck once again at how English progressives have so often been the friend of Irish progressives. From the 1790s to today. Because, whatever geographical unit you work out your ideals in, core values are shared.

This relationship is taking Karen to interesting new places.

> I'm doing a PhD now through the Anabaptist Study Centre. It's about nation and neighbours. Relating the Anabaptist story to the context of Ireland and Irish unity. The Anabaptists weren't perfect. But they were willing to stand with people. I think there is room in Northern Ireland for an alternative community, based on the Anabaptist core practices such as peace and reconciliation, the centrality of Jesus, simple living, multi-voiced community, interfaith relationships. So I'm focusing on those core values.

I love that Karen will be studying and talking about these ideas. Often when we think of religion and politics, our minds conjure the Paisley stereotype. But religion and faith have just as often driven political reconciliation in the North. While it's easier to identify religion's power to dominate and divide, it also has the power to heal.

* * *

Three hours after we sat down for coffee, Karen and I stumble out again into the daylight. Mascara a little smudged from a few tears. Karen would go home after this to receive more threats. I would go home and attend a loyalist anti-Protocol rally, desperate to understand the current unrest more deeply.

'Why do we care?' we kept laughing and asking ourselves. There are much simpler ways to live. But all of these conversations are already happening. And I don't think either of us have the inclination to sit them out.

Karen says:

> We need to have the courage, when it looks like violence is about to come. Because what is the alternative? That we live here in this cycle of wavering peace? Always wondering if things are going to collapse? Is this our future? Is this where we're still going to be in a hundred years? Or are we willing to push through it just a little bit? We have to try to find ways to live in a different Ireland, or a different UK, whatever the people choose. But I'm not willing to settle for this.
>
> As I get to this stage in life I'm asking what I want to pass on to my

children, and my grand-babies, or whoever comes behind. I want to put my shoulder to the wheel and do the work.

That's exactly it. And so, we keep going.

Karen and I did not talk about United Irish history at all. But, to me, Karen channels the spirit of 1798 in how she goes out of her way to create relationships. I would later bump into her at the first meeting of the United Irish Historical Society. Like so many of us, Karen was finding that 1798 was a space where people from different backgrounds were consciously trying to walk alongside one another. To see what goals we share. Dreaming of a better future.

Political Activism

Alternative Protestants are often to be found campaigning, protesting, volunteering, working for people's rights, shaping policy and politics in Northern Ireland. In this section, we take several snapshots of political activism amongst alternative Protestants. Roland Spottiswoode talks about his involvement in the civil rights movement in the late 1960s. We trace a line of socialism through time with trade unionist, Stephen Baker. Kellie Turtle explores feminism in the context of her family, and the modern struggle for reproductive rights on the island. Stephen Donnan-Dalzell gives us a window into queer activism. I explore Irish republicanism with Seán Napier. Maurice Macartney offers an alternative political analysis, based in environmentalism and the politics of Otherness. And Heather Wilson talks about how Protestants are integral to any new Ireland that the future might bring. While we do not dwell on 1798 in this section, its spirit is writ large.

18
Beatnik Aristocracy

Roland sends me a photo on WhatsApp. It's a Young Socialists' demonstration outside Belfast's City Hall on 24 August 1968. It was taken on the day of the first civil rights protest in Coalisland. The Young Socialists were protesting the Russian invasion of Czechoslovakia. Roland is in the photo, just behind a banner that says 'Support Czech Socialist Freedom'.

There's another photo in the *Belfast Telegraph* from that afternoon of Roland and Colin McAteer holding a Civil Rights banner, marching towards Belfast City Hall.

Later that day, twelve of the Young Socialists group travelled down to Coalisland, to march for civil rights with the locals. Yet another photo of Roland is snapped, this time by *Ireland's Saturday Night*, as he forces his way through a crowd towards a police cordon to pull his friend out of harm's way.

This was the beginning of a new phase of the civil rights movement in Northern Ireland, and you could feel it in the air. Bernadette Devlin-McAliskey later said that the Coalisland march changed her: 'When you go to something like that, all the pieces click into place […] you can feel where it's going, you can sense it, there's a power in it.' (*Irish Times* August 2018)

The next year – 1969 – Bernadette Devlin would go on to form the People's Democracy with Michael Farrell and others. Unsurprisingly, Roland joined too, a dramatic chapter in his lifetime of political activism.

You could ask what would lead Roland, a Protestant from an old ascendancy family, into the crucible of civil rights politics in the 1960s. But when you hear his story, you might also ask: how could he have ever stayed away?

THE GHOST LIMB

* * *

I have been writing to Roland Spottiswoode for six years now. Fraught political exchanges in times of trouble. Expansive folklore and historical dabbling in times of calm. We decided in the light of COVID-19, that we would stick to our forte and use email and WhatsApp to explore his experience of radical politics in the North.

Roland is an historian, folklorist, artist and publisher. One of the animators of 'The Snowman'. He runs Ardrigh Books from the Glens of Antrim with his wife Sara Craig Lanier. They publish rare and forgotten texts, specialising in works from the Irish Cultural Revival of the late 19th century.

Ardrigh is a reference to the north Belfast home of Francis Joseph (FJ) Bigger, an antiquarian, author and Irish cultural revivalist, who loops through Roland's stories seamlessly. Bigger is a larger-than-life figure. An Anglo-Catholic of the high Church of Ireland tradition, a Freemason, a Gaelic Leaguer, editor of the *Ulster Journal of Archaeology* and collector of cultural items relating to 1798. His home on Belfast's Antrim Road was a meeting place for artists, scholars, Gaeilgeoirí and political figures, known as the Ardrigh coterie. Although Roland was born in the wrong century to be a member, I often think of him as a time travelling part of that club.

The Spottiswoode family has a long history of establishment politics. In the seventeenth century, Roland's ancestor was the Lord Chancellor of Scotland for Charles I, and Roland still has a variety of aristocratic connections. Family members would later become involved in unionist politics. Roland's great grandfather was treasurer of the Belfast Conservative Association, which became the first Belfast Unionist Club in the 1880s.

But the Spottiswoodes have a history of alternative politics too. Two of Roland's ancestors were executed by the Covenanters for being Jacobites. Another, Maurice Spottiswoode, was a United Irishman and friend of Thomas Russell. From another relative, Roland 'inherited a little portrait of Napoleon, that hidden transcript of United Irishmen republicanism'.

More recently, Roland's grandfather, Charles Spottiswoode Jr. – Charlie – was a friend of FJ Bigger. Roland describes Charlie as 'a socialist, an anti-partitionist and a pan-European'. This politics flowed down to Roland's uncle, Billy Spottiswoode, who was in the Northern Ireland Labour Party. Billy talked to Roland about Irishness and socialism, leaving books by neo-Marxist

Frankfurt school writers around the house.

Roland's grandfather and uncle faced significant social sanctions as a result of their politics. Roland says:

> While being a Freemason protected Charlie from the worst of the harassment, it was still there. People regularly cut him off in the street because they knew he was in favour of reunification. After that, my uncle Billy knew what to expect. That those who dissented would be mocked, marginalised and socially ostracised.

Roland would soon go on to experience a more severe version of the 'velvet glove intimidation of unionism'. His involvement in the civil rights struggle in the 1960s made this all but inevitable.

* * *

Back to Coalisland on 24 August 1968, and the birth of the new civil rights movement.

The outward looking political dissent Roland identifies in previous generations of his family was very much alive in Northern Ireland at the time – in the counter-cultural politics of the 1960s, the inspiration of the civil rights movement in the United States, the solidarity with European and global socialist and pacifist movements.

> Before I joined the Labour Young Socialists with Cyril Toman, we'd been occasionally marching as anarchists against the Vietnam War and other pacifist causes. I'd been a regular at Terry Hooley's rooms on High Street, for Wednesday meetings about peace and nuclear disarmament.

All of these movements had Protestant members – Ivan Cooper and Inez McCormick amongst many others.

Whilst Roland was a member of the Young Socialists and People's Democracy, he held these affiliations lightly: 'It was such an anarchist thing. Everyone involved was free to act in whatever way they felt would be effective, under the umbrella. It wasn't like anything else I've ever been involved in.'

This internationalist political energy fused with the politics of Northern Ireland in very particular ways. You can see the fusing in the photographs. The Young Socialists' beatnik black polo necks and leather, mingling with the more traditional suits and ties of the local civil rights groups. 1960s bohemia meets bread and butter.

'One man, one vote', gerrymandering and housing inequalities were central issues for the emerging civil rights movement. Voting in Northern Ireland was linked to property ownership at the time. For example, in Dungannon Urban Council area (where Coalisland was) houses were built and allocated in a way that ensured two of three electoral wards would be unionist. In practice, this meant cramming Catholics (presumed nationalist voters) into the one remaining ward. This made it difficult for Catholics to get a house and led to serious overcrowding. Many working class Protestants lived in similar stark conditions. But gerrymandering added another layer of exclusion for Catholics, from both housing and voting rights.

The ground was being prepared for civil rights in Coalisland from 1963 by a group of young Catholic mothers, who formed the Homeless Citizens League (Keenan-Thomson 2010). They brought prams to Council meetings and protested about their inability to get a house. In June 1968, a Catholic family was evicted from a house in Caledon, which was then allocated to an unmarried Protestant woman. Austin Currie, the local Nationalist Party MP, and two others, then squatted in the house to draw attention to what was happening (Purdie 1980: 135).

I'm struck again by the crossover between the ideas and methods of radical European leftism at the time – in this case squatting – and the specific context of Northern Ireland. It strikes me as very United Irish, that outward focus and cross-pollination of thought.

Talking about the Coalisland march, Roland says:

> We didn't expect it to be anything other than just another demo. The march itself was very social, like so much else at the time, with a lot of singing.

They sang 'We Shall Overcome', which would soon become an anthem of the civil rights movement. As for the counter-protests:

> No-one really expected the Paisleyites to be allowed to block the march. Paisley had left the pacifist groups alone up until then. But then, there he was, fraternising with the RUC, blocking the road into Dungannon.
>
> We tried to avoid the early violence. Eventually, we went back to Belfast. We got the whole story from the locals who had stayed on until late,

blocking the road. After this, we knew we had a fight on our hands to stay demonstrating. On the way back, we talked about how the counter-protests could be used to get civil rights marches banned, which is what happened afterwards in Derry.

When I got home, my face had been in the papers and my uncle had been fielding phone calls from unionist family members all night. He was amused – he was in the Labour Party and didn't disagree with what we were doing. But he realised that the phone calls had a very bad feel. My mother was furious about him letting me 'mix with those Taigs in Tyrone'.

A civil rights march in Derry took place a few months later, on 4th October 1968. Until then, the Northern Ireland Civil Rights Association (NICRA) had been lobbying politicians and letter writing, but they were not making much progress. So when the Derry Housing Action Committee (DHAC) proposed a march, NICRA agreed.

However, after Coalisland, just like Roland and his friends anticipated, the threat of counter-protests led to the Derry march being banned. DHAC were keen for the march to go ahead. Which it did. But this time the RUC attempted to violently disperse the crowd:

The Derry march was an eye-opener for the violence. It was a direct confrontation between those who recognised that it was a legitimate protest and the ideas of some of the very paranoid unionists who saw counter-demos as a key way of blocking any civil rights presence on the streets.

Some say that by going ahead with the Derry march, we were being provocative and, in the final event, violent. But if we'd not marched, if we'd followed Betty Sinclair's moderation, the entire civil rights agitation would have become simply letters to MPs.[51] It would have fizzled out, I think. It was the brutality on the streets of Derry that exposed to the world what people were living under.

But things did fall apart very fast politically.

A few months later, on 4th January 1969, came Burntollet. The People's Democracy organised a march from Belfast to Derry, which was met with

---

[51] Betty Sinclair was a leading member of the Communist Party in Northern Ireland. She was a founding member of the Northern Ireland Civil Rights Association (NICRA) in 1967, but resigned as Chairperson in 1969 as she felt some members' tactics were counter-productive. See Purdie 1980: 153.

loyalist violence as they passed through Burntollet Bridge. Little police protection was provided for the marchers, and the loyalist group contained off-duty members of the B Specials.[52] Some of Roland's friends were knocked unconscious and injured.

> Until then I thought that we could be pacifist, and that we would 'overcome' through civil disobedience. The violence in Derry made me think I might get beaten. But Burntollet made everyone realise that we might be killed. That did not put us off, but it was a sobering reality check.
>
> After that my grandmother and my uncle (who I lived with) were threatened.
>
> An old friend of my grandfather, an inspector in the RUC, came and told me that the threats were serious, and recommended that I leave the North. I was accepted to Portsmouth for art school, then I went to Chelsea, then lived in London for a while, working in animation. All of that's another story.
>
> Occasionally, I sheltered deeply shocked refugees from the decline of Belfast's leftist politics into the Troubles. People targeted by everyone – the police, Provos, loyalists – who could not live in Belfast any longer.
>
> Left to my own devices, I'd have stayed in the North, but it was the threat to my family that really forced me out.

Even though Roland's grandmother was in her seventies and a lifelong unionist with many years of unionist activism under her belt, this made no difference when it came to the threats.

The political unravelling that came next in Northern Ireland is well-documented (Ó Dochartaigh 2004). A descent into violence that we would struggle to escape from for the next 30 years. It would be fair to say that over this time, a lot of the idealism of the early civil rights movement struggled for air, and the conflict took on a sectarian character.

Parallels can be drawn with 1798. How quickly the violent suppression of dissent led to the exile and silencing of Protestant radicals, and put serious pressure on anti-sectarian political collaboration.

---

[52] B Specials is a nickname for an emergency armed corps, the Ulster Special Constabulary. This was an almost exclusively Protestant force, and was disbanded in 1970. For a description of events at Burntollet from Ivan Cooper, see McKay 2000: 310-8.

Roland remains politically active today. True to his anarchist roots, he involves himself in local campaigns, for environmental protection or cultural preservation. Taking whatever action he feels is useful under the umbrella of his values.

Most of his friends from the early civil rights days remain fellow travellers. While there are a few notable exceptions who became more unionist and conservative in their politics, Roland says, 'most of them are still as radical today as they were back then'.

After moving back to Northern Ireland in 1994, Roland has channelled his energies into culture, music and history. He is currently working with Stiofán Ó Doireann on a book about FJ Bigger. Eight years, so far, of this labour of love, finely documenting the life and work of the man who played such a large role in his family's life. Roland says:

> I'd grown up with FJ Bigger as a constant presence in almost every aspect of culture at home. I took much of this for granted as a child. I only found out later that for most unionists, as a Protestant nationalist, Bigger was a bit of a joke. Either a joke, or a dangerous traitor.
>
> Bigger's memory is thick with encrusted myths, both positive and negative, and most academic work that discusses him, takes these myths as a given. Guy Beiner is an exception. Our research has stripped myth from myth, to reveal someone far more human and far more interesting.

By excavating the memory of FJ Bigger, Roland is leaving his own chalk mark on the wall. Revisiting the legacy of Bigger with a fine tooth comb is revealing a political imagination that was so much larger than a simple binary of orange and green. Far from an eccentric Lundy, Bigger is emerging as a layered, complex character who was, in Roland's words, an anti-partitionist, a dissenter, a pan-European. A vital link in our alternative Protestant chain.

* * *

Most people in this book come from working class backgrounds. However, a different kind of dissent comes through Roland's stories. More Marxist intellectual elite than roll-the-sleeves-up Labour club. But the synergy between the two is an important feature of our ecosystem. It is a dissent which traverses all social classes, each informing the other.

Ultimately, in all social classes, similar values are found amongst alternative Protestants. Internationalism, openness, solidarity and island. It's these values that take us together onto the same streets in protest. Voting for similar clusters of political parties. Advocating for equality, rights, environmental and economic justice in similar ways. Polo necks or trackies. Beatniks or millies. All part of this free-thinking tribe.

What also transcends social class is the silencing. Membership of a social elite offered Roland no protection from the threat of violence. Perhaps the main difference is that Roland had the means to get away.

But Roland came back. Like so many of us. In love with this place and stubbornly refusing to acquiesce with its sectarian strictures.

19

Bald's Yard

Stephen is waiting for me at the entrance to the Somme car park outside Newtownards on a freezing January morning. He doesn't want a cup of tea from the flask I've brought. He doesn't want to make small talk. The level of lockdown right now is high. Seeing another human in non-digital form is a rare occurrence. I think we are all vibrating with repressed conversation.

There is a deeper frustration as well. Last week, loyalist protests about the post-Brexit sea border ramped up. The 'thank you NHS' signs in our towns had been replaced with graffiti of gun crosshairs, protesting against British betrayal and DUP sell out. The DUP themselves were refusing to meet with north/south bodies – in what was only the second month of Brexit and a crucial moment in the COVID-19 pandemic. We didn't know it then, but street riots would follow.

As Stephen and I charge up the icy mud path to the Leadmines in a record four minutes, this is what he said.

> You were saying about the history of the United Irishmen. How history disappears and you hold it within yourself. And I think I've got to this stage where I just don't think I can hold it in any longer. I can't be private about it.
>
> When I got Marilyn Hydman's book [about socialist and dissenting Protestants] I knew some of them, I met others after. I found myself reading it and thinking, 'yeah, I agree with this'. You kind of think 'it's just me, and there's something odd about me'. But there are loads of us – all keeping it to ourselves.
>
> I don't want to make it sound like we're some kind of oppressed tribe. We're not. But there's no room, no way of talking about this politics, in public life.

THE GHOST LIMB

One of the good things about lockdown has been walking around places like this. We played here as kids, so it's not like I don't know it. But you look at things in a different way.

This was a lead mine. That means people worked here at one stage. There's a quarry over there. People worked there as well. There were mills in the town. People worked there too. Ards had a working class! There must have been socialists here. But there's no evidence of that socialist history. It's not marked or remembered anywhere. Every time we build something – a new road or a leisure centre – we call it Blair Mayne.[53]

What happens when you live here, is that unionist history is just thrown across this place, like a great big soggy wet blanket, and everybody has to live beneath it, kind of crawling around, trying to make sense of who the hell they are.

And recent events, from Brexit to coronavirus, the behaviour of the UK, the disintegration of the British welfare state over a number of decades. Suddenly, you go: 'I can't sit here any longer, pretending that this is alright. It's not good enough any longer.'

There's an element of age about it also. I'm just pissed off, having to constantly defer to this other history, this other politics. Always having to make sure that you don't encroach upon it or that you don't cause it any offence. Because even though it's dominant, it's fragile as well. And your small dissent might arouse it and make it angry. So you keep your head down and you don't say too much about it. You try not to draw too much attention to yourself.

I've just got to this stage, and I'm asking myself, 'is this what you bequeath to your kids? Just keep your head down. Don't say too much. Don't draw attention to yourself. Just learn to live with the powerlessness of this region. And your own lack of power as a citizen within it.' I've got to the point now where I feel like I want to be indiscreet more often. Instead of this constant self-censorship.

I don't think it's possible to put it better than this. The big soggy wet blanket is the stifled feeling that comes from constantly having to participate in a conversation that you don't get to choose. The bursting sense of wanting to

---

[53] Robert Blair Mayne, born in Newtownards in January 1915, was one of the founder members of the SAS, the Special Air Services of the British army.

talk about social class, economy and equality, but constantly being pulled back into the straitjackets of tribe. To so rarely see your own ideas reflected back to you in the public sphere. And to worry about the consequences of voicing your feelings too loudly.

Stephen and I walked for 11,000 more steps – the length and breadth of the Newtownards golf course, which commoners were allowed to roam during lockdown – getting under the bonnet of where these feelings come from.

* * *

Stephen Baker is an academic. A son of Cregagh and Cornwall. When new houses were built in Newtownards in the early 1970s, the Bakers moved out of Belfast. Things were kicking off politically, and his parents wanted to go somewhere quieter. They succeeded in that. Stephen had Catholic friends growing up, and there was an ease of life that came from not living on a sectarian interface. But he was keenly aware of the class dynamics around him.

The new Newtownards houses were seen as starter homes for the socially mobile. But for Stephen's family – whose mum worked in a factory and whose dad was a lorry driver – it was arrival at a destination. By the time he was a teenager, Stephen's best friend had moved away to a much bigger house. He noticed that his dad and his group of lorry driver friends also saw themselves as different from the others around them: 'I didn't live on a sectarian interface. But there was another kind of interface'.

While he didn't understand it at the time, Stephen says, looking back, that it was clear that his cultural capital was lacking, or different, from his friends. One of the neighbour's kids told him that he was going to be a lorry driver like his dad, while she was going to be a professional woman. While his eight-year-old self was delighted about being a lorry driver, the memory also stands out as being told 'you're not like me'.

Stephen's dad was a shop steward for the Irish Transport and General Workers' Union (ITGWU). So there was a sense of class politics at home. That said, Stephen describes his dad as a working class Tory, slightly to the right of Alf Garnett. So it was a mixed bag. There was everyday unionism in the house. The flag would go up for the Twelfth. They'd go out and make tape recordings of the Eleventh night marches and play them back after.

Things took off for Stephen politically in his twenties, when he had a job at a local department store. He began to notice that he and his friends weren't making any money, that their working conditions were awful.

> I'd no politics at this stage really. But a few of us got together and thought why don't we start a union. I got the idea from my dad's involvement, but had no clue how these things worked. So we went to see Eugene McGlone at ITGWU. I was appointed shop-steward because my dad had done it; maybe they thought it was hereditary.

They couldn't get the management to engage with them.

> The manager called us in one day and said 'you have driven a wedge between the management and the staff'. I said to him that maybe his wife's company car might have driven a bigger wedge. He was raging. He got spreadsheets out and started to show us where the money went. My mate was sharp and kept pointing to the large column of profit. He kept telling us, 'don't look at that bit'.

Another time when the union members were summoned by the director, Stephen suggested the director contact their union rep. The director said he'd already had a call about it, 'from someone called Eugene McGlone... I wonder what Lodge he belongs to?'

> It's meant to bring you into line. To remind you where your loyalties lie. But it had the opposite effect on me. I thought 'you don't have our interests at heart'. That was the decision made really, politically.

A lot of the shop's managers were unionists and Orangemen, who regarded Stephen and his friends setting up a union as disloyal. But a lot of the young guys who joined the union were in loyalist bands. 'They were at the bottom of the pile too – they realised just how bad things were.'

A new manager started.

> He called me in and said, 'you don't like it here. But I've good news for you. You will leave here. We won't sack you, but you will go.' I got a chance to do support for the Beautiful South gigs in Belfast and Dublin. I asked for some leave, and he wouldn't let me have it. I said, 'you know I'm going to do this anyway?' He said 'yes, and when you do it, I'll take that as your resignation'. And that was it.

* * *

The first time I heard Stephen play the guitar, he played an English workers' song, 'The Man who Waters the Workers' Beer'. Like so many socialists from Northern Ireland, Stephen was heavily engaged with class politics in Britain. The 1980s and Thatcher coincided with his political coming of age. Greenham Common, the poll tax and the miners' strike. He remembers a TV clip of a Conservative Party university society singing a song about what the miners' were going to eat for Christmas, maybe their pets. 'You just start to pick sides'.

When he was a teenager, Stephen wrote letters to Tony Benn.

> I'd say things like 'there are no socialists over here'. I thought I might be the only socialist in Ireland. I just didn't know anybody else at all. If you mentioned anything, maybe you'd seen Tony Benn on BBC Question Time, they'd say 'bloody rebel', so you just didn't mention it.

Tony Benn always wrote back. Often on House of Commons notepaper, maybe including an article he'd written for *Tribune*. But the British Labour Party told Stephen he was not eligible to join, sending him a poster of Neil Kinnock and suggesting he try the SDLP instead.

The Britishness Stephen associated with revolved mainly around popular culture and multiculturalism:

> It was about pop music, BBC dramas and Film 4. 'Boys from the Blackstuff.' It was about the literature of Stan Barstow and Alan Sillitoe and Keith Waterhouse, those kind of young English working class writers of the fifties and sixties. A cultural Britishness rooted in a welfare state, which was just starting to disappear as I was becoming aware of it.

Football was a big thing too. Stephen says he learned English geography through the football leagues. 'I could have pointed to Bolton before anywhere else in Ireland.'

With encouragement from his wife, Stephen went back to college, doing A levels at Bangor Tech, a degree and then a PhD at the University of Ulster.

He soon found himself lecturing in the Media Studies Department at Northampton University in the East Midlands of England. Stephen offered to run a film club, with his friend Paul Crofts, an independent socialist councillor for Wellingborough. Together they programmed films around the human rights calendar – Holocaust month, black history month.

Stephen and Paul also set up the Wellingborough Diggers' Festival.

The Diggers were people who had no possessions, and had been left destitute in the wake of the English civil war. They had to find a way to make a life. So they went to St George's Hill in Surrey, which was common ground at that stage. And they began to work it, and set up this early form of communism. But, of course, that couldn't be allowed to stand. So the landlords sent in mobs to wreck their commune.

When I look at someone like Gerrard Winstanley [an English Protestant religious reformer], his pamphlet, *The True Levellers Standard Advanced* (1649), the first line in it basically says, I've been reading the Bible, and I can't find anywhere that says that one man should Lord it over another. That's inflammatory. It's instantly revolutionary in that context – that intellectual and political challenge to the class system.

That's the tradition I come out of. I identified with a tradition of English socialism because that's what I was introduced to. I didn't know anything about Irish history, so I hadn't been able to identify with anything here I felt I belonged to.

Now, I know that these same ideas were moving through the United Irish. And then you've got the *Northern Star* newspaper in Belfast. And the Chartists have a *Northern Star* newspaper over in England too.

When I was younger, I'd thought of these movements as being kind of isolated. But they were all talking to each other. There was a political conversation taking place there. And I was just in one strain of it, with the Suffragettes, the Chartists, the Levellers and the Diggers, the emergence of a British Labour Party. But it was all connected.

At this point in his life, Stephen had been commuting between Northampton and his young family at home in Newtownards. So when a job came up in the University of Ulster, he went for it. And he got it. The dots were about to join up even more.

* * *

By this time, the feeling of being the only socialist in Ireland had long gone. Stephen had been involved with trade unionism and the May Day celebrations in Belfast. Early membership of Militant in Belfast, a socialist wing of Labour, had brought him into contact with radicals from all backgrounds in the North.

He read Irish history when he went back into education, and began to identify with James Connolly and with other socialist traditions on the island. The Green Party was in its infancy. The left/right politics he'd hoped to see open up after the Agreement hadn't emerged. But: 'I was starting to see that there were people like me everywhere'.

England was changing too. It was the countdown to Brexit. English nationalism was emerging. Anti-migrant feeling was rising. 'It wasn't the multicultural Britain that I was comfortable with. The shine came off it. I still loved it. But I wasn't the starry Anglophile that I was earlier, with my Jam records and Alan Barstow books.' He was finding that the English academics he knew hadn't a great appetite for talking about social class.

But most of all, Stephen just wanted to be at home with his family. He started to look at the Strangford Peninsula in a new way. It's a beautiful place to live. His kids joined the local football team. He started to feel knitted into the local community.

But he couldn't engage with his surroundings on the same terms as before.

> There were things that I wasn't comfortable with about the history of this place. My experience of Britishness in Newtownards was benign. The BBC, the Jam, the Smiths. I suspect if I'd been brought up in West Belfast or the Bogside, my experience of Britishness would be very, very different.
>
> And I can't ignore that any longer. I can't just say 'British multiculturalism and the welfare state, what have you got to complain about?'
>
> Personally, the reason I can't acquiesce with partition any longer is because it's clear that English nationalism doesn't care about us. And I mean all of us.
>
> Now that's something which I could have read in books and I could have understood at a theoretical and abstract level. But it is now something which I have experienced with Brexit. Not only does England not care about here, but in fact, the involvement of England in our politics isn't a positive influence.
>
> You've got to make decisions here. And in a sense I'm not that different to Brexiteers. The Brexiteers wanted a sense of sovereignty. And I don't have any here as a citizen. I don't think anybody else around me has any real sovereignty either. I have never voted for a party that's made up a government. Never, ever have I been represented by anybody I've voted for

at any level of government. That's shocking. And I'm just not happy to go, 'well, that's just how it is'.

I watched the Brexit debate. And nobody spoke to the kind of politics I had. The last time was probably with Jeremy Corbyn. Suddenly the BBC was obliged to give left socialist politics some public space. But as soon as they could get rid of him, they did. And they did it in the most brutal way.

The thing is, I will make a stand with English, Scottish, Welsh, Irish – any socialists or anti-racists anywhere, any time. This is not a politics of ethnicity for me at all. It's not about blood and belonging, as much as I love this place. It's an argument about democracy and politics and sovereignty and where power lies. What opportunities do I have to be part of a democratic debate about the future of this place?

I've been talking about unionist and loyalist identities all my life. I'm always holding my tongue and trying not to offend anyone. The self-censorship makes you have to think within a set of intellectual limitations. When you can't say what's in front of your nose, you end up bending yourself out of all intellectual and political shape in an attempt to work around this thing. And I just can't do it anymore.

I have no hostility towards unionism and loyalism. I suppose it's just saying, 'we want to talk about something else. There's a group of people here who have a different political perspective. And we want to be part of a dialogue. If you want to disagree with me, then let's debate it. But don't threaten me about it.' There's something politically and intellectually freeing about coming to this place.

When I listen to unionist arguments now, what I see laid bare is an allegiance to an archaic state. It's not democratic. And there's just nothing in it for me at all.

I go to Belfast all the time, to events about how to fund the public sector, how to develop a new economy, how to develop cooperatives. Really interesting ideas for our time. I rarely see unionists there, and I think it's a great pity.

Unionism could've made a convincing argument. They could have said, 'look at our social democratic tradition and welfare state; we're multicultural enough to accommodate your Irish identity'. That wouldn't have been a big ask. I could have lived with this, and suspect plenty of Catholics could have too. But they never built a consensus around it. David

Ervine made that argument. He was one of the best thinkers at the time of the Agreement. I wonder if he lived, would he have been sidelined.

I think for unionism, the more you sound that you're able to accommodate Irishness and Catholics within a kind of vision for Northern Ireland, the less unionist you sound. And you're a Lundy. And unionism kills itself in the end.

It's about having a sense of political agency. Unionism lives as a dependant. But I want to feel like a political agent. Why march up to the top of the hill and down again, just to hand power back to people who will betray you every time.

I think Scotland's growing sense of independence is agency at its best. When you look at the emergence of Scottish nationalism, it has announced itself in a working class Glasgow accent. The literature of working class Scotland is undergoing a renaissance. Obviously Scotland isn't perfect. But it's civic-minded. They're inviting EU migrants to stay there after Brexit. They're internationalists. They're looking outwards.

That's like the United Irish. They're influenced by events that are happening in Europe and America. And their ideas ripple out as well. This is nothing new. You can't treat culture like it's a preserve. You can't pickle culture in time. Culture is a living thing. You have to let new ideas in, and allow things to change, rather than seeing culture as something that is essential and needs to be preserved and protected from other people, which is what happens so often here.

I think it would be great if the North began to see itself as a potentially progressive force within a united Ireland. To have a bit of confidence about itself and arrive and say, 'you're not swallowing us. Things are changing because this is a new country and it's a new partnership.' And that's what I would be excited about. I want to make up a new social contract. I want to be part of that conversation.

That was us back at the carpark. And I haven't stopped thinking about his words since.

* * *

I look into the socialist history of Newtownards when I get home from the Leadmines. I find that an English company had owned the Leadmines, extracting the rich ore for export (Day and McWilliams 1991: 103). The town had a huge working class. Weavers were organising in Newtownards for better prices for their work in the 1790s (Gray 2018a: 15-6). There were tenants' rights groups in the town in the 1850s. There was a huge demonstration of the tenant farmers of Londonderry estate on Christmas Day 1880. Suffragettes attacked Newtownards Race Stand in 1914 to draw attention to their struggle for women's right to vote. On average, a third of people voted for the Northern Ireland Labour Party (NILP) in Newtownards after partition.

The local non-subscribing Presbyterian minister, Rev. Albert McElroy left the NILP in 1953 because it was too conservative, and started the Liberal Association. He was an early campaigner for Catholic civil rights. He advocated for the spirit of 1798, which he called 'that other Ulster Heritage', and was committed to breaking 'the Tory monopoly on the politics of Northern Ireland' (Beiner 2018: 487).

But the thing that sticks with me most is Bald's Yard. In 1842, there was a meeting in Bald's Yard to protest the corn laws, which had made bread far too expensive for local workers. One thousand people attended the meeting. The speakers and speeches were anti-sectarian, with Chartists, dissenting clergy and the local Catholic priest in attendance. They railed against the Tory government, asking why it can fix the price of bread, but not the price of wages or rent (*Northern Whig* February 1842).

Bald's Yard is in the exact location where Stephen worked in the shop. The very same patch of ground where he set up his own trade union nearly 150 years later. Probably within metres of each other. All that radical history under Stephen's feet. Hidden. Disremembered. As his teenage self wrote to Tony Benn, believing he was the only socialist in town.

These histories have always existed in Newtownards. Looping through time, generation after generation. They exist now still. Crawling around under the soggy blanket. Full of hope that there is a better way to live. And a growing reluctance to keep quiet about it.

20

Foremothers and Feminism

The last time I saw Kellie at Stormont was in October 2019. Westminster had just legislated to decriminalise abortion in Northern Ireland, and the DUP had recalled the Assembly – dormant for nearly three years – in an attempt to block it.

The foyer of Stormont was a blur of journalists, activists, MLAs, aides and advisors. Information was leaking out from back rooms to waiting crowds. At one point there was a rumour – whether true or not, I don't know – that some DUP MLAs might change their designation from unionist to nationalist, to get cross-community consent to block the bill.

Hours later, the political parties slowly filtered out to the TV cameras. The UUP did not fall in behind the DUP. Sinn Féin were also against blocking the legislation. The Green Party, Alliance and People Before Profit were always opposed. Colum Eastwood from the SDLP walked out to the foyer. We held our breath. The modern leader of what has been a pretty conservative Catholic party, said that they would not be getting involved with the DUP's political stunt.

It was game over.

The pro-choice activists, their friends and allies, collapsed in an exhausted, relieved heap. There would be many problems of implementation ahead. At the time of writing, abortion services have still not been fully commissioned in the North. But, for the first time in this place, young girls and women had the prospect of control over their own bodies and receiving healthcare at home.

* * *

Kellie Turtle is a feminist activist from east Belfast, and a close friend. We return to Stormont on a bright winter morning in 2020, to mull over that day and put it in context.

Some people are the first in their families to break the chain of conservative politics. Other people have foundations to build on. The foundations, in Kellie's life, were generations of strong women and feminist men, most of them socialists.

> My mum's paternal family were middle class, educated socialists from Belfast. They weren't religious. While the family came from a well off background, they were more hippies, and bohemian in how they lived.
>
> The working class socialism comes from her maternal side. Robert Atkinson Senior, my great granda, was a plater in the shipyard. My great uncle, Robert Atkinson Junior, was a trade union shop steward in the shipyard.

When Robert Senior lost his job at the shipyard in the early 1920s, he cooked and looked after the kids, while his wife went out to work. Margaret, his wife, was the breadwinner. She did domestic work, cleaning people's houses. 'One of her jobs was looking after elderly people in their homes, so it was an early type of paid care work, which was ahead of her time.'

While looking after the kids, Robert Senior began to write poems. He was one of a number of shipyard writers, including Presbyterian socialist Thomas Carnduff, and later Sam Thompson (Parr 2019). Robert Senior's poems often reflect on how it felt to be a stay at home dad (Hall 1993). How unemployment affected his sense of self and masculinity. The toll that his wife's work took on her body.

> *Her cheeks are plain', her hair's turned grey,*
> *Her han's are worn and rough,*
> *An' me with mine as soft as clay,*
> *I don't think it's good enough.*

Robert had been raised by his dad too. His mum died of uterine cancer aged 36 after having nine babies.

So traditional gender roles never really applied in Kellie's family. And these ideas of care and equality trickled down through the generations. From Robert Senior to Robert Junior. Through Kellie's great nana Margaret, who was the family breadwinner. To Kellie's nana Eleanor, a strong woman who grafted to get a job that allowed her to leave an abusive husband. To Siobhan, Kellie's mum. Then Kellie herself. And knowing Kellie's daughter, I don't think these values will be skipping the next generation either.

* * *

One of the reasons Kellie and I have come to Stormont today is to see George Walker – another of her great grandads on her dad's side – who is on the plinth of Edward Carson's statue. George was one of Carson's advisers in the 1910s. We thought this might lead to a conversation about how Kellie's story diverged from George's. But nothing is ever so simple.

George grew up in poverty in Lurgan, and lied about his age to get into the army. After stints in the Boer War and India, he came home and became involved in unionist politics and the UVF. Although this sounds like quite a traditional unionist identity package, family stories remember George as open-minded, anti-religious and non-sectarian. One of his motivations for political involvement was to resist the religious control by the Catholic Church which many Protestants expected to happen under Home Rule.

Kellie's family tell a story of when George lived on the Woodstock Road, in inner east Belfast. During the unrest of the 1920s, the Ulster Special Constabulary (USC) came one day to evict his Catholic neighbours:

> And the way my dad put it to me was that everyone knew in those days that the USC wouldn't just put people out, they might put them out and shoot them. So my granda ran upstairs, put on his UVF jacket, and stood at the door of the neighbours' house and said 'you won't be going in there'. There was a big standoff, and in the end they didn't carry out the eviction. I found it fascinating to hear he used his UVF credentials to stand up against a more oppressive institution.

Most Catholics, of course, did not have a uniformed UVF neighbour standing with them when they faced sectarian violence. But George's act of solidarity gives us a window into a history that has more layers than are usually remembered.

As Kellie and I walk up to the security barrier at Stormont, the irony of George's opposition to the Catholic Church is not lost on us. Arguably,

Protestants withdrawing from the debate about Irish independence allowed the Catholic Church an outsized role in the new Irish Republic, and gave conservative evangelicalism a foothold in the North (Collins 2017: 10-3). The consequences of which wounded Irish women deeply, both sides of the border.

You can see this when you look at suffragism in Ireland (Ward 1995; Cullen Owens 1984). Kellie tells me Edward Carson initially indicated that he might support roles for women in the provisional government of Ulster in the event of Home Rule. While the Ulster Women's Unionist Council played this down, the Pankhursts latched onto it (Kelly 1996).

> That's why the Pankhursts set up a satellite organisation of the WSPU [Women's Social and Political Union] in Belfast on University Street. They sent over a lot of English and Scottish radicals, and started having big meetings around Belfast.
>
> But soon after, Carson changed his mind. So the Pankhursts kind of declared war on unionism. They targeted a lot of unionist institutions, and caused a lot of damage. The WSPU University Street offices kept getting raided, and they found a few guns there. So they threw the women in Crumlin Road Jail. And the suffragettes consistently made the point that the UVF were openly marching with arms in the street, and nobody was touching them, while they were in jail. I found that interesting, them asserting that difference in treatment of the women and the UVF.

And there's the premonition of what was to come. How the new Northern Ireland, and its governing unionism, were a cold house for women. How women's rights were always subsumed by the national question. How certain types of male violence were tolerated, but women's response to their political condition was usually not. The modern parallels are inescapable. How the last time we'd seen each other at Stormont, Kellie was working to resist the DUP's reflex to control women's bodies. How the free-thinking Ulster that George desired collapsed under the weight of its own sectarianism.

* * *

We're right up to Stormont's steps now, at the top of the hill. Kellie is recalling a time when she worked at the Women's Research and Development Agency

(WRDA). The very first thing she did was to fill Stormont to the brim with women for International Women's Day.

> I had been talking with women for a good while about political participation. I kept hearing from them that they didn't even know where Stormont was. They couldn't imagine ever going there. It felt so inaccessible to them.
>
> So we coaxed them to open Stormont up for a day, for a big party of women, and their kids. The first thing I said was, if you're having the women, you have to have the kids too.

Four coach loads came. They took over the Long Gallery. There were art workshops for the little ones, while the women speed-dated MLAs. They were not shy with their questions.

> For women who had never been politically involved before, they gave those MLAs the worst time I've ever seen MLAs get. Because they had no airs and graces. It was 'let me tell you the 20 things I've been storing up to tell somebody like you'. And it was brilliant.

Although women have made progress in northern politics in recent years, Kellie says:

> There is a sense that all the protagonists of the history of Stormont, and Northern Ireland, were men. And it's still the case that women are struggling to survive, and rear kids, make sure there's enough money coming in, while also dealing with violence and abuse. We're nowhere near equality yet.

∗ ∗ ∗

'What about Repeal of the 8th amendment?' I ask Kellie. 'Has that shaped how you see feminism in this place?'

The 8th amendment of *Bunreacht na hÉireann*, the Irish Constitution, was repealed by referendum on 25th May 2018. This saw the Republic of Ireland legalise abortion with 67 per cent in favour of change. The campaign was emotional, as people told stories of bleeding out on Ryanair flights, or at home after taking pills from the internet and being too afraid to call for help. Stories of much wanted babies who doctors knew would never live being carried to full term by traumatised mothers.

The years leading up to the referendum were a seminal time for all-island politics.

> Until that two-year period leading up to the referendum, I didn't even really know people's names down south, and suddenly everyone's in working groups together. We were doing video calls before Zoom was a thing.

As the referendum approached, bus-loads of people, from all backgrounds in the North, travelled south to knock on doors and share stories about pregnancy, loss, violence, shame and trauma.

Kellie says it was the Belfast rugby rape trials when she fully appreciated how deep a bond had been formed. This was a legal case in March 2018 where a number of Ulster rugby players were accused of sexual assault. While they were acquitted, leaked WhatsApp messages and the graphic evidence given in court shone a light on a careless disdain for women that re-traumatised and incensed many across Ireland.

In cities all over the island, from Belfast to Galway to Cork, people rallied under banners saying 'I Believe Her'.

> The very quick reaction happened across the whole island in a way that it wouldn't necessarily have before, if it hadn't been for the Repeal movement. Those networks existed. It had been two years in the making, of the feminist movement on this island really solidifying.

There were tensions of course, as there are in all movements. When the 8th amendment fell in the Republic of Ireland, legalising abortion in the South but leaving it still inaccessible in Northern Ireland, two slogans emerged. 'The North is Next' and 'Now for Northern Ireland', each reflecting different constitutional orientations and language.[54]

I ask Kellie if she thought she was more pre-disposed than others to an all-island approach to feminist activism.

> I don't know. I've always had a consciousness of being on the island of Ireland. By the time I was an adult, we'd been on camping holidays to every county of Ireland, because we couldn't afford to do anything else. I could

---

[54] Nationalists often use the term 'the North' to refer to six of the nine counties of Ulster which make up Northern Ireland, while the official term 'Northern Ireland' is preferred by many unionists.

tell you all the main towns and car registrations for each county. But most of my friends had never been to Dublin.

The socialist consciousness in so many branches of Kellie's family, as well the hippies, led to a deliberate embracing of Irishness throughout the Troubles.

> Through the fifties and sixties, my grandparents were two Prods who lived on the Lisburn Road and sent their kids to Irish dancing. They called my mum Siobhan. My uncle actually said it at my nana's funeral, that raising the family with their socialist values and embracing Irish culture had been a buffer against the growing sectarianism.
>
> My mum was all about peace. She was a real hippy. There were doves all over our house growing up. Ban the Bomb and all that. I learned all these values from her over dinner conversations while watching the news.

Possibly because of these experiences, all-island feminist activism felt like second nature to Kellie. But the Repeal movement was an important shift for unionist feminists too, who played an important part in achieving change on the island.

It was Westminster politicians who ultimately legislated to decriminalise abortion in Northern Ireland in 2019. Stella Creasy, a Labour MP, led the way. And as ever, northern feminists move forward with whatever allies and levers of power are available in any given moment. There's something very United Irish about that strategy.

But Kellie has mixed feelings about this. On one level, she was delighted about making progress in abortion reform in the North.

> But I was also really upset about the way it came, with an English MP swooping in. Something you've dedicated a lifetime of activism to. I just felt very powerless.
>
> But here we were, just doing the messy work of trying to make progress, and thanking people that had helped us. Even if they left it late and can't necessarily be counted on in the future.

Standing at Stormont, the site of so many of these struggles, Kellie reflects:

> I think I would be the opposite of George Walker, from a pragmatic point of view, in terms of the Union. Maybe at the time, the loyalist in him felt

that he was just dealing with what was in front of him. I do get that.

But my idea around what political participation and what democracy should look like, I just don't think we can have a functioning democracy under Westminster. There's always going to be this glass ceiling.

It fell apart from me over welfare reform from 2010 onwards. We had really strong resistance to Westminster cutbacks from our local elected representatives. In their minds, they took it as far as they could. But we're still ultimately going to have the two-child cap on benefits, and whatever else the Tories come up with.[55]

That's when the scales fell from my eyes in terms of devolution. In terms of what I believe democracy should look like, I think on the island of Ireland, we have a better chance of doing that properly.

And I know that there are political elites in the Republic of Ireland as well. And the current government is full of them. You'd still have to grapple with all of that class politics. I just think it gives us more of a chance to affect change if we could do democracy in Ireland. But it's still going to be hard work.

Like Stephen Baker, Kellie talks about what the North could bring to the South. This is a significant reframing of the current narrative where the North often appears as a liability. Kellie sees things differently.

In some ways, I think we are more radical in the North. That's changing now. But it's the class dynamics. If you look back to the women's movement in the 1970s and 1980s, the southern movement had a lot of journalists and academics. Obviously there was grassroots stuff going on as well, but it was quite middle class.

In Belfast you've always had a different class dynamic. The women's movement here did have academics and middle class groups. But we didn't have time for ivory tower feminism, because things were always driven by working class women who were used to speaking up for themselves.

---

[55] In 2015, Westminster reform meant that social security payments would only be made for the first two children in a family, from those born in 2017 onwards. The Northern Ireland Executive decided to mitigate this policy, and top up social security payments to affected families. At the time of writing, these mitigations are still in place.

> Women here were really prominent in the trade union movement. There was the legacy of the housing activists in the 1960s, and the civil rights movement. All had a big place for women. By the time second wave feminism hit, women were ready for it.
>
> I'm not sure I see Ireland as progressive. It's liberalised for sure. But being liberal and being progressive are different things.
>
> I'd love to see if during this period of marking the hundred years of Northern Ireland, if there's any room for Protestant voices to say, 'actually, I think, maybe it's ok to call time on this thing. And that we have something really good to offer the rest of Ireland.'

* * *

When all is said and done, this is a story of intergenerational feminism. Women and men who found themselves taking on non-traditional gender roles. Who lived their lives in the orbit of the shipyards, the trade unions, socialism, hippiedom and boundary-crossing. Grey hairs and rough hands.

It seems fitting that we would stand at the statue of Carson and ask how far we have come since those days of heartache. How the legacy of partition impacted on women's lives, north and south of the border. How so many of the lives of the women in our families were shaped – and ended – by lack of choice and power over their bodies. Even retracing Kellie's feminism leads us to the written-down poems and statues of men.

> I feel like the women in my family just had a really hard time of it, and didn't really have a voice. They just did what they could. Maybe that's informed my feminist anger a little bit, my kind of need to have a voice all the time, because there's just no evidence of that really, throughout these histories.

But the ground has perhaps been prepared now for something new. Women across the island know each other better. We support each others' struggles. They are the same struggles. They are the same across Scotland, Wales and England too. But, on this island, north and south, our experiences have been shaped by a particular politics which gave conservative religion an outsized control over women's lives.

And so, we continue to help each other break free from this sectarian inheritance. Continuing the graft of our foremothers. A line we can trace from Mary Ann McCracken and Matty Drennan, through the suffragettes, through to Kellie and our 21st century sisters. A struggle which leaves us no choice but to keep going.

21

Cara Van Parke

Stephen and I talk online on a bright summer day, cute dogs jumping in and out of the call. It's the last conversation I have for the book. Both of us are struggling with the after-effects of COVID-19 infections and don't feel up to the walk.

When I first thought about writing this book, Stephen was top of my wish-list for people to talk to. I was interested in their involvement in queer activism in the North. And I thought it would be interesting to speak to a unionist, to see how the spirit of 1798 showed up in this tradition today.

But, by the time we sit down to speak, almost two years later, Stephen is no longer a unionist. While many factors led to this rupture, it was the pandemic that finished things off. The last few years have taken a toll on many of our politics, as well as our bodies and minds.

Stephen has had many ruptures in their personal and political lifetime. They're a fighter. Being a working class, queer kid from east Belfast, there weren't too many other options if you wanted to survive.

* * *

Stephen Donnan-Dalzell is a genderqueer, non-binary writer, activist and a drag artist – Cara Van Parke. They've worked in different jobs over the years – in youth work, as a trained counsellor, and now in addictions and mental health.

Stephen grew up in Cregagh and later Dundonald, on the edge of the Ballybeen estate. Their parents were unionists with a socialist streak. The family's socialism got stronger over time, as Stephen's dad became sick with Parkinsons, and their mum had to leave her job to care for him. As a result, there wasn't a lot of money to spare in the house. Everyone was at home a lot and the atmosphere could fray. But despite this, Stephen had a happy enough childhood.

Coming out as gay at 19 though, was not a good experience for Stephen. It was the late 2000s. It would be some years before the idea of marriage equality entered the political mainstream in Northern Ireland. Homophobia is still a huge problem in the 2020s. But ten years ago, it was unrelenting. Stephen says, 'I came out three days before Iris Robinson made those comments on the Stephen Nolan show'.

Iris Robinson was the then wife of then DUP leader, Peter Robinson. After a homophobic assault on a man in Newtownabbey, Iris Robinson said that the man should consider therapy to 'cure' him of homosexuality (Grew 2008). The previous week, she had told Radio Ulster listeners that homosexuality was an abomination. By 2019, these comments would inspire a sell-out show, 'Abomination: A DUP Opera' (*Guardian* October 2019). But in 2008, this catharsis was far in the future. Things seemed bleak, and Iris Robinson's comments contributed to an incredibly toxic and dangerous atmosphere for queer people in Northern Ireland. Stephen says:

> Iris lived just a few doors down from me at the time. My parents didn't take me coming out well. I couldn't believe the timing. Iris was talking about how gay people are no different than child molesters [*Belfast Telegraph* July 2008]. And then to hear those lines parroted back to you by your own family.
>
> If it hadn't been for the fact that there was a metro bus from Dundonald into Belfast, I don't know if I would have made it. I really mean that. Because I would get the bus into town and go to Gay and Lesbian Youth Northern Ireland; it's called Cara Friend Youth now. Meeting other people who were queer, my age, going through similar things, it saved me. I'd never met anyone like me before. A lot of these people were happy. They had stable lives. I never thought that was an option for me.
>
> I was dealing with a lot of homophobia at the time. Being sent death threats for being gay, being chased for being gay, being called all the names under the sun. My home life was incredibly hostile. Listening to people on the radio debate your existence and rights every day puts you in a bad place.
>
> When I was 19, I ended up moving away from home, and was homeless for a while. It wasn't a good time. But I got through to the other side. Having that community in Belfast was a life-saver. Literally.

Since those tough days, many things have changed for Stephen. They married William in 2019. A gorgeous bear of a man whose photos Stephen occasionally posts online. Family relationships have improved significantly.

> My mum loves my husband William to bits. She was at the wedding. And I got that acceptance from my dad before he died as well. I was watching a documentary on RTÉ with him around the time of the marriage equality referendum in the South. It was about a gay GAA player, Donal Óg Cusack.[56] Donal said he'd been made to feel worthless by his teammates, his fans, his family, his church and his friends. My dad asked me if he'd ever made me feel like that. And I said yes. Things were good after that. I really regret that my dad never got to meet William. I know he would have liked him.

***

Just as relationships in Stephen's family softened over time, the political climate for queer people in Northern Ireland has also shifted. The Assembly currently has three out gay MLAs, all from the Alliance Party, and there are more out gay councillors from a range of parties. There is still a long way to go politically, and trans rights are particularly under attack in the current moment. But the last decade has seen progress. It's hard to underestimate the role that the marriage equality referendum in the Republic of Ireland in 2015 played in this. A political movement that Stephen was at the heart of.

Stephen was young getting into politics. They joined the Alliance Party in 2012, running for the Council election in their own area – Castlereagh East – in 2014. The election took place in the aftermath of the loyalist flag protests, which Stephen's mum had attended. The flag protests erupted after Belfast City Council voted to limit the number of days the Union flag would fly at City Hall. Alliance abstained in the vote. But they became the target of loyalist anger. Alliance councillors received death threats, party members' offices and homes were attacked.

Stephen did not get elected in 2014, but their transfers got their running mate over the line, which they considered to be a job well done. But it was a different kind of activism that really grounded Stephen in local politics in the North.

---

[56] 'Coming out of the Curve', RTÉ 1, January 2015.

I was heavily involved in the marriage equality campaign in the North. I'd heard about gay marriage in Europe and Canada, but I'd never thought of it as happening here.

Originally, I helped Steven Agnew from the Green Party draft the first Assembly motion on marriage equality. That was a very big wake-up call. We realised that it was going to be a lot harder to get it through than we thought.[57] After that, I set up the Alliance LGBT network, to try and lobby for changes in the party.

Then I started working for the Rainbow Project in 2016 [an LGBTQ+ non-profit]. I worked as their campaigns communications officer, and my main focus was the 'Love Equality' campaign for equal marriage. It was my dream job.

I was only there for a year. I remember sitting in Stormont the day that we were presenting the new Equal Marriage Bill. There were representatives from Alliance, the SDLP, the UUP, the Green Party and People Before Profit. Sinn Féin sent their apologies as they were having a big meeting about something. We got the Bill signed off, and we were back in the office talking about how to take it forward. And then Martin McGuinness resigned.[58] That's what the big meeting was about.

Six months of work up in smoke, because there's now no Assembly. All of a sudden, the main focus of my job, which was to lobby MLAs, was gone. The funding was gone. And that was it.

We had so many ideas. We had plans for a launch on Valentine's Day. We even got a photo of Gavin Robinson from the DUP with a Valentine's Day card for marriage equality. Arlene Foster, the DUP leader, disassociated the party from it later, but it felt like we were making progress.

But then the campaign had to move to Westminster.

When the marriage equality legislation finally happened here in 2019, I just got a text from John at the Rainbow Project to say 'it's happening this afternoon', and I asked my boss if I could watch it on tv. It was so surreal,

---

[57] Between 2012-2015, legislation for marriage quality was defeated four times in the Northern Ireland Assembly. Late in 2015, the legislation finally passed, but the DUP vetoed it via a Petition of Concern.

[58] Sinn Féin's Martin McGuinness resigned as Deputy First Minister of the Northern Ireland Executive on 9th January 2017 over the DUP's handling of a green energy scandal, the Renewable Heat Initiative (RHI). This collapsed the Assembly, which did not return for another three years.

because there was all this hard work, and then all this hopelessness when the Assembly collapsed. And all of a sudden, it was done.

Don't get me wrong, I'm incredibly grateful. But it was surreal.

It wasn't like in the South when there was a definite moment. You could see the result of all your hard work and campaigning. Where people had decided to vote for your rights.

I remember sitting in Maverick [a gay bar in Belfast] the night it passed into law. I was crying. It was incredible. It was such a big part of my life. But I just wish we'd been able to do it at home.

I lost any motivation or inclination to be involved in local politics after that. I left the Alliance Party. A lot of my friends in Alliance got elected in, or were co-opted after, the most recent Assembly election [in May 2022] and I'm so happy for them. But I'm glad it's not me. I was talking to one of the new MLAs in Maverick after the election, and I asked what it felt like, and she said it felt crap. All that excitement and build-up to getting elected and she can't do her job now.

This moment that Stephen describes, of watching equal marriage pass through Westminster on tv at work, makes a big impression on me. I think of all the loss of talent from Northern Ireland's politics. It is very difficult to build a life or a political career in the midst of such a dysfunctional system of government. It is also difficult, as a citizen, to keep hopeful and engaged.

***

Moving out of party politics did not dilute Stephen's activism. In fact, it has given them space to re-evaluate some of their ideas. Stephen says:

I would have considered myself to be a unionist until relatively recently, probably until the pandemic. Not a strong unionist or a loyalist. I was never into the Orange Order or the marching bands. I just always believed that Northern Ireland was best served as part of the United Kingdom. But I don't believe that anymore.

I also don't believe that we'd be best served as part of the current set-up in the Republic of Ireland. So I wouldn't call myself a nationalist. I'm a socialist. I voted for People Before Profit at the last election.

If you want to call us alternative Protestants, I don't think you could call us the centre ground. I think we have really strong political positions.

I see myself as an Irish person. But in the same way that someone from Liverpool would be English, but they're *northern*. I'm Irish, but I'm *northern*. We do have a unique perspective here that isn't shared by people in England or in the South. And whether or not people like to admit that there's such a thing as a Northern Irish identity or not – it's real. Because for the last 100 years, we've had a very unique experience.

My first memory is a bomb going off. It was terrifying. I still live here in the Shankill, an area that's saturated by trauma, and the reminders of trauma – the murals, the tours. The violence has stopped, but the war is still going on in people's heads.

Despite this very distinctive northern Irish identity, Stephen does not think that the idea of Northern Ireland within the UK state is sustainable. The pandemic, for Stephen, underlined its failures.

When the pandemic came, I really struggled with the attitude of unionists when it came to cross border cooperation. They were waiting for the UK to make decisions, even though we share a land border with Ireland. We're a population of seven million on this island. We could have pursued a more effective pandemic strategy, maybe like New Zealand did. But at one point, Northern Ireland had the highest rate of COVID-19 infections in Europe. People died needlessly because we couldn't be flexible about practical issues.

The pandemic was the worst thing I can remember. In fact I don't remember a lot of it, because I think I just blocked it from my mind. The majority of people I work with have addictions and mental health issues. Mostly it's both. At the best of times, our welfare and criminal justice systems don't provide a safety net for people. During the pandemic, it was even worse. All the support networks just stopped. I don't know how people managed to get through it.

And everything since then has confirmed my move away from unionism. The current government sending refugees to Rwanda, clamping down on protest and dissent, how they treated workers during the pandemic.

I'm not even sure if it would have been much different if [left-wing Labour leader] Jeremy Corbyn won the 2019 election. Obviously, things would have been better. But I don't think that most English people can adequately interpret or represent Northern Ireland, or Irish people. And regardless of Corbyn's best interests, the British state is based on inherited privilege, the House of Lords, the monarchy. Socialism drives everything for me. And I just can't reconcile that with being imperialist or pro-monarchy in any way.

* * *

As I listen to Stephen talk about the marriage equality campaigns, and their move away from unionism, I keep thinking of the stories Kellie Turtle told in the last chapter. I ask Stephen if the queer community experienced a similar dynamic with marriage equality as Kellie identified with the reproductive rights movement. If it catalysed a sense of all-island solidarity in a similar way.

Stephen campaigned and knocked doors for marriage equality in the South. There have been many trips to Dublin Pride over the years. But while connections and relationships exist, Stephen describes a sense of being left hanging after marriage equality passed in the South. The northern struggle continued, but southern interest had waned.

However, Stephen thinks that island-wide solidarity has shown up in other ways.

> There's been a lot of solidarity when it comes to trans issues. The Irish feminist movement, north and south, hasn't become as transphobic as the British feminist movement.
>
> I think it might be because we're more down-to-earth in Ireland. Activist movements here are more aware of social class. Working class queer people are still working class. If you go down to Union Street [in Belfast's queer quarter] on Sundays for the bingo, it's all working class women from hen parties and caravan parks, coming down because it's their 40th birthday, or taking their grannies out. The performers and the drag queens are mostly working class. The bar staff are working class. People are there to have a good time, not worry about who's going into the toilets. There have been unisex toilets in the Kremlin [a gay nightclub in Belfast] since it opened in 1999; it's just never been an issue. I just don't think we've the capacity here to take on more conflicts. Life is already a struggle.
>
> Of course people will try to import these ideas. They did it with marriage

equality too, bringing in that American right-wing evangelical model. We have our home grown transphobes too.

But I don't think the community here wants to let anyone force a wedge between us. I've never experienced sectarianism in the queer community here. Even with abortion, the solidarity between the queer movement and the reproductive movement was immense. With the Irish language movement too.

I remember in 2016 there was marriage equality rally, a pro-choice action day, and an Irish language demo all on the same Saturday. And it just became known as the 'Day of Solidarity'. Because all the same people went to all the same things. It wasn't like 'there's the gay activists and there's the women activists', it was more, 'there's the community, coming together'.

Stephen tells a story about the moment Kellie and I spoke about in the last chapter, when the DUP recalled the Assembly to try to block Westminster legislation decriminalising abortion in Northern Ireland in 2019.

We were having an event in the Merchant Hotel to celebrate marriage equality passing. We heard the news and started to talk about what we could do. There were serious conversations amongst the marriage equality activists that we could go to Stormont and occupy the chamber, to try to stop this from happening. We didn't care if we'd get arrested. Because, if it was the other way around, we knew that the feminist and reproductive rights movement would have done the same thing. Luckily it didn't come to that. But we were ready for it.

It's that phrase – nobody is free until we're all free.

* * *

Stephen has been threatened repeatedly for their alternative Protestant political views. Told to shut up, both in real life and online. Sadly, threats are something Stephen was already used to as a gay and genderqueer person.

These journeys are connected for me, big time. When I came out, suddenly I went from being one of the flock, to being the enemy. All the homophobic abuse and death threats I got. I didn't fit in in the same way anymore.

However, despite receiving abuse from all angles, Stephen is not inclined to shut up. Each of these journeys has required a certain kind of grit, different kinds of unsilencing.

Stephen uses the word agitator a lot, and I like it. Stephen says they've a long family history of agitation. There's a family story about a Donnan who married a United Irish McCracken. There was Liam Tumilson, a socialist Protestant from Ballymacarrett who went to fight fascists in the Spanish civil war (Donnan-Dalzell 2020). There was Frederick G. Donnan, a chemist who helped forge passports for Jewish scientists to escape the Nazis before WWII. Also, there was Stephen's dad:

> The older my dad got, the more left-wing he became. The same with my mum. In 2011 there was a BNP [far-right British Nationalist Party] candidate standing in our area. The guy gave my dad a leaflet, and my dad tore it up in front of him. He said to the guy 'you're a bunch of neo-Nazis', and then went in and voted for the Green Party. I was like, 'what's happened to you?!'
>
> So yes, I guess the agitation runs in my family.

The Cambridge dictionary defines agitation as, 'the situation in which people protest or argue, especially in public, in order to achieve a particular type of change'. Stephen says:

> After being through all that, I've made it my mission to be a pain in the ass. People have done all they can to me, and I'm still here. And I'm not afraid of those people. But there are young people and kids who don't have the support that I was lucky enough to have. So I feel an obligation to fight for them. To be uncivil if I need to be. Nobody got their civil rights by being civil. I can't sit by and watch on.
>
> Sometimes people tell me I can be quite militant and aggressive. But I'd rather be that, than be someone who lets it slide. Because it almost killed me. And I can't bear the thought of somebody else thinking they have no other alternative.

I think about my young kids and their friends. And I feel deep gratitude to our queer community in the North, which has continually taken risks to protect, support and fight for the rights of the next generation.

Stephen and I make plans for me to bring my eldest to see Cara Van

Parke perform. Cara Van Parke is a gorgeous gender bending creature with bright makeup and facial hair, who Stephen describes as 'Ballyhalbert red carpet'. A loving tribute to working class culture and all the survivors of the conservative north. Stephen leaves me in no doubt of the mantra I have come repeat so often in this book, 'we exist'. We exist and we are not going anywhere.

22

Republican Planter

Seán was raised as Catholic in a mixed marriage family in Newtownards. He speaks fondly of the many British army servicemen in his family history, from the Duke of Wellington onwards. But Seán has seen the many faces of our politics, as both an insider and an outsider. He has often been on the receiving end of sharp sectarianism. And has come to identify as an 1798-inspired republican.

Seán's republican politics are confident and publicly visible. Maybe this is just the way he is as a person – confident. But I can't help but think that there is less dissonance between Seán's ideas and his chosen political tribe than for some others of us. This interests me, and we will go on to talk about it.

We're in his recording studio in Stranmillis today, Seán often pausing to show me old photographs or YouTube videos. Colm Ó Dóghair is coming later to talk about the 1798 Walking Tour they run together. Seán invites me to join in as a tour guide, although my crappy health will not allow it. He has built a sound-proofed studio to record podcasts and other media – Sweetstream Studios – from the Irish for Stranmillis, an Sruthán Milis. He invites me to take part in this too. There's an immediacy and warmth of invitation to Seán's world.

Seán lives and breathes 1798 history. His encyclopaedic 1798 posts on Twitter are how we first met. Later, we would bump into each other in real life at political events. Which is where I began to understand the depth of feeling behind his fascination with the United Irishmen. He says:

> Hopefully, one day I will see the ghosts of the United Irishmen come back. I've always wished for it. I know there are loads of them out there, waiting quietly.

1798 is much more than an interesting history to Seán. 1798 is what makes sense of his and his family's lives. I wanted to talk to Seán about how he relates to modern Irish republicanism in the light of these histories.

* * *

Seán grew up in a mixed marriage family during the Troubles. His story is one of integration and mixing. But also buried secrets and points of pain.

> My dad is a salt of the earth working class Protestant from Newtownards, and my mum is a farmer's daughter from Armagh. She was Catholic, and I was brought up as Catholic. I was baptised in St Patrick's Church in Newtownards. Same as Winnie Carney, James Connolly's secretary and friend.
>
> My Armagh family come from a strong, rural, traditional Catholic area. You've got what I call a 'Trinity' up there of the church, the GAA and politics. My Great Uncle Francie 'Alphonsus' was in the IRA from 1916 to 1922. I never knew much about it until the military records came out a few years ago. It was never really talked about.
>
> When my dad joined the family, it was amazing. He loved the culture and the simple country craic. He'd met my mum at the Queen's Hall in Newtownards. My aunties were training as nurses in Newtownards Hospital, so my mum joined them for a night out there. Mum's sister Phyllis was courting my dad's best friend at the time, a young Catholic guy called Paddy Cherry. Paddy was murdered by loyalists in Newtownards in 1974. He was shot outside the fire station, just because he was a Catholic. An easy target. My dad never forgot about him, and would take us to his grave when we were kids.
>
> Mum and dad got married in the early 1960s. They married in my mum's small county parish church. Not a single person from my dad's family came. Marrying a Fenian was a step too far. So my dad got Lundied out of his own family.
>
> My dad's father, my granda, never really spoke to us as kids when we visited the house. He just ignored us. We didn't exist as far as he was concerned. I remember going down to the house and my granda would come into the front room, he'd mumble a few words to my da and that was it. He'd barely speak to my mum either. I never knew him. Never had a conversation with my own grandfather.

> Dad didn't really talk about it that much. In a way, it never really bothered me and my siblings – we knew it was a load of sectarian nonsense. My mum just wanted us to get to university, get good jobs, and leave all that crap behind us. Which we did. My dad's influence made sure no animosity remained to poison future generations. But it's hard to completely erase it from your mind. Those echoes of sectarianism from the past lurk and linger.

Despite the disapproval of Seán's granda, there were plenty of other Protestants in his family who weren't sectarian at all. His granda's own father – Seán's grandfather – for a start. James Napier was a master mason and pipe player, who played in 'Lord Londonderry's Own Church Lad's Band'. He would go on to be a Grand Master in the Orange Lodge.

> James was still alive when my dad got married. And he said to my dad, 'Bobby, if you love her, it's fine, never mind what people think'.
>
> So it was complicated. The Orange Grand Master was fine, and my granda wasn't.
>
> My dad's mum was called Anne Reilly, and my dad was very close to her. A lovely woman. One of my own daughters is called after her. The Reillys were just a different family. There was never any issue there. Anne's father was in the 36th Ulster Division and killed in WWI in France. And going back further, one of her ancestors was one of the leaders in the 1798 rebellion in Ballynahinch/Saintfield. He was hanged in July of that year for treason. That might be partly where I get the spirit of 1798 from.

Seán grew up in the Glen estate in Newtownards, and describes his childhood as happy. Although the estate was mainly Protestant and loyalist, there was always mixing. Despite some low-level sectarianism, Seán says that dad never feared anyone in Newtownards, and that he was well known and liked in the town.

> My dad was in the British army. There's loads of it in my family. The family pedigree was the British military, the Orange, the Masons, the Black.[59]

Seán's dad was also a member of the British Legion. Between going to the Legion with his dad, school and Scouts, Seán grew up with a lot of Protestant

---

[59] The Royal Black Institution (or Black Preceptory) is the senior of the three loyal institutions centred on commemorating the Battle of the Boyne. The other two are the Orange Order and the Royal Arch Purple Chapter.

friends. But Seán says that 'the last thing on our minds in those days was religion'. He joined in with a lot of the life of the estate.

> I'd follow the bands, help gather all sort of stuff to build the Twelfth bonfire. I can understand the excitement of it, the inner blood and thunder feeling you get from the drums. Back then, I thought it was my tribe. But it wasn't.

*　*　*

As Seán got older, he began to realise that he was not accepted by many in the tribe. While he had known generosity of difference within his wider family and in Newtownards, experiences of sectarianism came to deeply shape his politics.

A story that his dad told sticks out.

> My dad was a (cable) jointer with NIE. He was working up in Tullycarnet, in loyalist east Belfast, connecting electric to the new estate in the early 1970s. One time he was working, a wee boy of eight or nine ran up to him, saying 'Mr, Mr, my dad shot a Taig'.[60] My dad couldn't believe that he was hearing this from such a young kid. He was a working class Protestant with a young Catholic family, living in the heart of a loyalist estate down the road in Newtownards.

Seán remembers the Third Force, Rev. Ian Paisley's loyalist vigilante militia, coming to Newtownards one night in 1981. Up to six thousand men walked loops around a dark Conway Square wearing orange armbands that said 'For God and Ulster' (*Time Magazine* December 1981). Seán was at Conway Square that night, a young child, 'shaken, yet excitedly fascinated'.

Later, Seán would learn that the United Irishmen marched through this same town square in 1798, until they eventually took over the Market House. This time, led by very different men of the cloth, Rev. David Bailie Warden, Rev. James Townsend and other Presbyterian ministers, who governed republican Newtownards via a French Revolution style Committee of Public Safety for a number of days (McCavery 1994; Allen 2004).

When Seán was eight, they moved to a little village in Armagh for a few years, near where his mum had grown up. It was a majority Protestant village surrounded by a rural Catholic population. There was one Catholic street in

---

[60] 'Taig' is one of a number of derogatory terms used by some loyalists to refer to Catholics.

the town. Seán's family moved to a Protestant street. 'Why not?' Seán says. 'We grew with Prods; they were sound.'

But the family experienced constant sectarianism in the village.

> It was there I really realised that there was a difference. Sectarianism gives you a blunt sense of who you are and who you are not. I've got two arms and legs. And you're trying to work out, 'why am I different?' Because I wasn't brought up like that.
>
> There were a load of part-time UDR guys in the village, aged 18 or 19. We couldn't believe how vicious they were to our family. One summer Sunday night, they unleashed hell on us. Our back garden ran onto theirs, and they threw bricks at us all night. All of us kids were under 12, hiding in the front room from a barrage of bricks and bottles. They were yelling at my father for marrying a Fenian, calling him a turncoat and a Lundy. A lot of them would be jailed later for terrorist offences. We hated the place. We weren't doing anything to them. Just being. Just existing.
>
> That's why I hate sectarianism so much, from any quarter. Being at the receiving end of it is traumatic. We went back to Newtownards soon after that, to the Protestant friends and cousins I grew up with. They just weren't like that. It was good to be home again.

***

Seán has a deep appreciation of the radical Protestant tradition. He calls his dad a 'radical Newtownards United Irishman'. While his dad often talked about WWI and WWII, he knew all about Betsy Gray and the United Irishmen of the town as well.

> My dad is the true sense of a Protestant Dissenter. That's probably one of the reasons why I am like I am. A lot of other members of my family are like this as well. They're Protestants, but have a sense of 1798 republicanism, and what it meant then and now.

We talk about the Quakers, whose politics are far from the PUL package. Seán tells me about 'mad Rab Bradshaw', who was a Newtownards Quaker in the early 19th century. When there was no room to bury Catholics in local church grounds, the Bradshaw Quakers gave some of their land to the Catholic Church for a cemetery, Killysuggan (Bigger 1902: 4-6).

Seán connects the radical Quakerism of the past to the radical Quakerism of the present.

> When I was living in London, it was the Quakers I always hung out with. Because all the big meetings, the revolutionary and radical meetings in London in the 1970s and 1980s were in Friends Hall in north London. All the republicans, the left, the Troops Out movement in the eighties, went to Friends Hall. Because the Quakers facilitated it. No-one else would.

We get to talking about James Connolly. Seán says Connolly was the early 20th century iteration of the United Irishmen. That's a line I'd trace too.

For Seán, the way forward is to embrace both parts of his identity.

> Napier is a very old Scottish name. Napier University [in Glasgow] and all of that. So I'm half Planter stock. There are so many other big Planter names in republicanism too – Adams, Morrison, Sands, Storey. This is part of our diverse history.
>
> For republicanism, it's a golden rule – if you're born here and you draw breath on this island, you're of the island. A lot of right-wingers don't like that. But there's no future in that kind of ethnic politics. It has no relevance.
>
> I describe myself more as a republican, than a nationalist. It's more comfortable. For me, nationalism is too confined. Internationalism is a much better concept.

This reflects the politics of most United Irishmen too. That democracy on the island of Ireland is a politics of choice, not a matter of DNA. Not something that is tied to Catholicism or a set range of cultural markers.

> Don't get me wrong, I love the music and sport, the culture, the full gamut. But I'm a republican. Republicanism seems more of a secular identity that loads of different people can identify with. There are all sorts of republicans all over the world. I just don't believe in monarchy, which is a big part of it.
>
> I have friends in the Orange Order in Newtownards, who I can sit with and have a pint. We talk about the Glorious Revolution and the radical freedom of thought it espoused, even Cromwell's republicanism. Both didn't work out well for Ireland. But it's another way of thinking about republicanism. As something that's about democracy and freedom.

Later, I will read Orangeman David Hume's book about 1798, where he describes Presbyterians as 'the first republicans in Ireland' (Hume 1998: 37-8). I like these open-ended definitions of republicanism. It's the way I see things too. I have come to think of myself as a Protestant republican. But there's an awkwardness there as well. I can hear on the tape that I sound a bit hesitant. Seán senses it. I've included the conversation from both of us below.

> *Seán:* I always feel as if some Protestants who really want to be radical believe that the space is crowded out with Irish republicans. They think, 'I'm a republican too, is there a place for me in there?' Yes, there is. But there's one big blockage. And I don't think it's the Church. I don't think smart radicals believe it's the Church. But what is that blockage?
>
> Is it the fact they think 'are you going to do unto us, what we did to you?' Is there an element of that?
>
> *Me:* I don't think so, no. Not that I've heard of. Not for me anyway.
>
> *Seán:* So what is the blockage? What is the fear?
>
> *Me:* I suppose I've come to identify as a Protestant republican through writing this book. There were a few blockages to get past. A fear for my safety and my kids' safety. You know, from being a Lundy. But that's also why I'm writing this, to try and break free from those expectations.
>
> I also have a sense of being politically let down by organised forms of republicanism. And I'm talking here as a feminist, as an environmentalist. I love all the community and left-wing politics that you get with Sinn Féin. But I often think that party politics can get in the way of those values. That's probably true of most parties. And it's not like republicanism is necessarily tied to any specific party.
>
> It's people in our families too. Most of us know people killed by the IRA. So it's uncomfortable for most Prods to just say, 'of course we're republican'. It's not that straightforward. Because the armed struggle devastated many of our wider families. We're really aware of the violence and bigotry that went on in our own families too, and aren't afraid to call that out. It's complicated.
>
> It's very difficult to talk about what the blockage is. But I think you're right. It is there. I'm hoping this book is a way to bridge and connect these two conversations.

THE GHOST LIMB

This conversation I have with Seán sticks with me. It's in the back of my mind the whole time as I write this book. It is of course not fair to ask Seán to speak for republicanism as a whole. He understands the obstacles on each side. He is the child of Planters, the son of a Dissenter and a Catholic mum who experienced the bluntest end of sectarianism in this place. He watched his own dad be Lundied. But he has never let go of his conviction that northern Protestants are diverse, nor of his hope that the radical spirit of 1798 will rise amongst Protestants once again.

He's just the person who happened to ask the golden question – 'what is the blockage?'

And I'm really glad he did. Because I have a feeling that these conservations, exploring in a deep and raw way what republicanism can mean in the North after the Troubles, might be a way to create change. For me to awkwardly stumble my way around the term, articulate my unconscious resistances. For Seán to listen and push back.

Maybe that's the way to summon the ghosts of the United Irishmen to life. By fully walking into, and embracing, these conversations. To connect up what has become disconnected. With open minds, and with honesty about what we've all been through.

23

The Woods

Maurice and I arrange to meet in the Clandeboye woods on a balmy autumn day. A dry stone wall that cuts through the woods is disappearing, piece by piece. Maurice walks past the wall nearly every day with his dog. Six months ago, he noticed that a few stones were missing. Each day, more stones disappear, until entire sections of the wall have vanished. The remnants, heaving with diverse plant life and critters.

I am glad I asked Maurice for a story, because what he tells me is not quite the same as other people in this book. It is a story of a dedicated 'Other'. A life driven by environmentalism and non-violence, community co-ops and the commons. Maurice refuses to accept the categories of Protestant and Catholic. He suggests to me that while the United Irishmen had the right idea in banding together, he would prefer to replace 'Irishmen' with 'Commoners'. To remove religious and national labels altogether.

His 21st century reimagining of 1798 intrigues me. With minds open, ideas buzzing, we set off to find the disappearing wall.

***

Maurice Macartney grew up in east Belfast, and moved to Bangor when he was 11. He thought people from Bangor spoke so politely that they sounded Canadian, and was told to speak properly in school so he didn't sound so 'Belfast'. A small early political revelation.

After school, Maurice did a few factory jobs, including several years working for Lowden guitars in Bangor, then in Newtownards. He says living and working so close to home prompted him to ask himself, 'is this all the diversity there is in the world?' He was curious and wanted to pursue the thought, travelling far and wide, with a million questions.

He went to Belgium, then to Warwick university, he lived in Coventry, spent time in Romania teaching English, did a PhD in Queen's University Belfast, worked in offices, worked for Oxfam, travelled everywhere he could get to, before finally settling back in Newtownards. This outward looking internationalism is something Maurice brought back from his travels, and is a defining theme of his stories.

We talk a lot about music. Maurice tells me that when he was working at Lowden guitars, he had his first encounter with Irish traditional music, which 'opened up my ears to another form of music and also relationship'. For a time, a Japanese luthier, Mitsuhiro Uchida, and his wife Izumi – master instrument makers – came to work in Lowden and became mentors to him. Later, while working at an Oxfam shop in Belfast, Maurice was asked to accompany Wilson Magwere, a singer from Zimbabwe, who was playing outside the shop. Maurice sat down beside Wilson with his guitar and they began to improvise music together. This began a lifelong friendship. Maurice joined Wilson's band, Magwere.

Maurice sees music as a portal for building relationships. He loves the improvisation that happens when people play music together – meeting people where they are at, each being shaped by the music of the other to create something new. Maurice thinks this is something that can be done in real life as well. I think this is a good thing to know about Maurice before coming into his world. Imagine him strumming a guitar or ukulele as you speak with him, inviting you to play along.

***

Maurice is a member of the Green Party in Northern Ireland, and is often their election candidate in Strangford. I have voted for him often. Land, environment and nature are central to his everyday life, as well as his politics.

Maurice walks through Clandeboye woods between Bangor, Newtownards and Crawfordsburn every day, and knows every inch of it. He shows me what deer prints look like. Tells me which farmers own which fields. Who used to play where. He knows the dog walkers and dogs who do the morning shift with him. He knows who has left suet pellets out for the robin. Pointing, he says:

> There's a little family of swans that lives on the lake here. Usually they have two, three, four cygnets a year. That was a moorhen over there. There's a

coal tit. A heron lives over there. Fish jumping in the river. There are nesting woodpeckers around here too. I'd usually see the deer once a week. Occasionally, I'd see a red squirrel or a pine marten.

But while Maurice experiences an intimate everyday connection with the woods, the woods are privately owned by the Clandeboye estate. We walk this land by invitation.

The wealth of successive families who have owned the Clandeboye estate came from the British Empire. The First Marquis of Dufferin and Ava was Viceroy of India. We walk past a monument, Helen's Tower, built by a Baron for his mother. Troops trained in the forest surrounding Helen's Tower for World War I. Little wooden crosses and poppies are pinned to its railings. Maurice says:

> I walk around here thinking about all kinds of things. How the paths we're walking on now are marked by all that bodily history, and the history of empire.

The wall that we've come to see was built as part of an outdoor relief scheme in the 19th century. Unemployed workers from the town lugged the stones here and built it by hand. Generations of local sweat and stories.

Maurice loves this section of the woods. Until recently, he wanted his ashes to be scattered here. But, where once the old wall snaked through the woods, now there are only piles of stones. We find a tiny section still standing.

> This is what's left of it. This is what it used to look like. Look, it's covered in moss, lichen, ivy, moulds, insects. It's a haven of wildlife. It had been here so long that nature had almost reclaimed it.
>
> Six months ago, I realised that a small section of the wall had been taken away. Every day as I walked past, more and more sections were gone.
>
> One morning I saw a couple of guys taking stones away. They worked for the golf course. They said they had permission. My guess is that it's being sold to a local developer.

I asked Maurice how he felt about it, and hear frustration in his usually calm voice.

> I felt really angry and upset about it. Because this piece of history can't come back now. It's extractive. This person has taken the stones of the wall away to use for their own purposes. I'm so sad it's been lost.

And of course, the disappearing wall is about so much more than these specific stones. It's about how we are living as human beings within our environment.

> Why are we the only species of animal that feels it doesn't need a habitat to live in? Even if you don't care about nature. There's an extractive violence to it.
>
> I went to a museum in Finland where there was a room displaying all kinds of hand tools. There was footage of guys working the forest in the 1920s. It showed how long it took them to cut down a tree, which was then pulled by a horse and floated down a river. There was bodily engagement, and there was a built-in sustainability, because it was such damn hard work.
>
> The next room had an exhibit of chainsaws and massive forestry machines. Cutting down trees within seconds with the flick of a thumb and finger, from the safety of a cabin, some distance from the wood. The trees become cubic metres of timber, just a commodity to be traded. You no longer have a connected, embodied relationship with the living forest.

Maurice tells me that he often sees large trucks coming into the woods now, to use it as a film set. Creating wealth that never reaches the surrounding community. Damaging wildlife, leaving a trail of detritus behind. That embodied relationship with the forest, broken.

* * *

Nature matters for Maurice, but it is not separate from people or politics. This comes across clearly in a short film he made about his family history, 'The Spirit Cellarman', titled after the job of his great-great grandfather (Macartney 2000).

Maurice's people, on his mother's side, were from the Isle of Skye, a north-western island of Scotland. In the film, Maurice visits the sites where his ancestors lived, and explores the social structure of clans and crofts. Traditionally, in Skye, clans owned the land. This was a communal way of living, where people had mutual obligations to one another, and had direct and meaningful stewardship of the environment. Maurice talks about dùthchas, a Gàidhlig word (similar to dúchas in Irish) that can describe heritage and belonging, and also a sense of interdependence between people, land, and nature.

THE WOODS

From the late 18th century, there were land clearances on Skye, as modern farming was introduced by new landlords. More money could be made from grazing sheep than renting to humans. The island's inhabitants tried to resist the landlords, and keep hold of the commons, but they did not succeed.

Maurice does not romanticise the past – clan politics could be bloody. But the concept of dùthchas speaks to the loss of people's relationship with the land, as well as the loss of mutual obligations.

Maurice's ancestor left Syke for Ulster in the 19th century, most likely as part of the Clearances. The family ended up living in east Belfast, steeped in Skye history, speaking both Gàidhlig and English, and, Maurice says, at odds with the idea of Protestant ascendancy.

> When you think of Scottish people here, you think of Planters. But it seems that he was an economic migrant, driven out by the Clearances. That complicates the politics here.

Once again, I am left pondering how much of our radical politics comes through a direct line from Scotland.

* * *

I have chalk in my pocket. I give some to Maurice, and he thinks for a moment while I mark out 1798 on the wall. We have to look hard to find enough surface to write on.

> Okay. I'm going to put this here. There's going to be a twist on an old slogan.

Slowly he chalks out:

> *1798 The Common Name Of Commoner.*

I ask him to explain.

> Wolfe Tone said that he wanted to substitute the denominations of Catholic, Protestant and Dissenter, with the common name of Irishmen. And I think, yes, while I'm with you in the first bit, if you're going to get rid of denominations as a way of coming towards each other, there doesn't seem to be much point in putting up a new one – the nationality of Irishmen. Because that's just substituting one denomination for another.

> To go back to my childhood in east Belfast, at some point, one of the teachers came to us and said that we had to fill in a form. They had boxes for the Protestant denominations and the Catholic denomination. It was the seventies, I can't remember if there was a box for Others, probably not.
>
> So you had to go and ask your parents what you were. This was somebody in authority saying, 'I'm going to ask you what you are and here's a list of the acceptable answers'. So you learn to put yourself into one of these boxes. And then you repeat that throughout your life. You repeat it for yourself, and you repeat it for others.
>
> You do it in the census forms and you do it when you join a company and fill in a monitoring form. It's built into the institutions of the Good Friday Agreement. You have to sign up as a Nationalist or Unionist or Other. But Other doesn't count as much.

I say to Maurice that I've come to feel that Otherness as a kind of absence. He doesn't see things this way at all.

> My email, Twitter handle and blog are 'jointhecoo'. COO stands for 'community of others'. I have a different way of thinking about community. It's not a bunch of people who simply somehow share an identity. There's no identity outside processes of identification. Ticking the boxes set out for you, and calling it a community, as if everybody in the one box shares some sort of core essential identity, misses the process, the action. Identification is something we do. It's something we are called to respond to. It's not just something that we are.
>
> Going back to the British Empire. Generations of children have been brought up seeing maps of Africa with straight lines. Thinking that's just the way Africa is, with European names stretched over. But those lines are the result of some guys sitting in a room with a ruler and a pencil. No Africans in the room. So you have to always question 'what did we do to make this reality?' It is not actually just the way things are.
>
> From early on, people are telling me I belong to this community and not that community. But my community includes my colleagues and work, my friends, my family, the people I buy my bread from in the market. People I go for a drink or eat with.
>
> It was a similar thing with church for me. People claiming your

allegiance on behalf of God. But they are humans, not Gods. The declaration of the Republic in 1916 is a good example, when it says: 'Ireland is entitled to, and hereby claims the allegiance of every Irishman and Irish woman'. But it's Patrick Pearse saying that, not 'Ireland herself', whatever that would mean. I think that there's something very interesting about this idea of someone speaking in the name of an off-stage entity, and claiming you owe it your allegiance, whether it's Mother Ireland, or God, or the Protestant community, or whatever else.

All of a sudden, your relationship with your neighbours, friendships, solidarity, community, become bound up in claims of allegiance. And then, instead of being faced with a choice between political projects – say, Irish unity or retaining the union, or remaining in or leaving Europe – you're faced with the choice of whether or not to betray your community.

I think that's what all of politics and history is about in the end. How to get people to combine together. It's effective to tell people they are already combined, by religion or nation. But it seems to me that there are other ways to combine.

This idea of combination is integral to how Maurice sees the world. Until recently, Maurice edited a writing and film project called 'The Combination' with Stephen Baker and Tanya Jones.[61] The name comes from the start of the industrial revolution, when workers began to come together in early trade unions, and the Combination Acts tried to outlaw them.

> They tried to prevent people from combining together because they knew there was a power in it.
>
> The idea of combination is that we can come together with people on some common task, or values, or some common ground without having to share an identity. We do this all the time. We're already good at it.
>
> Because you start by asking, 'how do I live as non-violently as possible with my neighbours?' And you start where you are, with the bunch of neighbours you have. For me, that could be in cooperatives, repair cafes, community wealth building, community ownership, community land buyouts.
>
> There's only so much you can do on your own. And I think that's why I like to talk about combinations. There's nothing humanly possible that we can't achieve if we combine together to do it. There is power in solidarity.

---

[61] https://thecombination.org.uk/

While Maurice identities strongly as an Other, he is less enthusiastic about being a Neither. Neither is defined by what it is not – a Neither is 'not Catholic' and 'not Protestant'. You are still adopting the terms of engagement which somebody else has set out.

Maurice doesn't want to convert anyone else to being Other. It just fits with his way of looking at the world to take people as they are, rather than categorising them. For Maurice, Other is a rich, inclusive space. The community of others is a place where 'you can come in with the strongest of identities, whatever your heritage, and work on common goals'.

* * *

Maurice uses the word 'relaxed' a lot. I like this. It's an interesting way to underpin a political orientation to the world. Rather than being loyal to 'Ireland' or 'the UK', Maurice just wants to live in a grassroots democracy where he can shape his life around his values.

He is disappointed that Northern Ireland is not yet a place where people can relax.

> With the Good Friday Agreement, the Union was secure as long as a majority wanted it to be. All that unionists had to do was to make Northern Ireland a place to live where most people could feel relaxed and happy. But that didn't happen.
>
> If you were different, you were regarded with suspicion, if not outright hostility. You were the wrong nation, or denomination, or orientation. You can't just love who you want to love. All the various kinds of restrictions and purifications, and the impulse to demand more loyalty from people, when all unionists really had to do was to make other people feel more comfortable, so that they can live their lives happily here. And they didn't do that. They chose denomination over combination.
>
> There's also a dynamic within the unionist movement, whereby anybody who gets a little bit too close to Others, let alone nationalists, gets accused of betraying their community. The problem with that is, unionism doesn't command a majority anymore. You're going to need Others. So, if and when it comes to a referendum on Northern Ireland, if you're going to get over 50 per cent, you're going to need to expand the combination you can call upon, not shrink and intensify it.

Maurice's search for alternative ways of doing politics ultimately led him to the Green Party in Northern Ireland.

> It was almost like a bolt from the blue when I first started looking into the Green Party. One day I read their website which said their four core values are sustainability, grassroots democracy, non-violence and social justice. Those values pretty much sum up my whole political outlook.
>
> I liked that the Green Party was not part of the binary reduction machine of Northern Irish politics. It had deeper values than green and orange. It was green in the environmental sense obviously. It was also red, with social equality, justice and support for the trade unions. And it was also about the rainbow, in the sense of diversity, gender, sexual orientation, all the rest of it.
>
> I remember early on I met Mal O'Hara and Anthony Flynn and others, who were deciding to set up an LGBTQ group and call it the 'Queer Greens'. It was so far ahead of every other political party in terms of that bold, radical assertion that 'I am not going to listen to your authoritative voice from on high telling me that who I should fall in love with, who I can marry'.

Maurice has been active in a lot of anti-racist work. He has worked with the Migrant and Minority Ethnic Thinktank, and Beyond Skin, a multicultural community arts collective. His approach with race is the same as religion. 'I just take people as they are, and don't ask them to be representatives of their culture, or carry that baggage with them'.

Island is a factor in Maurice's political hopes for the future, but not in a traditional way.

> The island is an ecological entity, where rivers and species traverse the border freely. We have an opportunity to take advantage of our island status as the climate changes. To think about our soil, biodiversity and food security. Many feel an emotional link to Britain, but this is not incompatible with how important the island is in our future politics.
>
> We all have to share this place, one way or another. My ultimate question in politics is: 'how do we learn to live together as non-violently as possible, for all our differences, on this, our one and only planet, and in this our corner of it?'

> I don't think that politics should be about leaving your heritage at the door. It's about leaving your violence at the door. You can be as Protestant, Catholic, African, European as you are. You just have to leave down your weapons and meet as commoners.

That magic key I slipped in my pocket, that fictive kinship that was so alive in the 1790s. Whoever finds themselves in this place is of this place. Here it is again, in the form of combination and commoners. And Maurice has added something even more beautiful. The idea of democracy as improvisation. Like playing along with music. Each person responding to the other, creating something that wouldn't otherwise have been possible.

* * *

Maurice and I talk for hours before and after our ramble in the woods. It takes a lot for someone in Northern Ireland to opt out so resolutely from the traditional discourse. At no point did Maurice ever define who he was, where he came from, his partner or her family, in terms of religious or political identity. The closest we have ever gotten, and in fits of laughter at my insistence, was Maurice saying that 'I am not Protestant or Catholic but, to be fair, I'm probably more not Catholic than I am not Protestant' because of his upbringing.

This is interesting to me, because my own journey in this book has been to redefine what Protestant can mean, rather than to reject the category. But I wonder if we are not so different. Both of us are rejecting terms that we didn't get to choose. I wonder if my solution is more short-term. Reclaiming and redefining the category of Protestant for myself, as a form of resistance. Maybe Maurice's solution is more long-term. Imagining a future where we do not reach for these categories when relating to one another. I don't know. But I will walk beside Maurice in this community of others any day of the week.

24

We Will Be the New Ireland

Heather Wilson is a member of the nationalist Social Democratic and Labour Party (SDLP) from a Protestant background. She's talked and written a lot about Protestants and Irish unity, and I love her perspective. I'm reading interviews with Heather online before we talk. I linger on a piece she wrote called 'Protestants and Unity: Moving Beyond Tokenism to Deeper Engagement' (Wilson 2018). And I realise, she's had this figured out for years. Heather writes about being a token Protestant in debates about a new Ireland. As someone who supports reunification, Heather understands why people are interested in her background. But in the piece she says:

> The *'unionists will be welcome in a new Ireland'* line can sound more like a condescending invite – misunderstanding the right to citizenship as a taxpayer whether you're called William or Liam – rather than any genuine outreach.
>
> To be clear, Prods won't just be 'welcome' in a new Ireland, they (we) will be that new Ireland. Whether you were christened in a Presbyterian church or confirmed in a Catholic one, the unity project belongs to us all – that is if you want to be part of it.

I think this really cuts to the heart of things. That if unity happens, Protestants will be full and equal citizens. You can welcome your guests. But family get the key to the front door.

* * *

While Heather feels that the SDLP are a natural fit with her values, it's probably not the route that some might have expected her to take. Heather grew up as a Methodist in Ballysillan, which is a largely unionist/loyalist area of north Belfast. I wondered when she realised that her politics might be a bit different to some of the people she grew up with.

> I guess I just always knew from studying Irish history at school that there was something inherently wrong about the way Northern Ireland was created, and how a minority of people were treated. That wasn't ok. There was an injustice done on this island that we've never recovered from.
>
> I started to articulate that out loud at the tail end of university. I wanted to join a political party. I actually tried to join Alliance at university, but I couldn't find the room! And then within a couple of years I was working for the SDLP. I know a lot of people from our background would land at Alliance. But I was always very comfortable with the SDLP. I think that was maybe meant to happen.

The last time I'd seen Heather was a few months before COVID-19 hit. Nearly every time I heard about what she was up to during the pandemic, it was helping others. Heather is very low-key. She wouldn't tell you this herself. But I kept catching sight of her in other people's photos, making up food packages, working in St Patrick's soup kitchen, helping the North Belfast Advice Partnership, delivering Christmas presents or Easter eggs. Heather finds these values to be in line with her political party.

> I really do think I have shared values with people in the SDLP in terms of social justice. I know traditionally the SDLP would have been seen as a Catholic middle class party, and that's fair enough. But I haven't seen that being at the front of their psyche when they're making policy decisions today. The opposite. I think they really do make policy decisions in a way that looks after people. Making sure that justice is done. The constituency offices of the best MLAs – from a range of parties – are always hiving. The social justice is hanging out of them. If I ever am elected, I'd hope to carry that with me.

Like many people in the North who live their lives outside traditional binaries, Heather had early experiences of social mixing. She says:

> I could easily have gone through life not meeting any Catholics until I was 18. Some middle class people find that hard to believe, but it really does

still happen today. But my dad's best friend is a Catholic. I also played sport when I was younger and that just naturally opens doors. One of my good friends still to this day, that I played with on a junior team, is Catholic.

Studying at Queen's University Belfast, Heather lived in the Church of Ireland/Methodist chaplaincy on Elmwood Avenue. This was an ecumenical space, where Anglicans, Methodists, Catholics and people from Charis (the religiously mixed charismatic church my mum and dad talked about in chapter 14) often came together for events and services.

> I think that softened the edges of what I understood Christianity to be like. And it also probably then softened my political views as well.
>
> I always remember those Charis guys, and all these mixed marriages at a time when it was very hard to do that. It made me think that there'd be absolutely nothing wrong if I did join the SDLP, or if that was my kind of politics.

'Are you a nationalist?' I ask Heather, hoping she can shed some light on how to find a good language to express our kind of alternative Protestantism.

> Well, I would always say I'm a social democrat first. But I guess by default if I want to see the reunification of Ireland, I am a nationalist. I don't overly like the connotations of that word in Northern Ireland, but I guess in reality, that's what I am.
>
> In some ways I'm a republican as well, in the natural sense of the word. But I remember once my mum heard me say that on the radio and she went through the roof. She got on the phone, saying: 'what are you doing?' But that's the Northern Ireland context isn't it, and the connotations it has here, as opposed to a Wolfe Tone kind of republicanism, which is what I'd relate to more.

This gets to the absolute core of the blockage I talked about with Will Jordan, Stephen McCracken and Seán Napier. It has come up so often in the book. The emotional way the word republican lands with many Protestants after the Troubles. But I think a lot of us also know that it's a concept worth spending more time with. To see if we can untangle it for the 21st century.

* * *

THE GHOST LIMB

There's not a Lundy amongst us who has not experienced pushback on account of straying too far from perceived PUL norms. Heather's experiences have been on the extreme end. Her family has been very accepting of her politics. She uses them as a sounding board to find out what issues people are having on the ground.

> But there have been some times when it's been complicated. When I ran for Council election in 2019, I thought it would be a good idea to have a family member as my election agent. But I didn't realise that it meant his details had to go on every election poster, including his address. They lived in the heart of Ballysillan at the time. Loyalist paramilitaries took the posters off the lampposts and I remember us both thinking, 'shit, we have to think about the implications of this now for all of us'.

Heather describes what happened next as poster-gate.

> Drama. They kept them for a year and put them on a bonfire the following year. Real perseverance. They really got their mileage out of them. I'm glad, because they're £6 a pop.
>
> As soon as I put the posters up on the Ballysillan Road in 2019, they took them down again. Billy Hutchinson [from the Progressive Unionist Party] said to me that he was sorry it happened.
>
> That was fine and the summer passed. But then the next summer in 2020, they were put up on the Tynedale bonfire in Ballysillan.
>
> But you know what they say, 'if you haven't made it onto a bonfire, you're not making an impact'.

Even though Heather is saying this as a joke, I don't really hear laughter in her voice. I don't know how anyone could ever feel ok about seeing their face on a bonfire. I swap her a story back, about my home address being put online. I try to package this up as a good anecdote too, but I'm not laughing either.

The strange thing though is how galvanising these kinds of abuse are. After the shock comes the grit. It hasn't made any of us decide to shut up.

What I found even more interesting about Heather's reaction to poster-gate, is how she continued to stick up for working class loyalist communities. Because of where Heather grew up, she obviously has loyalist friends.

Although Heather gave the Twelfth a miss the year her posters went on the bonfires, she usually attends the local parades with her family. Speaking to the *Irish News* (July 2020), Heather said:

> I know this behaviour is not reflective of loyalism as a whole, but rather a small, insecure minority, and whatever the constitutional settlement now or in the future, I will always be a genuine advocate for loyalism to have its full place in our society.

Like so many others in this book, Heather really does get loyalist working class politics. 'That whole Ervinian politics of the PUP, I understand it, I get it much more than I could ever get the DUP or UUP'. Like others, she found debates around the flags protests classist.

> I know that the people who put the posters on the bonfires aren't representative. And I get really annoyed when people talk about loyalists as if they're Neanderthals. I just don't think anyone should trample on others like that. I do think that working class people have been really let down, and if I can, at any point, play a role in cutting through that, in giving people better opportunities, and saying that there's more to loyalism than these elements, I think I have some sort of duty to do that.

* * *

It seems to me that a lot of what we've been doing in this book is talking about language. Alternative Protestant identities and the words that we might use for these. Heather pinpoints something.

> I was on a call the other day for the New Ireland Commission [an SDLP civic forum established in 2021 to discuss Irish unity] and somebody kept saying to me, 'you're part of the PUL community'. And I kept saying, 'I totally appreciate what you're saying, but that's just not something I consider myself to be part of. I just don't think the PUL community exists like that'. I'll take the P, but the UL isn't something I can relate to.

That's been a big part of the journey of this book too. Liberating the P from the UL. For me, it's been about radically re-defining what the P looks like. This project sets us on a future trajectory. It offers us the chance to unearth ourselves from traditional identities that have been proscribed.

THE GHOST LIMB

Heather is in her early thirties. It seems likely that Irish reunification, or some other kind of political reconfiguration on these islands, will happen in her lifetime. To my mind, she embodies the possibilities of what this could look like. Whatever it will come to mean, Heather will be the new Ireland.

Endings

25

The Past and the Future

This is a book about love. An indescribable love for the island of Ireland, its peoples, histories and cultures. In all of their beauty and pain. It is a love of saying the words, 'Catholic, Protestant, Dissenter, heathen, migrant and Other', and for those words to mean something real. Because they are healing words. Words which remove power from our sectarian binary.

This book is my aisling. Going walkabout in the 1798 Dreamtime to feel, talk, listen and try to will a new reality into being.

I finish writing this book feeling more whole as a person than when I began. As someone who has tuned in to their dislocated identity. Who has sat with their ghost limb and allowed themselves to feel its pang. Who has asked questions and found answers in the Dreamtime. Understanding why radical Protestant histories are still so often silenced, disremembered and spoken in code. I take the last steps of this journey as someone who has restored a personal sense of belonging. And who has found a community of people to walk beside – people who were there along.

Unexpectedly, walking this path has led me to embrace a Protestant identity. Where once I declared myself Other and Neither, my estrangement has lifted. I had felt that there was no place for me in the Protestant tent. That my Protestant identity depended on the acceptance of others. That the P was too difficult to disentangle from the UL. This was the dislocation that I came to feel as a ghost limb. A sense of uneasy belonging.

As I reached out in time and space, to radical ghosts and living friends, my world started to shift. I came to a realisation that a Protestant identity was mine if I wanted it. That this cultural tradition was my roots and my trunk. To cut myself off from it, was denying myself the opportunity to enjoy all it offers.

Retracing the steps of the United Irishmen, and all those who came after them, jolted me. Physically revisiting their locations – streets, cottages, pubs and landscapes – in Belfast, Moneyreagh, Six Road Ends, Antrim, Newtownards, Larne – made it real. Thriving little pockets of regional radicalism, then and now. Locating United Irish ideas in 21st century cultural, political, religious and linguistic subcultures gave me indescribable joy. 1798 became a living history. Nearly 20 years after returning to the North, I felt at home.

At some point during writing, I stopped carrying the chalk. I felt the urge to scrawl 1798 on trees and walls less often. I suspect I will return to it, if the ghost limb flares up again. But for now, I just know deep in my bones that we exist. We exist and we are everywhere. That even if you feel that you are walking on this path alone, we are with you.

We have always existed. This tidal force of alternative, dissenting, misfitting, radical, anti-sectarian Protestants. In most times and places on this island, we have not been the mainstream. There was a moment in the 1790s where a portal appeared, and we can imagine what might have happened if we stepped through it. It was an exceptional time of enlightened thought and co-operation across religious divides. 1798 was flawed in so many ways. The rebellion failed. But the spirit of 1798 did not disappear. It rippled down through time. Countless people have picked up the baton for their own generation. And now, it is our generation's turn to rise to the challenge. I wonder if it might be possible to open that portal again.

***

Disremembering requires deliberate action. As Will Jordan put it, the ideas of 1798 were almost thought-policed out of existence. Where families like Stephen McCracken's hold on to United Irish mementoes, but do not talk about them. A deeper silence took over. To the point where disremembrance can only be undone in the present by going out of our way. Making a conscious effort to retrieve social memory. Reaching out intentionally to connect with a huge cast of characters and ideas that have come before us.

THE PAST AND THE FUTURE

Some people are not rediscovering these histories for the first time. They were plugged in all along. Family members were links in the chain, passing on stories, books and memories. I think of Roland Spottiswoode, Kellie Turtle and Linda Ervine, where a critical mass of family members in each generation passed on experiences and knowledge. Or Angeline King, whose family are yarners. People who always had a strong sense of anti-sectarian Protestant identity, rich with layers and nuance.

Other people from strongly loyalist and unionist backgrounds have had different journeys. Families have sometimes split over politics. Sometimes these ruptures have sparked a reconnection with 1798 and alternative Protestant histories. Some families chose to accompany their children on their explorations. Many other families found it easier to maintain a silence around areas of contention.

The original title for this book was, 'Do Not Fear To Speak', after the 1798 ballad, as an encouragement and incantation. But I decided against it. Because, in comparison with other people around the world, most northern Protestants are people of considerable privilege. While there is most definitely a fear in speaking, I also did not want to position alternative Protestants in opposition to unionists. Because our traditions are part of one another. We share many values, particularly with left-wing unionists and loyalists. We are literally family.

That said, most people in this book have paid a price for being a Lundy. While the term Lundy – a Protestant traitor – has become an almost affectionate badge of identity for many, it has a barb in the real world. Election posters burned on bonfires, people being told to leave the country, get out of town, having to leave families, churches or faith groups, being sacked, being disinherited. Receiving threatening letters, messages and online harassment. Choosing to water down public opinions, hide personal details for protection. Everyone in this book has been Lundied in some way.

Marilyn Hydman's book on dissenting Protestants, published in 1996, contains even more chilling examples. An interviewee talks about a Protestant friend shot dead while asleep in her bed, a fortnight after marrying a Catholic (Hyndman 1996: 48). I note that almost half of Hyndman's interviewees asked to remain anonymous at that time. Nobody in this book chose anonymity, while being offered it. This makes me wonder if things have changed a little. Please let it be so.

THE GHOST LIMB

As I write, a number of prominent loyalists are themselves being Lundied to the point of receiving death threats. Many academics, journalists and business people are being similarly attacked for their stance on Brexit and Protocol issues. The generalised harassment, particularly of women, online and in real life, is well known. It strikes me that life is now so diversified, that it may be impossible to gate-keep old boundaries. Attempts to purify the tribe are more likely to diminish it. There is solidarity amongst the hounded.

Many times writing this book, I was asked why Protestants had forgotten their 1798 history. I asked it myself. But I learned that disremembering is different from forgetting, and that silence is often a rational reaction to turmoil. The Act of Union diverted much United Irish idealism into British reform, making political dissent even more dangerous in the aftermath of 1798. Partition wove unionism into the very fabric of the new Northern Ireland. Rotten Prods became suspect and were dealt with by force, alongside their Catholic neighbours. The Troubles were the most recent iteration of silencing. All of these political moments were underpinned, in different ways, by the threat of violence. It is hard to move out of the intergenerational trauma.

But even through the hard years, many alternative Protestants consciously followed in the footsteps of 1798. They lived their lives in defiance of expected unionist norms. Many paid dearly for it. Some had no choice but exile. We stand on their shoulders. This book is a small contribution to interrupting the silence once again.

I do not know how many people identify with the idea of being an alternative Protestant today. Most people I speak with have a sense of still being a minority within the wider Protestant community. Some feel very alone in their difference. As I begin to write and talk about the ideas in this book, I am struck by the messages I receive from others.

An older man tells me, 'I've been bottling up how I feel for nearly 50 years'. A woman who feels like the 'odd one out' in her family finds the concept of Protestant dissent liberating. A man who signs off 'a Katesbridge 56-year-old protesting dissenter', says that a light-bulb appeared above his head when he heard a radio conversation about alternative Protestantism. Another person tells me they don't talk about politics in their loyalist estate, but says, 'I'm glad I am not completely different after hearing your interview'. Another emails, 'I feel less of a misfit now'. A man who is a scholar of early and middle Irish says it's not safe to tell his neighbours about his interest in the language, and asks me to chalk something in Irish for him in his town. Which I do.

So many ghost limbs. So much dissonance. So much lies beneath the surface. And while I cannot tell you how many alternative Protestants walk this path today, it feels good to unsilence the feelings for my own self. To give words to the experiences of my friends.

Because when people come together and raise their voices, there is power in it. As Carol Coulter says in her preface to Marilyn Hyndman's book (1996: xi):

> [Dissenting Protestants] are a living contradiction of the notion that there are 'two traditions', 'two cultures', 'two nations' in Ireland or in Northern Ireland. Instead there is something much richer, much more interesting, a people with a multifaceted culture, varying, not only according to religious background, but also according to geography, class, gender and, above all, the choices made by thinking individuals.

Those last few words get under my skin. We are all born with loose identity markers. But, as human beings, we also have a great deal of power to make our own choices within the contexts we find ourselves. This is a politics of choice, not DNA.

While all of the people I spoke to in this book are politically engaged, none are (yet) elected to high office. The spirit of 1798, to my mind, requires both deep anti-sectarianism and an openness to the politics of island. Our current binary political system in Northern Ireland does not have much space for such open-ended boundary crossing. But I do not think the spirit of 1798 is absent in politicians from Protestant backgrounds. I have met many councillors at 1798 celebrations and similar cultural events. Sometimes things are said privately that cannot be said publicly. My sense is that the spirit of 1798 thrives quietly, locally, off the grid. Perhaps to enable people to fight within the narrower boundaries of what seems politically possible at this time.

And so, it feels politically important to tell these stories. So that those in power know that we exist. So that people know, when decisions are being made, that northern Protestants are even more diverse than might be expected. It feels psychologically important to tell these stories so that alternative Protestants feel less alone. So that we can see how we fit into a long historical chain. It feels important to tell these stories so that our Catholic neighbours can get under the bonnet of different kinds of Protestant lives. To see just how much we have in common.

We may not be the mainstream. Yet. Or maybe ever. But alternative Protestants have existed on this island for hundreds of years, keeping an imaginative space open, refusing to accept that we are two separate tribes. It feels important to keep celebrating this historical tradition. To reclaim space for the story of 21st century Protestant dissent. Out of healed past a healed present will grow.

* * *

Writing this book has changed me in other ways too. I thought I started out with an open mind. But walking this path has challenged me to go deeper. To cross more boundaries. Embrace ever more awkward situations and conversations. Find out that I am wrong about more things than I expected. I have much more to learn.

Some of this book has been about Protestants' complicated relationship with republicanism. Only a few people described themselves as republican, and even then, articulated a hesitancy in using this language around their families. At the beginning of this book's journey, despite many years of republican inclinations, I could feel this tension within my own self. This surprised me, given that I am clearly a republican in the 1798 sense of wanting deeper citizens' democracy on this island.

I have come to realise that some things do not have resolutions. We cannot change the fractures of the Troubles, our hundreds of years of painful history. We do not fully have a choice over all of our emotions. I think it's ok that we allow the meanings of republicanism to linger, creatively exploring the possibilities, and sensitively appreciating the sore points.

I finish this journey comfortable in my own republicanism. Aware of its history in Ireland. As dismayed by the armed struggle as I am by British state violence. Able to more clearly articulate my desire for a Second Irish Republic, with a new constitution, and what that could mean. Understanding why republicanism is not the norm for most northern Protestants. But confident that the values underneath us all – openness, solidarity, connection to this island – run deeper.

Some of the conversations in this book provide a worked example of how to move forward. From Rev. Karen Sethuraman, I take the lesson to stop over-thinking about republicanism, and to walk out into the world and be friends with republicans. A simple act. But one which can be hard to put into practice in a divided society. It requires going out of your way – to another part of town, to places where you might not initially feel comfortable, to a different part of your heart and your gut. Wherever you may land on the politics, friendship outside of comfort zones is never a mistake.

While writing this book, I also attended post-Brexit anti-Protocol rallies. I went to Twelfth of July parades. I tried hard to understand this fraught political moment. During this time, I had good conversations with loyalists about 1798. One was an admirer of United Irishman William Orr and had visited his homeplace in Ballycarry with other loyalists. A bandswoman and I discussed the shared history of songs.

At the beginning of this journey, I wondered if people who were drawn to the United Irishmen would share my politics. But I have come to understand that people relate to this history in different ways. For an Orangeman, conservative unionist, socialist loyalist or a Covenanter, the outworking of the politics of the 1790s can look quite different to my own (and to one other). But these are conversations that we enter as equals.

I tentatively mooted the idea of participating in this book to a few socialist loyalist and unionist friends. But as the writing took shape around the idea of a ghost limb, I realised that this was a different journey, and that it might take another book to explore it.

Many of the people I talked to were raised by, are related to, love and are loved by loyalists and unionists. I think about being introduced to Angeline King's Larne, and her Twelfth of July, which are so far removed from the stereotypes. I think about Stephen McCracken's trip to the Orange Order. And how walking towards awkward situations, choosing encounter rather than avoidance, can lead to unexpected goodness.

As the ideas from this book started to spill out into the real world, something else happened. When I wrote about my lost Irish language, northern Catholics contacted me to say that they identified with the ghost limb too. They remember Irish being spoken by grandparents and great-grandparents and associate deep pain with its suppression. I talk to exiles of all political persuasions who moved away from the North, often out of economic or political necessity, who describe feeling cut off at their roots.

Other friends articulate a different kind of ghost limb. On a hazy summer day, I walked with my friend Paul through a Holywood forest. We gave our daughters an old nail, and together they scratched 1798 in a fallen tree. We had just filled in the 2021 census. I had ticked my identity as Protestant and Irish. He had ticked Catholic, Irish and Northern Irish. He said this was partly as an act of reconciliation, to show how, in its centenary year, he does not deny the reality of the existence of Northern Ireland. And partly to express to the world that partition hurt him, and it is part of him now. This is a different way of feeling cut off from your culture and belonging. It may require a different kind of healing.

* * *

Susan McKay (2021) has talked about how, when writing her book on northern Protestants, her decision only to interview people from that background sometimes felt to her almost sectarian. I relate to this deeply. Sometimes it feels stupid for me to write a book about northern Protestants, when our present and future is so diverse. Some days I worry that holding on to this identity is not a modern act. And yet, other days it feels necessary.

Our history on this island, until recently, has been a story of two large cultural groups. It has mostly been a white history. It has most often been articulated by men. It's a history born out of religious traditions. The task is to find modern ways to connect with the realities of the past.

Lots of the people in this book have partners who are Catholics, atheists, and people from other religious traditions, who come from different countries, who have different colours of skin. Many of us are raising children in ways that – we hope – will make all of our labels porous, filled up with inter-cultural content. Some people in this book happily identify themselves as Other and Neither, and have not rediscovered their inner Prod. An equally future-facing journey. One that is still part of me, and which I may return to one day. Maurice Macartney's vision of a political future, shared between a community of others, each with their own culture, is a world that I would like to live in.

In many ways, I think a goal of many alternative Protestants is to live lives that blur and resist traditional boundaries. To cherish what we love about our Protestant heritage, but also to cultivate traditions that may be handed on to future generations as a broad set of values and ideas, which may sometimes come from Protestant faith, but are by no means tied to it. Modern values that can help navigate climate breakdown, technological change, multi-cultural futures.

My 11-year-old daughter pulls me into her room late one night. We have to decide what big school to go to. Once again, we are required to declare our religion on an application form.

'Am I a Protestant?' she asks.

'Not necessarily, I don't think', I replied. 'You go to a Catholic school. What do you think you are?'

'Neither', she says. 'I'm a scientist.'

I don't know if she'll be swept up in all this one day too. Or if her generation's multiply identifying brilliance will create new pathways of social memory. Maybe when she's older, she will write a book of very different stories. A re-invention of her own family's traditions, filtered through her future imagination.

I suppose the United Irishmen may have had this idea too. That the equality and unity of people they desired would be achieved in their lifetimes.

And yet, here we are, more than 200 years later, desperately in need of their wisdom. Given the trajectory of history to date, alternative Protestants may be needed yet. To keep raising our voices in resistance to the reduction of our humanity to a sectarian binary.

* * *

The constitutional question that is currently being discussed around kitchen tables across the island. What do 21st century alternative Protestants want?

I cannot answer this. Because we do not come to this conversation with a settled opinion. There is no alternative Protestant bloc of *x* per cent that can be counted up for a back of the envelope border poll calculation. We are not a club with an oath or a manifesto. We are various. Over half of the people I spoke with for this book would prefer Irish unity, some passionately so. I include myself in this. But unity in the context of radical reform. Not frying pan to fire. Others again are undecided. Their values run deeper. It is not yet clear where those values can best be realised.

What is shared, is frustration with the current inertia of Northern Ireland. Since the first Assembly election in 1998 to the time of writing, the Assembly has only been fully operational 59 per cent of the time.[62] And when it is functioning, it often staggers around in a state of crisis.

Our political health in Northern Ireland is heavily dependent on Westminster politics. Brexit laid bare just how little the needs and nuances of this place are taken into account in UK governance. This does not feel like a democratic way to live. I hear the political disillusionment and alienation amongst my friends and family. I think of the activists in this book who have to pivot quickly between jurisdictions to achieve change, lifting up and laying down their hard work as politics fluctuates around us. I wonder what ultimately happens when people feel such a lack of control over their own lives as citizens. I think of Wolfe Tone's description of Ireland being ruled from London as feeling like an 'amputated right hand'. Those words still feel relevant today.

A number of people in the book expressed a hope that people of the North would have more power as citizens of a new Ireland. Often this is countered by the fact that the South offers few solutions to the suffering created by late capitalism. The lack of housing, universal healthcare and the treatment of refugees in the current Republic of Ireland devastate lives. Nobody I know disagrees that serious work needs done. As Rev. Cheryl Meban says, 'every structure by its nature marginalises people'.

Yet it strikes me that so many of us are already involved in island

---

[62] The Assembly first met on 1st July 1998, and ran in shadow form until 2nd December 1999. It was suspended from 11th February – 30th May 2000; 10th August 2001 (one day); 22nd September 2001 (one day). It did not sit between 14th October 2002 – 7th May 2007 and 9th January 2017 – 11 January 2020. The Assembly sat without a Speaker or Executive from 5th May 2022 to the time of publication (November/December 2022).

politics. Across Ireland, feminists, environmentalists and trade unionists are already working together. Our churches are all-island bodies. Our Irish learners go to the Donegal Gaeltacht. The historical groups I am part of, have members from both north and south. These networks already exist. If you listen to independent media, you will find northern and southern voices already in conversation.[63] People with alternative politics are fighting together to bring the same values alive in our different parts of this island.

At the same time, many of us are shaped by, and love, British socialist traditions. Alternative Protestants in the North are deeply connected to activists, churches and families in Scotland, England and Wales. Many of us do not want a clean break with the UK, if such a thing was even possible. Our unionist families love being British. There is an urgent need for us to think creatively about how these connections and identities can be nurtured and protected in meaningful ways if constitutional change happens.

Some days, I fantasise about a north Atlantic archipelago, stretching down from Iceland and Norway through to Scotland and Ireland. A futuristic Viking Celtic co-operative. Some of us have started to talk about community wealth building and co-ops as a way to take direct political action, regardless of borders. Mostly though, alternative Protestants' minds are open. We want to be part of a creative conversation about the constitutional future of these islands. To ask questions and explore issues, without being bound by pre-ordained, ideological conclusions. Sometimes I wonder if current nationalist and republican politics is quite ready for all that northern Protestants might bring to this conversation.

A new Ireland is coming, in some shape or form. Because nothing ever stays the same. Brexit, Scotland, demographic change, technology, global economics, climate change, far-right mobilisation and war are all profoundly changing the political landscape in Northern Ireland.

Seas will rise. The earth will warm. Migrants will arrive. Exiles will leave. We will be connected and disconnected from each other in ways that we cannot even imagine. All of these things make traditional national borders

---

[63] For example, the podcasts of Left Bloc, The Echo Chamber, Trademark Ireland's A Workers' Guide to Everything, The Irish Passport, Louise McSharry's Catch-up, The United Ireland podcast.

less relevant to future politics. We need new ways of thinking to navigate crumbling empires, economies and ecologies.

As we saw during the COVID-19 pandemic, global problems often require local solutions. Staying at home was the key strategy for virus control. Holidays and free time revolved around exploring the island we were stuck on. As we dug down through the layers of where we live, many of us discovered new ways to be at home, new ways to connect to our environment. We will need to continue this work as the climate crisis changes our relationship with this island yet again. Focusing on the possibilities of geography as well as history.

The Irishness the United Irishmen envisioned does not run in the blood. All of us have the opportunity to opt into a fictive kinship, simply by embracing our lives on this island, and being creative about what this could mean. Alternative Protestants are the children of Planters, Scottish famine refugees and economic migrants. Married and tangled many times over with Gaels. We have never lived in monocultures. This is a good thing to remember when we think about the future. Vikings, Gaels, Scots, Poles and Eritreans. Whoever is on this island is of the island. We work our patch together. This is a choice that we can make every day.

Alternative Protestants stand in solidarity with all who share our ideals, from Glasgow to Cork, Paris to Palestine. It's an outward-looking orientation to the world. Most of us do not spend as much time thinking about local anthems and flags as much as bigger ideas of equality, healthcare, education, media independence, human rights. These values cut across all identities, tribes, religions and nations.

For United Irishmen, Irish self-rule was a means to achieve the goal of deeper democracy, not an end point in itself. If we think about the project of 1798 as a set of ideas and values, and can be visionary and imaginative about what this means territorially, this may provide a map for the future.

My deepest fear is that, as we move further into this century of climate crisis, people in Northern Ireland – in whatever form it exists – will hold on too tightly to old grievances. As resources become scarce, food supply less secure, as we take in refugees and adapt to new realities, that we look over our shoulders to see what the other lot are getting. That we are so limited in the practical action we can take in the North, that we cannot fix what needs to be fixed quickly enough. That our small democracy is too vulnerable to stasis. That our resilience will be found wanting. We must not wait for the flood to realise that it cannot be mopped up with a flag.

My deepest hope is that as our world changes – ecologically, digitally, economically, socially – we see how much we need one another. That all we have is our neighbours and we need to be better at it. The roots of anti-sectarianism may be hidden from view, but they run deep through the earth beneath our feet. Through time and place. These roots can anchor us, if we let them. We have all the tools we need to dream a new reality into being.

*** * ****

This is ultimately a book about hope. Because having these people in your life is the antidote to despair. Watching your friends and people you admire living brave, counter-cultural lives. Refusing to accept brokenness as our final destination.

As I wrote this book, I watched the people in it move mountains. Set up schools, win policy changes, write books, run food-banks, strike for fair pay, save landscapes, change debates, shape thought, learn languages, record histories. I have watched them dig deep as they were challenged time and again. And I have watched them hold strong. In Rev. Cheryl Meban's words, they've stubbornly kept their toe in the door. Never allowing this imaginative space to close over. To take opposition as an opportunity. To convert despair into change.

I started this book by asking, where did the spirit of 1798 go? Who are the keepers of the flame?

And *here* is the spirit of 1798. Living, breathing, campaigning, organising, writing, telling stories, busting a gut. We might not be the mainstream. But we exist.

It turns out that we are the keepers of the flame. Maybe you are a keeper of the flame too. Here on this island, or in your own time and place.

The 1790s were a vital time. Politics was full of both heat and light. Passionate debates were happening in pubs, kitchens and street corners across Ireland, just like they are today. It was not a coherent time. People had different ideas, and many changed their thoughts over time. I feel like we may be in a similar era right now. The energy, the fear, the contradiction, the hope.

Excavating the ideas of 1798 offers us the opportunity to reimagine the future in different ways. To ask new questions about what it means to live on this island. To dream another existence into being.

We have a job to do. We are unearthing ourselves. Finding our voice.

We exist.

Our roots are deep.

We are ready to help shape the future of this island.

26

The Betsy Gray Café

This book ends as it began. With hospitality, friendship and stories. On an autumn afternoon, 20 friends and neighbours gather in Ballygrainey Orange Hall car park opposite the new Betsy Gray café in Six Road Ends. We are here to talk about local 1798 histories. Protestants, Catholics, Dissenters and others. Of all political shades. Ulster Scots ones and Gaeilge ones. Swapping scraps of research. To preserve the stories, and to see what they might tell us.

I organise the Six Road Ends event with my friend, Bill Kirk. The gathering sees many people in this book coming together. Seeing them together gives me joy. Bill brings his friends. Jane, who runs the café, brings her friends. And we are more connected through telling these stories than we were at the beginning. I say to my friends, old and new:

> If you're here today, there is probably some invisible cord that pulls you towards 1798 history. This will be different for all of us.
>
> I was born here in County Down. Although this landscape shaped me in so many ways, I always had a strange disconnection from place. I think that came from living in places that wear their British and unionist culture so loudly. Cultures that I enjoy aspects of. But which I didn't think had room for someone like me, a northern Protestant who still believes in the United Irish ideals. Who still holds a torch for the unity of Catholic, Protestant and Dissenter.
>
> And then something changed. Bill left a book of 1798 sites for me at the pub. The journey began. I met others of you at the school gate, online, through politics. All through this time, you and other neighbours lent me

books. People would phone with some small brilliant mystery about our alternative history. And I would jump in the car and follow the trails.

I slowly started to realise that these radical histories were right under our feet.

And as I found out more about local United Irishmen and women, I started to feel at home again. I came to feel like a tiny link in a long historical chain. And that everyone I had met along the way was maybe part of that chain too. I feel like I've found the spirit of 1798, here, with all of you. Its spirit is alive and well.

After the event Lisa and Seán and I thrash out the old debate, of how republicans and radical Protestants can approach 1798 differently. Seán talks about the need to talk about 1798 with celebration and pride. Lisa and I talk about hiddenness and safety. It does not get resolved. But I think that every time we have this conversation, we come closer to some kind of understanding.

As we pack up the chairs, I overhear two neighbours talking.

You're a great storyteller, is that your job?

No, I was a prison warden. On the night of internment, I interned every one of those boys.

May God forgive you.

I had no choice. They were bucking the boys out of helicopters. I was doing my job.

My friend was an internee. It changed his whole life. He could never get over what they did to him.

I write this as the 25th anniversary of the Good Friday Agreement approaches. 1998 was a time when the air was filled with raw, hopeful energy. People's pain was writ large then, as it is now. But we decided to sit together in the same room with it. Because this created space for radical empathy, which in turn allowed magical things to happen. We need very urgently to sit down together again. To tell stories, take risks, really listen, not turn our face away from others, and prepare to be changed by what we hear. For this remains the only path to healing.

I have come to see 1798 as a meeting-point in the present. Exploring this history is one of many ways we can get back in the room. Every 1798 event I have attended has included Protestants, Catholics, Dissenters and others. Nearly every event has seen raw and awkward conversations emerge. Ideas batted around, disputed, revised, added to. Real connections and friendships formed. I think that certain types of people are drawn to this history. Curious and brave people. People who love democracy. Who love their neighbours, even when they may not agree with them. People who are reaching for roots and wings. And I, in turn, am drawn to all of these people. For being open-hearted and minded enough to go walkabout in the Dreamtime, to step into the unknown.

And this, a chairde, is where this story ends, and where new stories will begin. The Orangemen think the Six Road Ends event is interesting, and invite us to use their Hall for the next meeting. The year after the Betsy Grey café, we put on a United Irish play in Newtownards Town Hall. Friends organise a festival in 2022 to commemorate the 1792 Harpers' Assembly, with Irish and Scottish harpers. Reclaim the Enlightenment are campaigning with Sinn Féin, the Alliance Party and others to win the Assembly Rooms back for the people of Belfast.

Stephen Baker emails me after reading an early draft of this book. He says:

> I've often felt that there is a post-1798 melancholia in the North. A sort of community of mournful heritage enthusiasts longing for what might have been. But that's changed now. This feels like a moment of opportunity. It's also the start of something. The excavation, the recovery, the digging is necessary work. But we can't hang around in graveyards forever paying our respects to the ghosts of dead generations. When we've done our excavations, what do we begin to build?

And that is what this journey has always been about. Looking back. Being present. Imagining futures. Creating new stories of what is possible. Asking what do we want to build.

Bibliography

Agnew, Jean (ed). *The Drennan-McTier Letters 1776-1820*, 3 vols (Dublin, 1998).

Allen, Harry. *Men of the Ards* (Donaghadee, 2004).

Andrews, Liam. 'The very dogs in the streets will bark in Irish: The Unionist Government and the Irish language 1921–43' in Aodán Mac Póilin ed. *The Irish Language in Northern Ireland* (Belfast, 1997), pp. 49-94.

Aylward, Gladys. *The Little Woman* (USA, 1970).

Baraniuk, Carol. *James Orr, Poet and Irish Radical* (London, 2019).

Baraniuk, Carol. 'Who fears to speak of '98?' Tracing a trauma narrative in the Braid Scotch poetry of James Orr (1770-1816)' in *The Honest Ulsterman*, February 2021.

Bartlett Thomas (ed). *Life of Theobald Wolfe Tone* (Dublin, 1998).

Bartlett, Thomas, Dickson, David, Keogh, Dáire and Whelan, Kevin. *1798: A Bicentenary Perspective* (Dublin, 2003).

Beiner, Guy. *Forgetful Remembrance: Social Forgetting and Vernacular Historiography of a Rebellion in Ulster* (Oxford, 2018).

Belfast Media Group. 'Who fears to speak of '98? Certainly not the new group behind United Irishmen Visitor centre plan', 31 August 2020.

Belfast Telegraph. 'DUP's Iris Robinson: Gays are more vile than child abusers', 21 July 2008.

Belfast Telegraph. 'Census 1911: Belfast's Shankill had as many Irish speakers as Falls', 2 April 2012.

Belfast Telegraph. 'Woman who quit Presbyterian Church over same-sex ruling urges others to examine their support for institution', 12 June 2018.

Belfast Telegraph. 'Presbyterian Church distances itself from Mid Ulster Pride event', 20 January 2020.

Belfast Telegraph. 'Thomas McCabe, the Presbyterian Radical', 20 June 2020.

Belfast Telegraph. 'Push for Belfast City Hall anti-slavery crusader statue as councillor says current symbols mainly "white, Protestant and male"', 4 May 2021.

Belfast Telegraph. 'Holy Cross 20 years on', 3 September 2021.

Bigger, Francis Joseph. 'The Bradshaws of Bangor and Mile-Cross, in the County of Down' in *Ulster Journal of Archaeology*, Second Series, Vol. 8, No. 1 (1902), pp. 4-6.

Cadwallader, Anne. *Holy Cross: The Untold Story* (2004).

Campbell, Mary. *Sea Wrack, or, Long-ago tales of Rathlin Island* (Ballycastle, 1951).

Clyde, Tom (ed). *Ancestral Voices: The Selected Prose of John Hewitt* (Belfast, 1987).

Coigly, James. *The life of the Rev. James Coigly: An address to the people of Ireland, as written by himself during his confinement in Maidstone gaol* (1798).

Collins, Peter. *Who Fears to Speak of '98: Commemoration and the Continuing Impact of the United Irishmen* (Belfast, 2004).

Collins, Peter. 'Aftershock: Retreat from the Enlightenment', in Reclaim the Enlightenment, *Celebrating Bastille Day in Belfast in 2017.*

Courtney, Roger. *Dissenting Voices: Rediscovering the Irish Progressive Presbyterian Tradition* (Belfast, 2013).

Crowley, Tony. *Wars of Words: The Politics of Language in Ireland 1537-2004* (Oxford, 2005).

Crozier, Rev John A. *The Life of the Rev. Henry Montgomery LL.D., Dunmurry, Belfast; With Selections from his Speeches and Writings* Vol. I (Belfast, 1875).

Cullen Owens, Rosemary. *Smashing Times: History of the Irish Women's Suffrage Movement, 1889-1922* (Cork, 1984).

Curtin, Nancy. 'The Transformation of the Society of United Irishmen into a mass-based revolutionary organisation, 1794-6' in *Irish Historical Studies* xxiv (96), (1985).

Curtin, Nancy. *The United Irishmen: Popular Politics in Ulster and Dublin 1791-1798* (Oxford, 1994).

Dáil Éireann, *Joint Committee on the Implementation of the Good Friday Agreement*, March 2021.

Dawson, Kenneth L. *The Belfast Jacobin: Samuel Neilson and the United Irishmen* (Kildare, 2017).

Day, Angélique and McWilliams, Patrick. *Ordnance Survey Memoirs of Ireland, Parishes of County Down II 1832-4, 1837, North Down and The Ards*, Vol. 7 (Dublin, 1991).

BIBLIOGRAPHY

Devlin-McAliskey, Bernadette. 'Left Behind by Good Friday', *Jacobin*, 25th April 2016.

Dickson, David, Keogh, Daire and Whelan, Kevin (eds). *The United Irishmen: Radicalism, republicanism and rebellion* (Dublin, 1993).

Dolan, Terence Patrick. *A Dictionary of Hiberno-English: The Irish Use of English* (3rd ed., Dublin, 2020).

Elliott, Marianne. *Partners in Revolution: The United Irishmen and France* (New Haven and London, 1982).

Eydmann, Stuart. 'Sounds across the Moyle: musical resonances' in William Roulston ed. *Antrim and Argyll: Some Aspects of the Connections* (Belfast, 2018), pp. 97–140.

Gahan, Daniel. 'The Scullabogue Massacre, 1798' in *History Ireland* 4:3 (1996) www.historyireland.com

Ganiel, Gladys and Marti, Gerardo. *The Deconstructed Church: Understanding Emerging Christianity* (Oxford, 2014).

Ganiel, Gladys and Yohanes, Jamie. *Considering Grace: Presbyterians and the Troubles* (Dublin, 2019).

Gibney, John. *The United Irishmen, Rebellion and the Act of Union, 1798-1803* (Belfast, 2019).

Graham, Joe. 'Mallusk Co. Antrim', www.rushlightmagazine.com

Gray, John. 'On Progress', in Reclaim the Enlightenment, *Celebrating Bastille Day in Belfast in 2017* (Belfast, 2017).

Gray, John. *The United Irishmen and the Men of No Property: The Sans Culottes of Belfast* (Belfast, 2018a).

Gray, John. *Cave Hill and the United Irishmen* (Belfast, 2018b).

Gray, John. *Mary Ann McCracken 1770-1866* (Belfast, 2020).

Greer, Roy. *Con O'Neill: Last Gaelic Lord of Upper Clannaboy* (Belfast, 2019).

Grew, Tony. 'Police to investigate Iris Robinson over homophobic comments', *Pink News*, 7 June 2008.

Guardian. 'Abomination: the riotously high-camp opera about DUP homophobia', 18 October 2019.

Hall, Michael. *Idle Hours: Belfast working-class poetry* (Newtownabbey, 1993).

Hayward, Richard. *Ulster and the City of Belfast* (Ballycastle, 2015 ed.).

Holmes, Andrew. *The Shaping of Ulster Presbyterian Belief and Practice, 1770-1840* (Oxford, 2006).

Holmes, Andrew. 'Protestant Dissent in Ireland' in Andrew C. Thompson ed. *The Oxford History of Protestant Dissenting Traditions, Vol. III, The Long Eighteenth Century c. 1689 – c. 1828* (Oxford, 2018), pp. 119-38.

Hume, David. *The Spirit of 1798 and Presbyterian Radicalism in Ulster* (Lurgan, 1998).

Hutchinson, Wesley. *Tracing the Ulster-Scots Imagination* (Ulster University, 2018).

Hyndman, Marilyn. *Further Afield: Journeys from a Protestant Past* (Belfast, 1996).

Ingram, John. *Sonnets and Other Poems* (London, 1900).

Irish News. 'Loyalists "charge" United-Irishmen-tour bus', 6 August 2014.

Irish News. 'SDLP rep from unionist background 'disappointed' after posters placed on bonfire', 14 July 2020.

Irish News. 'Unionist man's love for the Irish language brought to life in animation', 3 March, 2021.

Irish Times. 'The Lost Story of Northern Ireland's First Civil Rights March', 24 August 2018.

Irish Times. 'Presbyterian Church trying to retrospectively justify homophobia', 23 February 2021.

Jordan, Glenn. *Not of This World?: Evangelical Protestants in Northern Ireland* (Belfast, 2001).

Keenan-Thomson, Tara. *Irish Women and Street Politics 1956-1973* (Dublin, 2010).

Kelly, Vivien. 'Irish Suffragettes at the time of the Home Rule Crisis' in *History Ireland* 4:1 (1996) www.historyireland.com.

Keogh, Daire. *The French disease: The Catholic Church and radicalism in Ireland, 1780-1800* (Dublin, 1993).

King, Angeline. *Snugville Street* (California, 2015).

King, Angeline. 'The Band Stick' in *Children of Latharna* (Larne, 2017).

King, Angeline. *Irish Dancing: The Festival Story* (Leschenault, 2018).

King, Angeline. *The Dusty Bluebells* (Larne, 2020).

Lingard, Joan. *The Twelfth Day of July* (London 1995; originally published 1970).

Lyttle, Wesley Guard. *Betsy Gray or Hearts of Down* (*Mourne Observer ed.*, 1968).

Mac Póilin, Aodán. 'Irish in Belfast, 1892–1960: from the Gaelic League to Cumann Chluain Ard' in Fionntán De Brún ed. *Belfast and the Irish language* (Dublin, 2006), pp. 114–35.

BIBLIOGRAPHY

Mac Póilin, Aodán (ed). *The Irish Language in Northern Ireland* (Belfast, 2017).

Mac Póilin, Aodán. *Our Tangled Speech: Essays on Language and Culture* (Belfast, 2018).

Mac Siúrtáin, Will. 'On The Trail of the United Irishmen of Belfast', www.anseisiun.blogspot.com/

Macartney, Maurice. The Spirit Cellarman: Clans, Clearances and the Commoners, https://www.youtube.com/watch?v=t4VHIPCsT0M

Madden, Richard Robert. *The United Irishmen: Their Lives and Times* (3 Vols, London, 1842, 1843 and 1846).

Magan, Manchán. *Thirty-Two Words for Field: Lost Words of the Irish Landscape* (Dublin, 2020).

Maume, Patrick. 'Richard Lyttle' in James McGuire and James Quinn eds. *Dictionary of Irish Biography: From the Earliest Times to The Year 2002* (Cambridge, 2009) https://doi.org/10.3318/dib.004981.v1

McBride, Ian. *Scripture Politics: Ulster Presbyterians and Irish Radicalism in Late Eighteenth-Century Ireland* (Oxford, 1998).

McCavery, Trevor. *Newton: A History of Newtownards* (Dundonald, 1994).

McCracken, Stephen and O'Ruairc, Colum. *United Irishmen – Emigres of Erin* (Mayo, 2020).

McCoy, Gordon. 'Protestant Learners of Irish in Northern Ireland' in Mac Póilin ed., *The Irish Language in Northern Ireland* (Belfast, 1997), pp. 131-70.

McCoy, Gordon. *A Gaelic History of East Belfast* (Belfast, 2019).

McKay, Susan. *Northern Protestants: An Unsettled People* (Belfast, 2000).

McKay, Susan. *Northern Protestants: On Shifting Ground* (Belfast, 2021).

McMahon, Eamon. 'Celebrating Bastille Day in Belfast, in 2017. Why?', in Reclaim the Enlightenment, *Celebrating Bastille Day in Belfast in 2017.*

McMillan, Rev. William. *A History of the Moneyreagh Congregation 1719-1669* (Moneyreagh, 1969).

McNeill, Mary. *The Life and Times of Mary Ann McCracken 1770-1866* (2nd ed., Kildare, 2019).

McSkimin, Samuel. *The history and antiquities of the county of the town of Carrickfergus, from the Earliest Records to 1839*, ed. Elizabeth J. McCrum (Belfast, 1909).

Millar, Alan. 'Whar is Campbell?' in *Ullans,* Nummer 15, Ware 2018, pp. 48-54.

Moriarty, John. *Dreamtime* (Dublin, 1999 edition).

Nic Lochlainn, Sorcha. *Long Forgotten Gaelic Songs of Rathlin and the Glens*. https://antrimhistory.net

Northern Whig. 'Repeal of the Corn Laws: Meeting in Newtownards', 22 February 1842.

Ó Buachalla, Brendán. 'From Jacobite to Jacobin' in Bartlett et all eds. *1798: a Bicentenary Perspective* (Dublin, 2003), pp. 77-95.

Ó Ciosáin, Niall. 'Gaelic and Catholic?' Review of Nicolas M Wolf's (2014) *An Irish-speaking Island: State, Religion, Community, and the Linguistic Landscape in Ireland*, 1770-1870, *Dublin Review of Books*, July 2015.

Ó Cléireacháin, Pádraic. 'Feiseanna Remembered' in Eamon Phoenix, Pádraic Cléireacháin, Eileen McAuley and Nuala McSparran eds. *A Century of Gaelic Culture in the Antrim Glens* (Belfast, 2015).

Ó Dochartaigh, Niall. *From Civil Rights to Armalites: Derry and the Birth of the Irish Troubles* (London, 2004).

Ó Snodaigh, Pádraig. *Hidden Ulster: Protestants and the Irish Language* (Belfast, 1995).

Ó Tuama, Pádraig. *Feed the Beast* (Rhydwen, forthcoming, 2022).

Ó Tuama, Pádraig and Jordan, Glenn. *Borders and Belonging: The Book of Ruth: A Story for our Times* (Norwich, 2021).

Orr, James. *Collected Poems* (Belfast, 1936).

Packenham, Thomas. *The Year Of Liberty: The Story of the Great Irish Rebellion* (London, 1997).

Parr, Connal. *Inventing the Myth: Political Passions and the Ulster Protestant Imagination* (Oxford, 2019).

Patterson, David. *The Provincialisms of Belfast and the Surrounding Districts Pointed Out and Corrected* (Belfast, 1860).

Patterson, William Hugh. 'On Some Ancient Sepulchral Slabs in the Counties of down, Antrim, and Donegal' in *Proceedings of the Royal Irish Academy. Polite Literature and Antiquities*, Vol. 1 (1879), pp. 273-6.

Purdie, Bob. *Politics in the Streets: The origins of the civi rights movement in Northern Ireland* (Belfast, 1990).

Rodgers, Nini. *Ireland, Slavery and Anti-Slavery: 1612-1865* (London, 2007).

Roulston, William. 'The origins of the Reformed Presbyterian Church in Ireland' in *Familia, Ulster Genealogical Review*, 24 (2008), pp. 90-8.

Smyth, Jim. *The Men of No Property. Irish Radicals and Popular Politics in the Late Eighteenth Century* (Dublin, 1992).

Smyth, Jim. 'Freemasonry and the United Irishmen' in David Dickson, Dáire Keogh and Kevin Whelan eds. *The United Irishmen: Republicanism, Radicalism and Rebellion* (Dublin, 1993), pp. 167–75.

Stevenson, John. *Two Centuries of Life in Down, 1600-1800* (Belfast, 1920).

Stewart, ATQ. *A Deeper Silence: Hidden Origins of the United Irishmen* (London, 1993).

Stuart, Douglas. *Shuggie Bain* (London, 2020).

Sweeney, Kevin. *The Irish Language in Northern Ireland 1987: Preliminary Report of a Survey of Knowledge, Interest and Ability* (Belfast, 1987).

Switzer, Catherine and McDowell, Sara. 'Redrawing cognitive maps of conflict: Lost spaces and forgetting the centre of Belfast' in *Memory Studies* Vol. 2(3) (2009), pp. 337-53.

Tierney, Mark. 'Charismatic Renewal' in *The Furrow* Vol. 26, No. 11, 1975, pp. 643-51.

Thompson, Hugh C. 'Rev. Richard Lyttle: A Home Rule Protestant' in *Familia: Ulster Genealogical Review* Vol. 2, No. 2 (Newtownards, 1986).

Time Magazine. 'Northern Ireland: Unleashing the Third Force', 7 December 1981.

Tone, Theobald Wolfe. *An Argument on Behalf of the Catholics of Ireland* (1791).

Ward, Margaret. *Unmanageable Revolutionaries: Women and Irish Nationalism* (London, 1995).

Wilsdon, Bill. *The Sites of the 1798 Rising in Antrim and Down* (Belfast, 1997).

Whelan, Fergus. *Dissent Into Treason: Unitarians, King-killers and the Society of United Irishmen* (Dingle, 2010).

Whelan, Fergus. *May Tyrants Tremble: The Life of William Drennan* (Kildare, 2020).

Whelan, Kevin. *Tree of Liberty: Radicalism, Catholicism and Construction of Irish Identity 1760-1830* (Cork, 1996).

Whelan, Kevin. *Fellowship of Freedom: The United Irishmen and 1798* (Cork, 1998).

Winstanley, Gerrard. *The True Levellers Standard Advanced: Or, The State of Community Opened, and Presented to the Sons of Men* (1649).